Readers' Thoughts

This is a serious book, thoroughly thought out and meticulously written in a logically organized way. It deserves a careful read. If you truly want to delve into your inner self and perhaps arrive at the root of some of your longest standing issues surrounding your belief in your value as a person, give it a read. I found when I spent the time to read it carefully and consciously ruminate on what it had to say, it led me to answers I had been seeking. While this must necessarily be an ongoing process going forward, the book's provided blueprints for pursuing these goals make a seemingly impossible task doable. Greater happiness, peace of mind and love for yourself and others is worth every bit of the effort you put into it. It has earned a home on my bookshelf of books of real value, so thanks Anne.

—**Gina Reeder,** *Patent Paralegal Contractor, Artist*

This book was amazing from beginning to start! It has an amazing message that anyone would find helpful in their journey in life. It really helped me devise a plan on where to start my personal healing and learn to value myself.

—**Allison Bertram,** *Entrepreneur*

I think what makes this book so appealing is that Boudreau's approach is personal and comforting. She's been there. She acknowledges the pain and how hard it is to change. But it is possible. I loved the information on replacing negative messages with positive. I knew the power of affirmation but did not realize the tremendous override of negative comments that is going on constantly in our heads. And it was another reminder from the universe to spend time in reflection, which is another way of saying be mindful of not only your actions, but your thoughts. I recommend!

Neuroplasticity—I'd say your book is right on point on so many levels and so very brilliantly written. Thanks for sharing that level of vulnerability. You may very well have just disclosed the recipe so many who have experienced betrayal, trauma, and addiction too, and who need to address trust, anger, resentment, forgiveness, and redemption--just to touch the surface. Thank you so very much!

—**Steven Brown**, *Principal Consultant, Network Infrastructure*

This book holds an inspirational message for anyone looking to release the beliefs and misconceptions that hold them back in life. Chronicling the experiences of people that have allowed their self-worth to be broken by circumstances and simply stopped trying, this book weaves together their stories and wisdom that provides empowering advice to overcome doubts and setbacks that prevent you from living your best life. I would like to thank the author for her poignant, proactive, accessible guidance to becoming a better me.

—**Cali R**, *Orlando*

Self-worth is such a vital yet oft times neglected aspect of understanding the human soul. A Human Mosaic explains in a very understandable and thought-provoking manner how to use the Author's research and life experiences to greatly improve your life. Highly recommended!

—**Joshua Kingston**, *Investment Advisor*

A Human Mosaic

A Human Mosaic

HEAL, RENEW & DEVELOP SELF-WORTH

ANNE BOUDREAU

Published by Deeds Publishing in Athens, GA
www.deedspublishing.com

Printed in The United States of America

Library of Congress Cataloging-in-Publications data is available upon request.

978-1-947309-63-0

Books are available in quantity for promotional or premium use. For information, email info@deedspublishing.com.

First Edition, 2019

10 9 8 7 6 5 4 3 2 1

To Patricia, Alan, Rick, Lucas, Sophia, and Colin

Contents

Preface

A Human Mosaic: Heal, Renew
& Develop Positive Self-Worth

You deserve to feel spectacular.

If you have been living with negative thoughts that have blocked your ability to be joyful, to revel in the beauty of each day, to love your life and know that you are on earth for a reason, to believe that your life matters, this book is written for you.

You *are* spectacular. But no one can convince you of this, you have to believe it yourself. And, for this to happen, you must choose to take the reins of your life and commit to self-change by building your inner strength and stamina, and creating a space of peace within you. Only *you* know how you feel about your innermost self. The value you place on your life affects the quality of every relationship you have and impacts everything you do.

The subject of self-worth has always intrigued me. As a young girl, I would quietly observe the complex and volatile relationships around me with a mixture of curiosity and fear. The rise and fall of emotions in the universe in which I grew up was a mirage of perplexing disparities.

As most of us do, I grew up outwardly-oriented, meaning my center of gravity was directed toward my environment, how people responded to me, and what I achieved relative to others. I relinquished an enormous amount of energy and many years of my life seeking praise, approval, validation, and acceptance. It didn't take me long to realize that I was

1

on a never-ending search for something—anything—to cling to for security and sustenance.

When I learned that there is a difference between self-esteem and self-worth, it became clear to me that what I lacked was self-worth, not self-esteem. Although the terms are often used synonymously, they are not the same, in fact, they are the opposite of each other. Self-esteem, or what I refer to as the "outside you," is about what you do in the world, your talents, profession, athletic ability, social life, how you look, how much money you have, your external actions. A person may have confidence in their competence, however, still feel inadequate. Self-worth, conversely, is the value you place on yourself, how you feel about yourself internally, or the "inside you," your innermost core being.

One of the motivators for writing this book emanates from my core belief that people are inherently good. Every human being enters the world with a fertile mind that is unencumbered by prejudice, hatred, or a propensity to be violent. Infants are wholly innocent. Their only needs are to be fed, cared for, and nurtured. Within the first year of life, a child's sense of trust is formed, and during the next few years their identity is shaped.

A young child observes and absorbs everything in their surroundings; their minds thirst for information and stimulation. Yet, they don't always receive the nurturing or love they need to feel secure, confident, and trusting. Infants cannot choose who takes care of them after birth. They are totally dependent on others to survive. The majority of us have not been raised by adults who understand the vital nature of teaching a child to believe in themselves.

I have spent nearly seven years researching, interviewing, and examining self-worth from every conceivable angle. When I decided to change how I felt about my inner self after decades of self-condemnation, I could not find any material that taught me *how* to build inner strength. So, I chose to create my own program for intensive self-care and repair. I relied heavily on Carl Rogers' book, *On Becoming a Person*, and on other psychologists and philosophers whose focus is on the internal dimension of a person. I also interviewed many experts and individuals who have endured tremendous suffering as a result of low self-worth. A heavy amount of due diligence was involved in writing about a subject as highly complex and deeply personal as how one feels about their inner core self.

My revelatory moment came when I learned about neuroplasticity, our brain's capacity to change at any age or stage in our lives. It is amazing to know that our brain is not hard-wired as we once thought. This scientific evidence proves that our brain is changeable and adaptable, that it can form new neural pathways at any point during a person's life. This is a truly significant point to embrace, especially for those of you who think you cannot change, *now you know you can;* all you have to do is retrain your brain. This is the golden ingredient to the process of change — our brain will allow us to heal, renew, and rewrite the script of our lives.

My mission to help others heal and build self-worth intensified over the last several years as our world's climate shifted dramatically; not just the global climate as in the dramatic weather we have experienced, but also in terms of the condition of our lives. The prevalence of low-self-worth today is staggering and is manifested in the rise in hostility, bigotry, racism, bullying, irrational violence, drug overdoses, and suicides, all of which have exponentially escalated since I began writing this book. I have always understood that those who propagate fear and terror, who malign and abuse others, are deeply troubled themselves.

Each of us can help change this challenging climate. One person at a time. The title of this book, *A Human Mosaic,* is symbolic of the way we develop and change throughout our lives. We never remain the same from moment-to-moment, day-to-day. We are dynamic, multi-dimensional beings whose parts differ in size, shape, and color as our energy shifts throughout our life. The facets of who we are represent our uniqueness as human beings, and it is our uniqueness that contributes to the magnificent tapestry of our world. We each have a pivotal role in diminishing the negativity that exists by modeling behavior that is nonjudgmental, accepting, compassionate, and loving. We can create a movement of optimism and love that will spread to others.

This begins with you, as you evolve to be the best and brightest version of yourself. With an internal reservoir of strength, stability, stamina, and unconditional love, you will have the capacity to survive raging waters that might otherwise drag you down. Self-worth is the lifeline that will keep you afloat, that will enable you to heal from illness or loss, that will fill you with the resilience to recover from and transcend any challenge. When you build positive self-worth, you will develop self-trust, self-respect, and self-love, which will resonate to others. And, then you can share your loving self with the world.

You are A Human Mosaic—The distinct, beautiful blend of multi-colored facets that comprises you.

> To live a meaningful life is our soul's desire.

In Gratitude

A special thank you to those who shared their wisdom and knowledge with me, particularly Dr. Richard Boyatzis, whose research provided me a nexus of understanding about what truly drives thought and behavioral change.

To my amazing editor, Judy Kirkwood, thank you for your wonderful effort and for loving the subject matter. You took what amounted to volumes of writing and reviewed, dissected, pruned, and added precious material to make it all fall into place.

To my publisher, Deeds, thank you for going on this thrilling adventure with me. Cheers to many more!

To my husband, Rick, my Rock of Gibraltar, you are without a doubt, the most genuine, kind, and loyal person I have ever known. I am deeply grateful for your unwavering support, especially during the challenging periods. Your belief in me is etched in my heart, mind, and soul.

To my oldest son, Lucas, your constant encouragement during these years...and years...of writing has meant so much to me. You have taught me things about life from an entirely different perspective, one I had not known before you entered my life. Your voice and energy have inspired me when I needed it most.

To Sophia, my Soul Daughter and lovey, you are the child who was called an old soul even before you could speak. Your wisdom and shining intellect combined with a strong dose of common sense are special gifts that you share with everyone you know. I have valued your opinion heavily during this illuminating journey.

To my youngest son, Colin, I am forever thankful to you for pushing me forward with your motivational boosts and loving heart. You have grown from a boy into a man in the span of time that it took to complete this book. What an extraordinary young man you are, touching all of our lives in uniquely beautiful ways.

To my mother, Patricia, my confidante, you are my go-to person for sage words, truth, wisdom, and unconditional love. Your resplendent love is the melting pot that brings us all together as one. You are my closest friend and the most meaningful support system, for this I am eternally grateful.

To Sharon, my sister-friend, we have been through a lot of highs and lows during the last thirty years, supporting one another through each one; our friendship is stronger than ever. Thank you for all of your support and standing by my side.

To my dear Amy, you have been a shoulder to lean on and are the most selfless, generous person I know. You are my own loving Mother Teresa, and for you I am deeply blessed.

To the Reader

How you value yourself—your sense of self-worth—is the foundation for the quality of your life. The greatest gift you can give yourself, and the world, is to accept who you are. If this has been difficult—no matter the reason—it is possible to change the way you feel about yourself at any age or stage of your life. You deserve to feel amazing about who you are, to believe that your life matters, and that you are here on earth for a reason.

Live your most fulfilling, meaningful life by learning how to love, honor, and care for yourself through building positive self-worth; by creating inner peace for yourself that will flow out to others; and by committing to practices that will lead to enduring transformative change.

I did it and so can you.

Introduction

When I finally decided that enough was *ENOUGH*, that this way of living had to end, I was stark naked—pale, frail, pill-filled—Zoloft, Effexor, Lexapro, in that order, Ambien nightly, with liquor-for-my-meal-plan, anchored to my bed, and to borrow my youngest son's phrase, in perpetual "Lala land." I had been that way for a long time after my father died.

But, on this particular morning, sweet Amy, my dear, dear friend for decades, stopped by unannounced (she knew I would be there because I never left the house). Ringing the doorbell multiple times, she switched to knocking, then ringing, then knocking harder. I tried to ignore it. I was alone and not expecting anyone. I never answered the door these days, nor the phone; I was hiding. Pulling the comforter over my head, I hoped the noise blasting at my brain would stop. Loving, tenacious Amy, however, was on a mission. The phone rang, guess who? Amy. "Huullow," I answered in a low, hoarse voice. "Open your damn door or I'll huff and I'll puff, and I'll kick your door down!" "Okay, okay," I responded. As lousy as I felt, I knew Amy too well, she would never give up.

I threw on my mother's light blue sweat shirt over baggy gray sweat pants and slowly made my way down the stairs to the front door. Every step was a conscious effort. "Hurry up!" She yelled through the window by the front door as she watched me; that huge smile of hers melted everyone who was fortunate enough to know her. "What—are you ninety-nine years old or something?" She mocked me as I reached the door and opened it. "Oh, my fricken... Oh my, mother of…goodness gracious, shit almighty…I'm so sorry sweetie, but you look like death. I don't want to be mean, but you look like you've been in a concentration camp." She looked at me pitifully. I stood still as she marched past me, her arms were filled with baskets and trays, with a large bag hanging from her shoulder that was over-flowing. She placed them on the island in the kitchen and returned to her car a few more times to retrieve other stuff. I would have felt overwhelmed and self-conscious had it been anyone but Amy. She is in her own category of special.

Amy is my Mother Teresa, the name I fondly gave her when we were in our twenties. She is someone on whom I rely for strength and wisdom. Amy is love and all things good in one human being. And, she is dependable in ways that many people in my life have not been. Amy says what she means and means what she says. I count on her for the absolute and blunt TRUTH, which means a lot to a person when they're down. Everyone else had been soft on me because they knew I was suffering, but Amy has a knack for telling you how it really is — something real and raw without hurting your feelings. Quite a remarkable gift, one shared by very few. She could say, "You're a lazy bitch," and follow it up with, "Dear Anne, there are times when we all need to be lazy and nurture ourselves. I understand how you feel."

Amy looked at me with tenderness as I sat my boney body down. She was speeding around my kitchen, handling platters labeled with preparation instructions—heat to 375 degrees, covered, for forty-five minutes—and doing what she does best—taking over when you need it most. "Darling," she looked at me with her large, jade-green eyes and said, "I love you, but you look horrible. Now let's fix this…this *situation* by filling you with lots of comfort food and a large dose of Amy's honey pie." Her "honey" pie had multiple meanings, both literal and figurative.

When Amy finished organizing her extravagant feast, taking plenty of time to explain what I—or someone—needed to do with the dishes she had prepared, she gave me her impassioned speech on how to regain my health. "I'll do my best," I responded in an effort to end the loving lecture. I knew that she meant well, but I was having trouble listening to imperative statements such as, 'You need to take care of yourself.' 'You have to eat and sleep better.' 'How long do you think you'll feel this bad?' Really? There is a timeframe for grieving? This one, though, was the kicker, the one that really turned me upside down: 'Your father is in a better place.' *Better* place? Better place for him? For me? No, he would rather be alive. And, I want him back.

After Amy left, I walked straight back up to my bedroom and looked at myself in the mirror. A person with a long, thin, gaunt, strained face and NO eyes was looking back at me. Where were my eyes? It was a strange, unsettling feeling not to be able to identify with my reflection. Yet, as detached as I was, I noticed something. I was feeling something, even though what I felt was disturbing. It was, at least, a feeling. I had been mourning my father's death for so long that I had lost sight of who I was. I was disconnected with myself and my life.

What struck me right then was that my beloved father's death triggered a deeper anguish within me. Losing my father, my soulmate and best friend, was dreadful, but I lost more than my father. I lost the one person in my life that I believed loved me unconditionally. I lost my safety net. Who was I without him to prop me up, to give me the praise I desperately craved? My dad had been my sage mentor and lifelong protector. He was my hero and the conductor of my life. My lifeline was cut when he died. The image I saw in the mirror that day reflected a lost soul.

I crawled back into bed and tried to nap, but the words, *lost soul*, kept murmuring in my brain. Shivering under my comforter, I realized something profound about myself. It was not a matter of being lost, or that my soul had vanished into lala land. The truth was that the foundation supporting me throughout my life had shattered. I was fractured in so many places from the intense fall that I had no perspective of who I was any longer. Or did I ever? My father's death stripped me to the bone, and all of my facades and defense mechanisms died with him.

Later that evening, I thought about the depth of sorrow I felt. My father would no longer be here to lean on, to love me unconditionally, to be the apple of his eye. No longer did I have someone to prove how successful, intelligent, and knowledgeable I was. Yet, if I had been trying all my life to please my father, striving for excellence to win his praise and admiration, who was I? Was I *that* person or was I *trying* to be *that* person? Would I have achieved all that I had without a father who pushed me? What is my motivation in life if I don't have my father's ever-present interest and unfailing support to depend on?

Something was stirring within me. I was beginning to awaken, to slowly allow thoughts to enter without frantically squelching them. As I began noticing the thoughts, I asked myself questions that would be pivotal to my healing, and, to the rest of my life. Why had I been living in the grave with my father? What was I afraid to unearth? What was I hiding from? I was—at long last—opening the blackout shades in my brain and allowing light to enter.

I realized something quite remarkable. I knew that the only one who could help me was me. At that moment, I made a decision. I refused to continue attending my own pity-party, to be sad all the time—little orphan Annie, a defenseless victim, and the target of others who fed on my fears and insecurities. I wanted to be free of the arrows piercing me in the most vulnerable areas of my body and brain, continually reminding me of who I wasn't, what I couldn't do, or hadn't done. I recognized at that point that I had never lived in harmony with my inner core self. My father's passing and my response to losing the pillar of strength, the lion of my life, exposed significant issues about myself that I had long been suppressing.

This was the intersection of my life. I had to choose which way I would go, whether to continue as I was or change and bring myself back to life. The fact that I had three young children gave me the inspiration. Enough was enough. It was time to start living again. I didn't have my father to be my navigator any longer, to lean on as my crutch. I accepted that this was a path I had to walk myself.

Part One: What Is Self-Worth and Why Is It so Important?

The work to build my self-worth began that day. I decided that I would invest the time and effort to develop practices to heal my wounds and rewrite the narrative of my life so that I could live with inner peace and joy. The result of my effort is what you will find in this book. Please do not feel you have to do everything I did to heal. You may choose which practices you like best and which are a better fit for your personality.

The most important step you can take to transform how you feel about yourself is to develop your own internal pillar, your inner source of strength and sustenance, and become your own best advocate and friend. There will be challenges during your life, however, by building self-worth, you will have the resilience and inherent power to heal, recover, and renew.

I believe wholeheartedly, dear reader, that if you travel this journey with me, it will change your life.

You Matter

"You yourself, as much as anybody in the entire universe, deserve your love and affection."
Buddha

You have one life. One life. That's all, at least here on earth.

Every facet of who you are and how you live your life is filtered through your internal sense of self: how worthy you believe you are, the value you place on yourself as a human being. How you feel about yourself is the lens by which you view everything in your life—so your lens needs to be sharp and clear. Every relationship and interaction, your mental, emotional, physical, and spiritual health is permeated by your belief about yourself.

You may not know what your purpose is yet, but we each have one. We all have something to contribute to the grand scheme of things. Being alive gives you the freedom to pursue anything you desire, to define yourself anyway you wish. The energy we collectively contribute to the universe has meaning and substance. Each one of us has a role to positively impact our world.

Robert F. Kennedy said that each time a person "stands up for an ideal, or acts to improve the lot of others, or strikes out against injustice, he sends forth a tiny ripple of hope, and crossing each other from a million different centers of energy and daring, those ripples build a current that can sweep down the mightiest walls of oppression and resistance." You have the power within you to affect change in the world in ways you may not even realize.

But first, you must believe in yourself, feel at peace with who you are, and stop oppressing your own abilities. Learning to like who you are — LOVE — who you are, is worth striving for because it will change your life. Believing in yourself, knowing that you are going to be fine no matter what, frees you to pursue things you never would have thought possible.

When you discover, accept, and own yourself as you are—instead of devaluing yourself because of past experiences or comparing yourself to others' successes or expectations of you—you will lead a purpose-driven life that is more satisfying than anything wealth or external accomplishments provide.

Self-worth is the belief that you are worthy. That no matter what happens—and a lot happens in life—whether it is good or bad, when you make mistakes, feel sad or joyful, when you fail or succeed, you know unequivocally that your life matters. That you matter.

It sounds simple. But it is a hard concept to grasp for many of us whose self-worth was damaged by parents, caregivers, or bullies when we were children. Some who struggle with self-worth may have been born into environments that devalued them. Even if we reached early adulthood with our self-worth intact, family expectations as well as cultural cues for what is "normal" can affect how we see ourselves. And with aging and enduring challenging events, we are given a whole new set of challenges to our self-worth.

Far too many people live their entire lives not knowing that they can transform themselves. They believe that they are stuck as they are, with sharp thorns that are constant reminders of painful events. This is not the case. Anyone can change. You have the ability to release these wounds and replace them with positive thoughts. You have the power to alter your thoughts and impact your behavior. Each moment of each day offers a fresh template, an opportunity to learn new ways of thinking and feeling.

Change is difficult and can feel overwhelming. That is why so many people give up on their goals. Don't walk away and abandon the one life you've got by giving up on it. You can design your future any way you wish if you connect with your inner core being and live in alignment with who you really are.

Building your self-worth so that you can feel strong enough to be yourself, to act on your beliefs and intentions, and meet the goals you set for yourself, is the most important mission of your life.

Why is this the most important mission of your life? You are here on earth to evolve, to learn, to treat others with kindness and compassion, and to form meaningful bonds with those you care about. When you suffer from low self-worth, your intrinsic energy is depleted by the negative thoughts that are occupying valuable space in your brain. These internal thoughts erode the natural beauty of your life by clouding your vision and blocking your ability to live with joy. When you feel inadequate, you are not able to enjoy the moment-to-moment pleasures of being fully aware and present to your life. Even life's big events are diminished by how you feel about yourself.

Having gone through the process of uncovering, discovering, and recovering my own self-worth, I will walk you through the steps as we move into the sections in this book. Humans are designed to be lifelong learners when we operate at our optimum level. It is never too late to change.

"The most common way people give up their power is by thinking they don't have any," said Alice Walker, African American novelist, poet, and activist. It is time to claim your birthright, your reason for being.

The fact that you were blessed to be born is meaningful and significant.

Let us begin.

My Own Search for Self-worth

"The wound is the place where the Light enters you."

Rumi

Who am I to be telling you that your life matters and that you can change?

I am someone who has very possibly walked in your shoes, who has given up multiple years of my life to internal suffering and decided to do something about it. I am you, my friend. Our circumstances may be different, but if you are reading this, there is a good chance you grew up questioning your self-worth or became challenged later in your life due to troubling events.

Since I was a young girl I have made self-worth my area of study because I had to do something about how I was feeling. My lens by which I viewed the world was damaged, but I didn't know why. Why was I distrustful, insecure, and forever seeking to be loved and accepted, despite my academic, athletic, social, and business accomplishments? I was the person everyone thought was confident, independent, sophisticated, intelligent, and successful—the woman who had it all. This is how it appeared on the outside.

The outside me, how I behaved outwardly to the world, was the external manifestation of my incessant need to prove to myself—and everyone in my life—that I was successful. Why was "success" so critically important to me? Success was actually the window dressing—it was what was behind the success that mattered most to me—in my mind, success meant I was liked and admired. Success to me meant that I was valuable, smart, an integral component of society. It was the surest route to receiving acceptance and praise. I was consumed by the need to be needed, a starving tiger doggedly seeking whatever scraps of recognition and affirmation I could find.

How did I get here? When and why did I turn against myself?

A Brief History

I have been writing this book since I was a child. I have refined what I have to offer in terms of guidance through years of study and interviews with experts. I have learned an immense amount by coaching people just like you—and me—to value themselves, to trust themselves, to live authentically as who they are, and not as who they think they should be.

When I was six years old, I started keeping a diary in which I would analyze everyone I knew. Eventually I had 31 diaries. My father realized I was not only a precocious writer, but that I was delving deep into people's characters. Even at such a young age I wanted to be a psychiatrist. My father, who believed in pulling yourself up by your bootstraps and carrying on—did not favor psychiatry or psychology—gave me the book *The Making of a Psychiatrist* (1972) by David Viscott, thinking it would turn me off from psychiatry. I was not equipped, of course, to understand such a sophisticated work, but I pretended to take it in. I was thrilled he was taking seriously my fascination with the minds of people and what makes them who they are. Studying others led to facing—and solving—my own difficulties with self-worth.

Let's back up for a snapshot of my upbringing. I was born in Santiago, Chile, where I lived until I was six. Dad was a global executive with Ford Motor Company at the time. He and my mother had previously lived in Belgium, Scandanavia, Cuba, and Puerto Rico, and led a glamorous international existence.

My two brothers and I had the privilege of living in several countries which exposed us to many cultures. But in my early years, this meant I was often left with maids who perceived me as another chore on their list.

Several early traumas stand out. You may know how it feels when you are very young and the tightwire you're straddling suddenly breaks. The fall is hard and fast, but the complications afterwards are long-lasting and deep. Routine events are processed in our brain with a minimum of detail, but emotional or traumatic experiences are recorded with vivid detail and clarity. As a hypersensitive child living in a volatile environment, I have always had incredible recall of past experiences.

At the age of three and a half in Santiago, I remember the tangerine-tinged sunlight as I sat cross-legged on the floor of my bedroom. I had two small, raggedy baby dolls in my lap that our live-in maid, Elena, had given me. I looked around my room trying to find something more exciting to do.

Puffs of gray dust and black cat hair underneath the chair next to my bed caught my eye for a moment until I remembered something. When I couldn't fall asleep at night—which was most nights since I was always energetic and full of curiosity—the maids or my mom would give me baby candy to soothe me. It was kept on top of my bureau.

I pushed a chair across the wood floor and climbed onto it. I opened two of the bureau's drawers that were at waist level and used them as a ladder to boost myself to the top. There it was! I grabbed the bottle, opened it easily, as there were no child safety locks then, and began pouring the little tablets into my hand. I ate them one by one.

After finishing the entire bottle, which only took a few minutes, I sat looking around my room. I'd never seen it from that vantage point. Rays of sun drenched the room in a yellowy-orange color that reminded me of the taste of the baby candy.

Footsteps approached after a while. Elena peered in, saw me perched up on top of my bureau, empty bottle still in my hand, and shrieked. She screamed for her sister, Graciela. Seizing me from the bureau, Elena gripped my arms as Graciela called my mother, who was at the Prince of Wales country club playing golf.

My mom's close friend, Sheila, drove us to the hospital in a panic as my mother, who held me tightly on her lap, trembled and wept, while she blamed Elena and Graciela: "How could they? Leaving her alone long enough to swallow an entire bottle! They'll be fired! They'll be gone by tonight!"

At the hospital, I watched the doctor holding a long plastic tube in his hands before he stuck it down my throat. My mother's fingers were spiked talons pinning my arms down by my side. Other hands were all over me, forcing me down into the mattress. I felt like I was sinking, drowning, until waves of nausea catapulted me back into my body, my vision blurred, and everything went black.

Elena and Graciela were not fired, but certainly treated me differently after that incident. I was told over and over that I was very naughty and greedy to take so much baby aspirin and get them in trouble. But I never heard anything said to the maids about leaving me alone for so long without checking on me.

All I knew was that I had done something terribly wrong, behaved badly, and that Elena and Graciela suffered as a result. Their transgression became my burden. Why hadn't I been more careful? I must try to be better.

We moved to Rye, New York, when I was six, so my father could work for David Rockefeller in Manhattan. Perhaps because of my intelligence and my old-soul nature, I was inordinately close to my handsome father, who treated me like an equal. He was brilliant, had gone to Yale, had several business degrees, and spoke seven languages. I enjoyed his company more than anything else in the world.

My mother was jealous of our relationship, and I don't blame her. It was hard to reconcile my mother's justified feelings of betrayal about my father's numerous affairs and his denials, even though I knew he was lying to her. I watched my mother suffer for many years with numerous nervous breakdowns.

To the world, being born into my family appeared enviable and I knew I was fortunate that my parents were wealthy, and that they stayed together, as dysfunctional as that was. That's why it was so important for me to be smart, strong, and accomplished, the golden girl. And, above all, never question my good fortune.

Next, we moved to Akron, Ohio, where my father took on various high-level positions with Goodyear. I hated living there.

I was bullied for sixteen months. Nothing was done by anyone to stop it or address its impact upon me. My self-worth was shredded. My innocence and trust had already been replaced by a world-weary acceptance of how things were in my family. But this was beyond my comprehension. I was a young girl on the cusp of a breakdown. I was so good at being good, however, no one suspected.

What happened: I had a friendship with two girls who lived in my neighborhood and attended school with me. A new family moved to town with a daughter who was older than me. I adored her as she was mature and more interesting than the other two girls. Because I began spending my time with the older girl, the other two turned against me. I knew they were mad, but I didn't realize the extent of their anger until the three of us were at a sleep away camp for two weeks.

The terrorizing began the moment my parents dropped me off. The girls took my toothbrush and dipped it in mud, sprayed deodorant all over my blanket, hid grotesque things under my covers, stole my pillow case and wiped it with mud and shit—probably their own—and many other disgusting acts. They turned the entire cabin of campers against me, telling them lies about me, whispering to one another and pointing at me. When I wrote my parents letters describing their behavior, they found my letters and tore them up. They came up with new and heinous ways to torture me every single day. When Parents Weekend came, I told my parents everything. My mom begged me to return home with them, but I was not going to cave in to the girls' bullying. I handled it in the stoic way I knew my father would want me to.

I stuck it out for the entire session, immersing myself in sports, excelling in archery, tennis, horseback riding, and every activity to escape their terror. I handled the bullying as best I could by ignoring it and internalizing what was deeply painful. I felt as if my heart was being torn apart by their vicious fingers; I was an alien who had no place of comfort.

Outwardly strong, the taunts penetrated into every cell of my body. It went on after the summer into the school year. The two girls turned all the "popular" kids against me, telling them things like I ate my boogers while picking my nose and I didn't wipe myself after I peed or pooped, and other terrible lies. They loathed me, but I never understood why.

The worst part was the loneliness. You think that maybe this is it for your life, your happy feelings are dead, and you're now damaged goods. How was I to know that I could heal or find support to lean on? That dreadful time in my life eradicated any innocence left in me. My ability to trust was annihilated, and I became highly self-critical—not surprising after being unfairly maligned.

Bullying back then was not an open topic of discussion as it is today. What took place that summer and the following year was never addressed by anyone. I was expected to move on, to get past it, without any knowledge of how to manage the lesions inside of me. I held onto the humiliation for decades and didn't trust anyone, even as I advanced in my career in communications and marketing.

Today bullying is a widespread problem, exacerbated by social media. Children have not been taught how to handle the onslaught of disturbing comments directed at them. Unless you have been a victim, it is hard to understand the terribly deep and painful wound it causes a person's psyche, as well as the long-term injurious effects. I experienced less radical forms of bullying later in my life, more accurately described as maltreatment from people I worked with or knew socially, including blatant sexual harassment.

Even as an adult, I did not know how to handle unjustified smears or unpleasant advances from men, other than immerse myself at work and suck it up. The painful splinters that festered inside of me occupied too much meaningful space, yet I carried on the only way I knew. Deal with it. Leave it unexamined even though you are miserable.

My dad's death in 2002 was cataclysmic for me. After being hit by the drunkest drunk driver that ever drank, he lived a few more years, until a cardiologist screwed up on a minor procedure that left him brain dead. Taking him off life support was something I refused to consider but was over-ridden by his living will and my family's boxing me into a corner I never saw coming.

I plummeted into a depression that lasted more than two years. When I began to awaken from the greatest heartache I'd ever experienced, I was not the same person. I saw a frail lost soul in the mirror, 98 pounds of fragility. I had a husband and three children. I knew I could not survive if I continued to internalize my suffering. I also knew I could not blame my adult struggles on the pendulum swings of my chaotic childhood. My system of disconnecting the external me from the internal me that had begun in my childhood had been my standard operating procedure my entire life. I gave it a name, my *Outer-Inness*. I viewed myself, my entire existence, from the outside in, based on what people wanted me to be, and what I thought I had to be to be accepted and liked. This outwardly focused mindset developed from my birth forward. What I once believed about myself internally was supplanted by what I thought I needed to be to please others and be accepted.

As a young child, I didn't have the coping skills to manage my internal anxiety and insecurity, as few of us do, so I contrived my own interpretation of events, especially those I considered hurtful. When what was happening around me was threatening, I'd channel it inwardly, as a protective mechanism. I became adept at hiding my emotions and never permitting myself to appear vulnerable or insecure. In fact, I went overboard to present an image of strength. I played the role of the person I believed I *should* be—smart, vibrant, outgoing, confident—storing how I really felt about myself in a place where no one would uncover my true identity.

How I felt internally did not align with my external attitude and behavior. You might recognize a similar pattern within you when you do something that doesn't feel right. Internally, you feel out-of-step with your actions; your external behavior is not congruent with your core values or beliefs. My outward persona and my inward, private trove of thoughts were not in sync.

This divide between who we are internally and how we behave externally creates a tension within us that perpetuates our low self-worth. It creates constant friction that stems from being out of harmony with our innermost self.

You will experience subtle signs such as when you have second thoughts about a decision or action, or you might experience as I did a physical symptom such as anxiousness or discomfort. It shows up differently in each person. Some people have told me that their inner tension does not permit them to live in the moment, to feel fully engaged in their activities. Others avoid making decisions as they are not sure what is best for them. Some notice that their temperature rises, or their hands shake. My inner tension manifested itself very early in life through severe stomach aches. This was my ongoing physiological response to emotional duress for decades of my life. *These mental, emotional, and physical symptoms are signals that alert you to the fact that you are conflicting with your authentic nature.*

Where do these mind-draining issues originate? We aren't born into the world feeling confused about our identity.

Discord between our inner and outer self develops early in life. It is a result of societal expectations placed upon us by our earliest role models in tandem with the way we interpret these expectations. When who we are in our inner core being differs with who we think we ought to be, our identity is obscured by colliding messages in our brain. This internal disparity causes the tension inside of us.

It's not that my situation was graver than many others who have suffered. The fact was that I needed to feel better about myself because my past experiences and how I felt internally had cast a dark, ever-present shadow on my life, always lurking, even during presumed "happy" moments. And, I couldn't find a viable source to help me reconcile what I was feeling.

I had always been a problem solver. But, this problem—that was ruling my life and robbing my joy—was one that eluded me. The only way I knew to handle my inner turmoil was to suppress it with as much force as I could muster. With time, it became an automatic pattern in my brain to restrain my inner thoughts and emotions and allow only my outward self to exist in the world.

What we suppress never disappears. It stays inside of us creating unnecessary tumult. This was not how I envisioned my life to unfold. I was filled with contradictions that caused unrelenting anxiety and doubts. Confusion about who I was and who I wasn't, what was real and what was fictitious, eclipsed my days and disrupted my nights.

How are you supposed to live "in the moment" or "be present" to your life when you aren't sure about who you are, and, frankly, are more concerned with who you should be? It is not possible to live with self-awareness and self-understanding if you're not living as your true being. As you age, you learn to live with this friction inside of you because you don't think there is anything you can do about it—this is just the way it is, even though it never feels quite right.

Who was I really? I didn't feel like an authentic human being. It was not that I was living as an imposter, quite the contrary, I was battling with myself to sort through the ambiguity of living with conflicting thoughts. I felt as though I was a mathematical fraction, the denominator was the outside me, the larger value, the one I portrayed to others, and the numerator was the real me, my innermost self, which I kept hidden. If I were portraying myself as someone other than "me" was I even a good person? These questions filled me with increasing internal anxiety. How could I live, as the expression goes, the best possible life, with these thoughts cycling and recycling through me?

I struggled with the question of what I was worth because in my mind, I didn't know whether I was worthy or not worthy. If I didn't know who I was, then how could I live a fulfilling life? Was I only worthy when I was on my A-game, doing everything to the best of my ability to please everyone in my life, performing for others to receive the applause that I craved in order to measure up to my own inordinately high standards? Was there anything special about me that wasn't a product of my attempts to be thought of as special? And, if anyone learned that I wasn't the outside me, that I was only a fraction of what I portrayed, would I even be loved?

This was a profound existential dilemma. Not knowing who you really are is a strange and isolating space in which to live. What felt worse was being aware that my behavior was incongruent with my core self, but I didn't have the courage or knowledge to do anything about it. This mindset resulted in layers of internal discrepancies—as though I was trapped in a never-ending maze within another never-ending maze.

Although successful on the outside, I felt trapped by superficial, judgmental, societal modes of self-evaluation. How could I truly know myself when my entire perspective was from the outside in? I was only as good as my last accomplishment. This was a tenuous way to live for four decades of my life. It took a lot of ups and downs—a lot more downs—to make me understand that nothing outside of myself would heal the wounds inside of me.

After my father's death, when I began coming out of my grief, I realized that I based how I felt about myself on my "performance" in life: what I did well, what I didn't do well, how I looked, how smart I was, who liked me and who disliked me. As I performed for others, and also for myself, the admiration I received that kept me afloat was like a co-dependent narcotic that fueled my duality. The more I succeeded, the more recognition I garnered from others, the greater my addiction to be a high achiever. The narcotic was a powerful form of self-disguise. An addiction that dominates your life stunts your mental, emotional, and spiritual wellbeing.

I was vulnerable to anything and everything that flew in my direction, whether it was aimed at me or not. This meant that I could be feeling wonderfully on a particular day, yet if I came across someone who was rude—even if it didn't have anything to do with me—it ruined my day. Up and down...up and down...with no neutral ground. My interpretation of what I thought someone thought about me took precedence over how I felt about myself. Even though I realized that if I permitted every comment or action to topple me I would never feel stability, I didn't do anything to change.

Honestly, I didn't think I could change. No one ever told me that a person didn't have to suffer throughout their life because of past trauma. I thought I was a done deal.

So, this was it for me? This was a startling realization for someone who had always viewed herself as introspective and deep, and well versed in psychology and human behavior.

Clearly, this was an unhealthy approach to dealing with my emotions. It intensified dramatically after my father's death because no one knew me as well as he did. Moreover, it was unsettling that my Outer-Inness was not apparent to anyone. No one close to me had any clue about the carefully manufactured veneer I had polished for many years.

I had been to psychologists, but it had not been effective for me. One renowned psychotherapist to whom I was referred fell asleep—well, he nodded off, long enough to start snoring—during my two-hundred-dollar session! Evidently, my issues were too trivial to hold his attention. When he realized he had slipped into a comfortable snooze, he shook his head and looked at me with half-open, bloodshot eyes, and, without apologizing, told me that his typical clients were psychopaths, pedophiles, and schizophrenics. Silent pause. *What an asshole,* I thought to myself. He could have made that clear to me prior to the appointment and the long drive to his musty, gloomy office. Suddenly the chair on which I was sitting felt uncomfortably hard. At that point, Dr. Sleepy started yawning—the biggest, deepest open mouth-tunnel I'd ever seen was in my face, disrespectfully breathing disinterested, foul air my way. "I see," I said. "And, by sharing this information with me, I'm supposed to feel better?" He FELL ASLEEP while I was talking. The ultimate rejection.

So, that was the end of my patience with seeking guidance from someone else. I know many amazing psychologists and psychotherapists, however, I did not find the magic chemistry with the ones I encountered.

I found no process or system to follow that helped me feel differently about myself. There was no book, model, mentor, seminar, pill, drink, procedure, friendship, husband, sibling, parent, child, exercise, or hobby that could teach me how to build positive self-worth. I realized only I could transform my opinion and belief about who I was so that I could live without the tension of my Outer-Inness.

Although there were plenty of articles on things one could do—setting goals, having purpose, being intentional, having gratitude, focusing on strengths, meditation, exercise, proper nutrition, and numerous other action steps, these were not addressing my internal thoughts. I had a whistle blower inside of me that stole my joy and was a constant reminder of who I wasn't. I couldn't figure out what I could do to soothe my pain and feel that my life was meaningful.

One day when the awful turmoil within me was eating away at my soul, I was in my office and noticed Carl Rogers' book on my desk, *On Becoming A Person*, which was one of my favorite texts in a psychology course in college. I began re-reading it. I highlighted every single part that applied to my personal experience. I truly believed Rogers was talking to me directly through his prose. Then I turned to Carl Jung's, *Memories, Dreams, Reflections*, and this quote jumped out at me:

"Your vision will become clear only when you can look into your own heart. Who looks outside, dreams; who looks inside, awakes."

I copied this quote and taped it onto my desk as a reminder of how important it is to one's life to be in tune with your soul.

I didn't ask others for help. I didn't have anyone I believed understood me well enough to seek their advice. I began my own existential and spiritual submersion to adjust my perspective of my self-worth. As a professional, I was strategic, creative, and innovative. Why not put those skills to use in my quest to deprogram and retrain myself? As soon as I realized I could figure this out and find a way to transcend the inner tumult by replacing it with peace and beauty, growing from the inside out, I began to feel better.

This process of change would be my Soul Detox, a holistic journey of healing, in which my mind, body, and spirit would be cleansed by releasing toxic thoughts and negative memories, enabling me to open up and freely take in all of the spectacular opportunities and blessings that life has to offer.

I prepared a framework for myself, which I share with you in this book, that enabled me to take the negative experiences that had occurred in my life and release them from that fortress in my brain. Using that same framework, I replaced the negative thoughts with practices that generated positive thinking in order to enlist my brain in changing my life.

The Impact of Experiences on Self-Worth

Just as our brain stores new skills through repetition when we are young, such as how to crawl or jump rope, it also has the capacity to hold onto negative thoughts and patterns of behavior. With enough time and repetition, these thoughts and actions are etched in our neural pathways and absorbed into long-term memory where they remain for as long as we allow them. We know from an abundance of research on the human brain that negative thoughts and habits have a damaging impact on our brain and affect our overall health. With this base of understanding, I realized that negativity can be released and transcended by new patterns of thinking and feeling. I discuss this in more detail later in the book.

On a brighter note, positive experiences also factor into our development. Favorable, loving interactions and experiences have a positive and powerful impact on our self-worth. These instill us with comfort as well as appropriate coping skills to deal with those not-so-pleasant aspects of life. Every interaction and event—positive or negative—contributes to how we feel about ourselves.

Your time and investment in building your self-worth will change you in ways you never imagined.

One beautiful outcome is that our past suffering can become a conduit to compassion for ourselves and others. There is nothing more satisfying than to live in the world as your true self, knowing that your life has value and worth.

Let's walk together on the path to self-discovery and self-understanding, self-acceptance, self-trust, and self-love, so that we are capable of creating a healthy awareness of ourselves, which is intrinsic to positive self-worth.

Part One: What Is Self-Worth and Why Is It so Important?

Note: Before diving into the process of developing positive self-worth, it is important that you have a basis of knowledge about what is involved in learning to fully accept and love who you are and reconnect with your innermost Soul Self. These next series of sections are the building blocks that are necessary to establish the foundation prior to beginning The Practices, the daily applicable exercises to retrain your brain and build healthy self-worth.

Part One

What Is Self-Worth and Why Is It so Important?

Defining Self-Worth

"Peace comes from within. Do not seek it without."
Buddha

What is self-worth? At the most basic level, self-worth is how you view your innermost self. It is the belief that you are a good person who should be treated with respect. Self-worth is the lens by which you view everything in your life. Your opinion of yourself pervades into every aspect of your life.

Why is self-worth so important? Every facet of who you are and how you live your life is filtered through your internal sense of self—how worthy and lovable you believe you are—the value you place on yourself as a human being. How you feel about yourself affects the nature of your relationships. Your sense of who you are not only impacts you, it also affects everyone with whom you interact. It affects how you feel in the morning and when you go to sleep at night. It has a heavy bearing on your energy and enthusiasm, what you accomplish at work, how you respond to critical comments, how fast you heal from injury, and how you handle life's challenges.

We are not raised to think about nurturing our inner core self; we are characterized by others by our behavior, our external self. With time, we learn to view ourselves by our external self, what we do, not how we feel and think.

A gripping example illustrating the dichotomy that develops between our internal and external self became public when an enormously successful athlete chose to discuss his personal experience with low self-worth.

Several years ago, I read an article in *Sports Illustrated* about how Michael Phelps suffered from a deep depression during which he contemplated suicide. How could this phenomenal gold medal swimmer—the best ever—feel anything but confident and assured? After years of rigorous training, winning many medals, and being considered the world's greatest swimmer, he was thinking about ending his life. As famous and decorated as Phelps was, when he was away from the spotlight with time to reflect on who he was and how he felt about himself, the thoughts he'd kept to himself left him feeling hopeless.

Phelps spoke about his feelings, stating, "I had no self-confidence, no self-love." For Phelps, despite all his success, when he wasn't in the public eye competing and winning, he was overwhelmed by a sense of despair from years of blocking his "negative emotions," as he called them. Phelps was open about his struggle with low self-worth, which in my eyes dignified him further as a heroic human being. The fact that he was candid with the world about his mental and emotional challenges enables others to understand that anyone, even someone seemingly superhuman, can suffer with low self-worth. Phelps had won eighteen gold medals after the London Olympics, and was considered the world's greatest athlete, yet in his core being he was dealing with the heavy burden of unworthiness. His extraordinary talent was a result of his competitive drive and his athletic ability. These were derived from his self-esteem, what he was capable of achieving, but he lacked self-worth.

It is striking that a person appears one way outwardly but is inwardly suffering. None of us know how someone truly feels about themselves, how they value their innermost core being. Siddhartha Gautama, known to the world as Buddha, the spiritual leader and teacher who lived in the 6th century, B.C., once said: "Peace comes from within. Do not seek it without." None of us find lasting comfort or fulfillment outside of ourselves. The seed of our inner joy must be planted within. It flourishes when we learn to nurture ourselves through self-acceptance, self-trust, and self-love—the blooms of self-worth.

Human beings share more similarities than differences. Unfortunately, in our current world, our divisiveness has escalated to an unnerving hostility; an increasing number of people define themselves by issues that are not organic or natural to their nature. The truth is that we are all connected to one another through the evolution of time. We share human qualities that are not defined by values or beliefs. Self-worth is one of these qualities, an intrinsic aspect of who we are and integral to our lives.

Low self-worth has no boundaries. It affects people across the board, regardless of age, gender, socioeconomic status, religion, ethnicity, or culture. It is a common issue among peers, family, colleagues, politicians, actors, athletes, those who appear to have it all, and those who have nothing but the cardboard on which they sleep. Although some are able to conceal it better than others, the negative tug on their psyche is ever-present. Today, with all the volatile issues we face, the importance of healthy self-worth is ever more crucial to short and long-term well-being.

Whether derived from your upbringing and environment, or your personal experiences, low self-worth will make you feel inadequate, unfulfilled, and dissatisfied with life—no matter how successful you are outwardly. Many of us suffer as a result of a distorted view of ourselves based on an overly critical mindset instilled early in life. Anything less than perfect is not acceptable. Low self-worth can also come from comparing ourselves to others and disparaging our own talents and abilities as not good enough. These inner critical thoughts create a negative image within us that blocks our ability to live with joy and feel true peace. But that image is not real.

This distorted image is not who you are but is a false self-perspective you have acquired through life's ups and downs. Think about wearing a pair of eyeglasses with the wrong prescription. You try them on, wear them for a while despite the fact that they don't allow you to see clearly.

Soon you realize you must get the proper prescription that will enable you to see without straining your vision. This makes all the difference in the world. When you don the new eyeglasses—crisp, clean, focused vision gives you self-assurance that you won't be driving in the wrong direction. Why would you choose to live with a view of yourself that is blurred by false beliefs and misguided notions? The fact is that you can remove this self-perspective anytime you desire and opt for vision that is unmarred and luminous.

> A vital point to understand is that you are responsible for your thoughts, and your thoughts are just concepts or ideas floating inside your head. These thoughts are not neccesarily real or truthful. You can choose to change them any moment you desire.

The essence of you exists in your soul, the infinite energy that is you, unencumbered by your critical mindset. Understanding that you have the freedom to transform these negative thoughts within you is the first step in the process of building healthy self-worth.

A Note on the Difference Between Self-worth and Self Esteem

Self-worth is often confused with self-esteem. A person can be proud of his or her achievements (self-esteem), and still feel a lack of internal ful-fillment (self-worth). An easy way to remember how the two terms differ is to think about them this way: self-esteem is about your skills. It relates to your confidence in your competence. It is the outside "you": what you do and how well you do it, how you feel about yourself externally. Self-worth is based on how you feel about yourself internally. It is the inside "you": your soul, or innermost core being. Your self-worth is your field of energy, your spiritual center, and is intrinsic within you.

When someone compliments you on a speech you have given, for example, and you feel good that you made a positive impression or touched someone with your words, knowledge, and interpretation of the subject, that's self-esteem. When you feel good about articulating your words, knowledge, and interpretation of a subject in a speech because you feel confident and centered inside and conveyed what you wanted to say no matter how it was received, that's self-worth.

Self-esteem is never enough to replace self-worth. It leaves you vulnerable to events that are not within your control—those unstable, inconsistent issues that arise in everyday life. Living in alignment with your true inner core being—your Soul Self—and enjoying inner peace and equanimity that stem from healthy self-worth is the most meaningful tribute to you, your loved ones, and the universe.

> The essence of self-worth is to know that your life matters.

Transformation Tenets

◇ Self-worth is the value you place on your innermost self.
◇ Low self-worth impacts every facet of your life.
◇ The distorted image of low self-worth impedes your ability to live with inner joy and equanimity.
◇ No external achievement fills the void of low self-worth.

A Human Mosaic Vignette

A Story of Self-Discovery

A few years ago, a former colleague named Sam telephoned me to see how I was doing. After a lengthy conversation, he asked me if I would be willing to coach him. I wasn't expecting that question, but of course I agreed. I had heard from mutual friends that he was extremely successful, running two companies that he created from scratch. Sam is brilliant and amazingly creative in solving complex engineering-related problems.

We met the following week at a coffee shop. Sam is a gentle giant, six feet eight inches tall, and has the softest voice that echoes from his large frame. He looked nervous as we caught up and shared stories about our past work experiences, including his new sizable endeavors. Sam described the evolution of the two companies he founded, one of which was already exceeding projected revenues. But, as we know, money—even an overabundance—doesn't solve personal issues. In fact, at times, it intensifies the issues.

"I know this may sound strange to you, Anne, but as much as I have accomplished with work, I still struggle with a problem that I cannot overcome, no matter what I read or try to do. I am miserably uncomfortable meeting strangers. And, gosh, if I am attending a conference and I walk into a large room filled with people, I become panic-stricken. I have tried all sorts of exercises, but nothing has helped," Sam said in strained words.

We began working together shortly thereafter. Sam is exceptionally disciplined with business matters but has zero discipline about his life outside of work. He was perplexed by the degree of anxiety he held inside and had no clue where it originated. We spent time exploring his childhood and teenage years in an attempt to uncover something that might have occurred in his past that may have contributed to his mental angst.

After several sessions and homework assignments that I developed, Sam shared a story about his high school and college years. "I never fit in with anyone. I was made fun of for my height, and I couldn't play basketball since I wasn't coordinated, so I was pretty much alienated. I spent tons of time by myself. One year I went camping alone, for a very long time, several weeks in fact. I called it my 'controlled homelessness,' because I didn't feel at home anywhere, really. I knew that nature had no way of hurting my feelings or breaking my heart. It was the most peace I have ever felt, yet I was lonely," Sam admitted.

After about nine weeks of working together, and several sessions of role playing, Sam was projecting signs of confidence, indicating that he was much more at ease with strangers since we began working together. I still sensed reticence in his demeanor but knew this was normal. It takes time to change long established patterns of thought. Sam was leaving for a huge convention where he would give a speech, so we spent time working on talking points and practicing strategies on giving a powerful talk.

Shortly thereafter, Sam flew to the convention. The next morning, I began receiving a flurry of texts on my phone: "I need encouragement. I didn't realize there would be more than three hundred executives in the audience. HELP. SOS," his text read. I guided him with deep breathing exercises for several minutes until he said he had calmed down. He needed time to prepare for his speech. We discussed the importance of setting a great tone at the very beginning of a speech, so he needed to be calm and assured that what he had to say was important. I gave him tips for ridding himself of the butterflies and then we ended our conversation.

During our next meeting, Sam said his speech came off without a hitch, and he was thrilled. Then he became somber while changing the subject. He told me that ever since he was a child, he had always felt out of place. This emotion intensified as he grew older and caused a startling alarm to go off in his brain anytime he was in a new place with people he didn't know. "I would think to myself, I'm different, I'm not social, people don't like me, nor are they drawn to me," Sam stated. When we dug deep enough into his early childhood, he recalled being teased by a group of popular kids. They were mean, hurling comments at him that wounded him. He believed he was forever labeled a misfit.

Once Sam was able to understand the root cause of his low self-opinion, he could begin the work to heal himself. If no one, especially parents, teach a child to know they are worthy, to feel they matter, to stand tall in the face of adversity, and believe in themselves no matter what others spew forth, they will be unprepared to deal with bullies whose goal is to injure. Moreover, when a person feels unworthy and they don't know why, it creates ongoing anguish that remains inside of them, sometimes for their entire life. This is what happened to Sam. But, now that he knew what it was that made him feel like an alien, he could begin letting go and learning a new way of thinking about himself.

If you dig deep enough, in a safe environment, you will find a root cause for your low self-opinion. There is a reason for your suffering. And, there are many avenues to help you heal and grow beyond it to a space of comfort and wellbeing. As Sam said to me, "You become your own voice of reason, and learn to lean on yourself during tough times."

The Power of Journaling

"Fill your paper with the breathings of your heart."
William Wordsworth, English Romantic period poet

Before we move further, I highly recommend that you begin keeping a journal, whether it is a physical book, or if you prefer, you can use your computer, tablet, or phone. The most important point to remember is to keep an ongoing record of your thoughts during this period of time.

Now is the time to begin acknowledging your thoughts as they come, listening to them without shoving them away, writing down how you are feeling. Let your words flow out of you without trying to focus on grammar or complete thoughts. This is a practice to take your internal thoughts and put them into words, a process that is highly beneficial as you travel along your quest to build positive self-worth. It is one of the simplest and yet most effective methods of releasing stress and attaining peace of mind.

I have spent all my life detailing my most personal thoughts, emotions, and reflections in journals from the time I was six years old. What I have personally gained from the process of journaling is knowledge of an intimate friend. That friend is me. I have learned so much about myself from writing that I would not otherwise have learned. Writing frees my voice and my soul to tell the truth. I can't always accurately interpret the messages I have written down. Sometimes their value does not emerge until much later. But the act of writing has always given me solace and peace.

Note to Reader: If you notice any extreme thoughts or emotions prior to or while engaging in writing, please seek professional help. The purpose of journaling is to decrease stress and increase focus and energy, so if you feel any trepidation about this exercise, please hold off and seek guidance from a professional.

I have always been drawn to writing as my natural form of self-expression. But anyone can tap into the power of journaling. If you think you are not the type to express how you feel in writing, just try it. Start today. At first it may feel forced, laborious, and strange. But as with all these practices, the more you do it, the easier it is.

Writing about your thoughts is more effective than recording them for clarity and cleansing. When you put your thoughts onto paper or on a computer, you experience an unearthing of information that might otherwise continue to lie dormant in your brain, or that you try to ignore. The act of writing legitimizes what you are experiencing. When you see your thoughts in print, they become real. These aren't delusions or imaginary thoughts, obsessions or fabrications. This is a meaningful exercise as when you see what you feel, you gain insight about the issues that you may have been blocking. You are quite literally and figuratively taking thoughts from your brain where they have been nesting, and concretizing them on paper or computer. Writing also allows you to detach from your emotions, to get separation, and with separation comes perspective, which leads to a better understanding of whatever you are facing. Writing is a practice of self-care; by writing you are honoring your thoughts and emotions.

Journaling is a tool in and of itself to organize your thoughts and record events to which you can always refer. Writing about what you are feeling is also an invigorating experience on its own, in that you are capturing your thoughts, summarizing them, labeling them, and at the same time working through what they mean—their significance and ramifications in your life. My journals were life savers for me. Being able to write down what I was feeling served many functions. Keeping my thoughts in a private place gave me a sense of peace and freedom that comes from letting go without judgment or scrutiny. Writing is also a steadfast confidante during difficult times when I feel uneasy about something. It is fascinating to go back to a journal that I kept when I was in my teens and read excerpts that transport me back to that age with remarkable vividness.

As soon as you begin to form a ritual around journaling, you will find that it is a cathartic practice that helps to detox your soul by liberating your mind of all that you have been storing. When you become accustomed to writing, you will feel emotions of relief and relaxation, as though you have just lifted heavy weights off your shoulders, or have taken a hot shower, or a walk in a beautiful garden on a breezy day. You will form a new positive habit that will support your growth and development and be a companion to you in the future. Another byproduct of journaling is that one day in the future, you will be able to look back at your writing and feel tremendous pride with the commitment you made to yourself to build your inner self.

Susan Sontag, an American writer, filmmaker, philosopher, teacher, and political activist, said "In the journal I do not just express myself more openly than I could to any person; I create myself. The journal is a vehicle for my sense of selfhood." That is what I found as I journaled my way from low self-worth to healthy self-worth. It is the most direct practice in this book. You only have to be able to write; not write well—just write.

Since our work in building self-worth is inwardly focused, being able to express yourself in writing is a venting mechanism, a release valve, that will give you an understanding for how you are feeling in the moment and as you go from day to day. It will also enable you to recognize subtle changes in your behavior.

Within a few short days, you will begin to notice that you will look forward to writing about your accomplishments or any setbacks you might experience. You will feel less encumbered by issues that in the past caused you irritation or upset you. You will have access to perspective that you can review when you need to, and plenty of inspiration to keep going forward. Write for insight, clarity, momentum, as a creative outlet, for free expression, catharsis, stamina, memory, mindfulness, healing, recovery, and rejoicing. Let it all flow out of you, unrestrained.

Writing is an unparalleled vehicle to measure your progress and evaluate what is working and what may not be working. You will be able to look back at your writing and note the growth and transformation that has taken place more easily since it is tangibly captured. I cannot emphasize enough how valuable it is to express your thoughts in writing.

Check out these undeniable benefits of journaling:

◇ Aids Reflection and Detachment. Writing is in and of itself an opportunity to pause, reflect, and detach from your inner drama. Writing about your thoughts is a cognitive action that requires translating and transferring content out of your brain and into the open. Writing down your thoughts and feelings makes them concrete instead of abstract.

◇ Promotes Freedom of Expression. You have the freedom to say anything about yourself—in any fashion—with the confidence that you will not be judged or scrutinized. If you are concerned about privacy, keep your journal in a locked box or in a password protected file on your computer.

◇ Promotes Self-Understanding and Self-Discovery. Your writing can provide amazing clarity and insight into who you are at any given moment. If you are honest, your words will provide fundamental clues to the process of building self-worth. They will also guide you when you get off track and reinforce why you are committed to this process of discovery. You will learn to listen to your thoughts and release them without fear. As you unveil the thoughts onto paper, you will find that you gain greater understanding and respect for yourself and the work you are committed to doing.

◇ Dissipates Emotions, Tension, and Anxiety. Journaling provides a superb dumping ground for unloading everything that troubles you. It is the perfect place to vent. Afterwards, you can recover, reorient, and reinvigorate yourself without having to answer any questions from anyone. Writing takes a tremendous burden from your brain and releases it.

◇ Enables Healing. Many emotional issues that hide in our brain, once expelled, release internal stressors and issues that create anxiety within us. Journaling is a marvelous mode for reducing stress.

◇ Increases Memory. There is a direct correlation between what we think and what we write that strengthens memory. Just as you wrote vocabulary words on notecards to memorize them as a child, when we express ourselves in writing, we are more apt to remember and use that information as fuel in the future. You are helping your brain remain attentive and active.

◇ Constitutes Mindfulness. When you write, you are in the present moment. Writing regularly becomes a kind of meditation. You notice things in your surroundings, as well as in your mind, descriptive details that you would not otherwise absorb. You become an active participant in your life.

◇ Acts as an Inventory. Journaling is an opportunity to take stock of how you are feeling and how you are doing. It is an important time to check-in with yourself during which you can note where you are now versus where you were and where you want to be.

◇ Harnesses Your IQ and EI. Writing in general has been proven to increase your cognitive skills as it improves memory and recall by firing neuron cells in your temporal lobe, strengthening those pathways in your brain. We've already mentioned the wonderful emotional benefits derived from writing. Our Emotional

Intelligence (EI) is refined and enhanced through our awareness of what we are feeling, and the influence these emotions are having upon our lives.

◊ Inspires Tenacity and Self Discipline. Expressing ourselves is a tremendous motivator, driving us toward keeping up with and achieving our short- and longer-term goals. Writing is also a discipline for which you set aside time and focused energy.

◊ Supports Commitment. As you work to build your self-worth, journaling will be a positive pillar of support and strength to turn to whenever you need reassurance, reflection, detachment, or rejuvenation to maintain your commitment to yourself.

◊ Long Term Sustenance. The beauty of writing is that there is no end to it. It is always available to enrich your life at any age or stage.

A character in Bram Stoker's gothic novel *Dracula* says about writing in her journal, "I am anxious, and it soothes me to express myself here. It is like whispering to one's self and listening at the same time." When you write, what you write goes back into your brain when you read it over. Write anything you want in the beginning: fears and frustrations are fine. But once you make journaling a habit, use it to your brain's advantage. Use it to feel calm and peaceful. Use it to understand who you are, and then use it to celebrate who you are. Use it to develop your skills of observation and description. Use it to amuse yourself. But do it. Write. Write. Write.

Protect your Privacy. Whatever modality you use for writing—paper and pen or computer—safeguard your journal from prying eyes. It is for you and only you unless you choose to share a part of it with someone you trust.

Choose a Time and Place for Writing. The classic place for a journal is on the bed stand, which suggests writing before you get up or before going to bed. But if you share a bed, you might not feel as safe and free. Some people find that writing at a table in a coffee shop with the ambient noise in the background makes them feel more private.

Date Every Entry. You will be so glad you did. You can track your progress in building self-worth, and later, when you journal out of habit and love of writing, you can more easily locate entries you want to review.

Write Quickly and Without Hesitation. If you attack the page, or the keys, and keep writing, you may be able to outrun the dreaded internal critic, as well as writer's block. Letting your words pour out also lets spontaneity have the first word, which can be both surprising and entertaining. Later, you can slow down and let your thoughts direct the writing. But for beginners, especially, dive right in! Don't worry about writing in sentences. Use bullet points and list thoughts.

Be in the Moment. If you are lost for words, start with what is going on at the moment. What happened today? How are you feeling right now? Keep writing. Eventually you will break through to what is really on your mind. Do not go back and rewrite or edit.

Be Honest. Write your truth. You are not on trial. Tell it the way you feel it.

Re-read what you wrote. Consider this wonderful quote by John Dewey: "We do not learn from experience, we learn from reflecting on experience."

> Journaling is an opportunity to express yourself honestly, without judgment, and with confidence that your words will support and enrich your work to build healthy self-worth.

Transformation Tenets

◇ Writing is a simple and quick way to unload your emotions and gain distance from them.

◇ Writing is a process that unearths information that you might normally ignore or suppress.

◇ The act of writing legitimizes what you are experiencing.

◇ Writing is cathartic, energizing, reduces anxiety, provides clarity, improves recall and cognitive functions, and enables healing, recovery, and resilience.

Why Self-Worth Matters

"We can never obtain peace in the outer world
until we make peace with ourselves."
The Dalai Lama

As often as I had heard this quote, I never understood how meaningful it was until I faced the fact that no matter what I did or who I knew, how many wonderful friends I had or how physically fit I was, none of it brought lasting contentment. Of course, there were spurts of good times, but those would dissipate, and I would find myself right back to the same spot of disenchantment.

You know how it feels when you are looking forward to a party, a trip, or a new job. You feel energized during that wind-up-time as you prepare for your adventure. There is a spark within you that is fueled by anticipation, the thrill of what could happen. This spark lasts for a period of time, but then you realize the party or new job was not what you had hoped for—the disappointment stings you, and you go back to square one, feeling dissatisfied again. Or, you fall madly in love and marry, believing that this person is the one who will change your life, heal your wounds, and fill all the holes in your heart. But, after several months or years, the chemistry dims, the arguments are more frequent, and what you had thought would be your panacea, disintegrates into strain and strife.

Onward goes the search for what is missing. It's got to be out there somewhere…but it's not "out" there. It is within you. If you have heard this expression multiple times, which most of us have, there is a reason why it keeps reappearing. It is shouting at you to listen to those fundamentally important words: Look within for truth, meaning, peace, and unwavering love. You may not believe it now, but you will find that fulfillment and love for which you thirst when you learn to accept yourself by building your inner world, rather than continue relentlessly seeking gratification and peace in the outer world.

Without positive self-worth, no matter how much you achieve in your life, you will always be seeking to fill the emptiness and dissatisfaction inside of you. That's what I did. Despite success and many other attributes of happy, productive people, I was not happy on the inside.

Throughout the last decades, I asked myself these questions repeatedly as I tried to uncover what was continuing to make me feel bad about who I was.

Why am I distrusting?
Why do I fear rejection?
Why do I feel the need to be the best in everything I do?
Why am I working overtime to please others while ignoring my own feelings?
Why am I on a never-ending quest to fill the void in my life?

Many of us live our lives trying to mask self-doubt and self-loathing by spending money, seeking new relationships, getting a divorce, pursuing weight-loss or plastic surgery, buying a larger house, demeaning others with critical remarks, bullying, gossiping, portraying ourselves as omnipowerful and invincible, always searching for something bigger, better, trying to force thoughts and behavior that still don't improve the way we feel. But none of these external actions heal our internal struggle to define and accept who we are in our true inner beings.

My research and reflection have convinced me that the "bad" that happens in our world comes from those who are fearful and distrusting, insecure and jealous, dominating and destructive—all of which stems from low self-worth. Raising humanity's collective level of self-worth by tending to our own needs to feel fulfilled and happy is the only viable solution to rid our world of what is inhumane and destructive. If we all worked on our self-worth, the world would be a better place for us personally and as societies, cultures, communities, and nations.

As much as we can be a positive force of energy that radiates to others, we cannot control what happens in the world. There will always be disappointments. We will always make mistakes, lose our way, suffer sorrow. Yet if our self-worth is healthy, our ability to manage challenges will be rooted in stability, the certainty that we can work through them.

Had I understood this monumental concept much earlier, perhaps some of the struggles I faced would not have had such a significant impact on me. I wasted so much time on self-deprecating thoughts, feeling inadequate, taking what someone said or did as a personal affront, and not standing up for myself. Somehow, I believed that it was what I deserved. I preferred to internalize my emotions rather than show what I perceived to be "weakness." Although I could always carry on with work and keep up with other professional or social pursuits, these thoughts robbed me of my personal energy. My actions did not reflect the negative image of myself that I held inside. That was my private shame.

One learns from experience and, particularly, from mistakes. Since there were no other resources available that were targeted to my needs, I decided to teach myself how to navigate my mind to a place where I could recognize my own self-worth. When I got to that place, here is what I found.

When you have healthy self-worth...

When you have healthy self-worth, you feel centered and steady. When you don't, things feel out of balance, unsteady, as if you are sliding down a slippery slope with nothing to grab onto that could break your fall.

Healthy self-worth heals, strengthens, sustains, restores, and redefines who you are. It allows you to forgive, permits you to experience the beauty in life, and fills you with inner peace even as the world is in tumult around you.

Healthy self-worth provides unwavering support, fills the void in your heart, and replaces the internal unrest that has followed you through life.

Healthy self-worth is your lifeline when you are being challenged with the loss of a loved one, or when a loved one hurts you.

Healthy self-worth is in all ways positive, powerful, and provides energy, optimism, and vitality when you need it the most.

Healthy self-worth is soulful, spiritual, and reflects self-knowledge.

When you have healthy self-worth, you can project that love and compassion for yourself out into the world as a powerful, positive force for change.

Part One: What Is Self-Worth and Why Is It so Important?

Where Does Self-Worth Come From?

"Every word, facial expression, gesture, or action on the part of a parent gives the child some message about self-worth."
— Virginia Satir, American psychologist and family therapy pioneer

Have you wondered what caused your feelings of low self-worth? By the time we are in our teenage years, we don't ponder that question, rather we fixate on what is wrong with us, and why other people don't treat us the way we want to be treated. We spend valuable time wondering why this person is saying crappy, unfair, stuff about me on social media. Why am I the target of people's anger?

The way you feel about yourself begins forming very early in your life. After birth, infants immediately form new neural pathways in their brain based on how they are treated. The way we were raised has a substantial effect on our self-worth, as do our past experiences. We acquire personality attributes and other strengths and deficits from the genes passed down by our parents and grandparents, but the environment in which we are raised has the greatest impact upon our self-worth—how we value ourselves and whether we feel our life matters.

How you acquired your sense of low self-worth does not have to overshadow and consume your life. Life is about self-discovery and self-understanding. Every day of our lives affords us the opportunity to discover more about who we truly are and develop a clearer understanding of ourselves. We are able to examine the origin of our thoughts and emotions, and to gain clarity about who we are and how we wish to be in order to live the healthiest, most fulfilling life possible. Each day offers a fresh template, an opportunity to learn new ways of thinking and feeling, which we will discover as we journey forward.

It was well into my quest to heal myself that I discovered a fact that had never occurred to me, one that consumed me for a while because it shattered a stigma that had been entrenched in my brain. All the years that I spent blaming myself for how I felt melted away in streams of tears when I finally understood this truism: No child is responsible for his or her low self-worth.

Now I understood that I was not the cause of my low self-worth, which gave me an odd sense of relief, although I was also aware that my constant recycling of self-critical thoughts did not help matters. I was resolved to find a way to develop healthy self-worth, knowing only I could change myself.

Newborns do not lack self-worth. An infant's brain is not yet molded by experiences and relationships at birth. We didn't come into the world with low self-worth. We came into the world wired to trust our first adult caregivers. In fact, self-trust is an important precursor to self-worth, as you will read in the next section. If an infant's needs are ignored from the beginning of life, it will grow into a child, and then an adult, with low self-worth. Learning to trust is a basic developmental stage. Those who were denied the nurturing we all deserve at the beginning of life have a very hard time of ever establishing healthy self-worth, and usually have a spectrum of related health issues.

Similarly, being subjected to verbal, emotional, or physical abuse is crippling to any child's self-worth—clearly through no fault of their own. My third grade teacher, Mrs. Barnes, never liked me. Anyone could be talking during class, but it would be me that she singled out. What did I do? I was smart. I was obedient. I spoke fluent Spanish, did all my work quietly and was respectful. Could it have been that she had issue with my parents? My dad was a handsome, wealthy business executive and my mother was as stunning as Marilyn Monroe. Perhaps these factors caused her to dislike me. I would assume that being a straight A student would earn any teacher's respect. But this was certainly not the case with Mrs. Barnes, who was inexplicably hostile.

I was also singled out by being assigned to tutor a boy while sitting on the floor facing the classroom for all to observe and ridicule. It felt as though we were ostracized because we were different from the rest of the kids. I felt bad for the boy, who was disheveled and shy, with greasy, matted blondish-red hair. He wore the same brown plaid flannel shirt four out of five days each week and smelled like spoiled milk—that sour-acidic stench made me sick to my stomach. We were both clearly in pain, but for different reasons. He tried hard to follow my lead as I tutored him, struggling from attention issues that made it tedious for us both. It was torture to have all the children watching our progress as if we were literally a floor show. We were paying for something in Mrs. Barnes's psyche, but neither of us knew what it was.

The not knowing is perplexing to a child, causing them to think it is something about them that is drawing the negative attention. As an adult with perspective on my side, I am able to clearly understand that Mrs. Barnes's apparent dislike of us was rooted in her own personal issues that she projected onto us.

A child doesn't know how to tackle the impact of abuse and bullying, especially if it comes from an authority figure. Parents and school staff are often oblivious. In our current world, the prevalence and high status associated with social media, and the impact it has upon a child's perception of herself in relation to her peers, is a dangerous platform for self-judgment that too often leads to low self-worth. Families, together with educators, must develop stringent guidelines to stop bullying across all communication technologies, as well as in school, out of school, during sports, and all extracurricular activities. This is imperative to prevent the crippling of self-worth of generations of children. We must also recognize that those who are doing the bullying, the perpetrators, are just as damaged as the victims.

Some individuals with low self-worth had happy, stable childhoods, and only began to doubt their self-worth and value in the world as a result of unwise choices, traumatic events, or toxic relationships at work or at home. Whatever the source of your internal wounds, the responsibility to change is in your hands. No one but you can truly uncover what is buried inside of you. The thoughts that prevent you from feeling strong and healthy will continue to intrude on your life until you choose to look inside of yourself and reconnect with the real you—your true nature, not the image you have of yourself or what others think of you.

Your self-worth is developed over time as a result of your experiences, whether they are positive or negative. Self-worth doesn't reflect whether you are a good or bad person, whether you are kind and compassionate or self-centered and insensitive. It isn't rooted in how popular or successful you are, whether you are a surgeon versus a plumber or a mathematician, student, or street vendor. Your self-worth is rooted in a much deeper realm that is hidden from view: your pure energy and your life source, which I call the *Soul Self,* the most sacred you.

Blaming your childhood and parents or your spouse, your colleagues or your eight-year-old foes for how you feel today will not remedy you in any way. This approach only intensifies your negative emotions, and the issues remain. When you stop blaming others for how you feel about yourself and choose to assume responsibility to engage your brain to heal and grow, the anger and hurt, and frustration and resentment towards others will begin to diminish. You will not feel burdened by your past, rather, you will be invigorated to live with self-sustaining inner strength.

No one volunteers to be a victim. We are only responsible for making the choice to pursue healthy self-worth as adults once we know it is possible.

It is possible.

I know because I have developed healthy self-worth after decades of punishing myself for not being perfect, and, therefore, not good enough. Before I researched how to develop my own self-worth, I wanted to find a way to stop the incessant banter in my head demanding me to strive for "perfection." This internal tyrant fueled an astounding amount of mental and emotional strain resulting in physical symptoms, typically the chronic stomach aches to which I had grown unpleasantly accustomed. The need to be "perfect" is an unhealthy perspective that generates tremendous pressure, especially upon children and teenagers who judge themselves by this fallacy. Human beings, in fact all living organisms, have variations even among their paired features such as eyes, hands, lungs, ears, feet, kidneys. Nothing about us is symmetrical or the exact same shape or size. Our worldly endeavors do not lead to perfection, only to transitory satisfaction. Our personal characteristics don't translate to perfection as there is no single metric by which this elusive objective is evaluated.

> The state of perfection does not exist for any single human being or any living organism, period.

There is no rank, no measurement, no universal judgement system that qualifies and categorizes us in the world. When I finally realized this fact, a two-million-ton weight fell off my weary head. I discarded the "P" word from my vocabulary—permanently—as it served no purpose other than to disillusion, disappoint, and occasionally, depress. And, I understood with all my heart that what allows us to open our eyes to the world and truly *see* one another is precisely because no single human being is alike. Each one of us has a distinct fingerprint that touches the world, our own singular brand that is one of a kind, never to be duplicated. Every facet of who we are as human beings is beautiful due to our differences.

Before I reached this place of understanding, I had to endure a series of challenging experiences. When I was hired by a CEO of a global corporation in my twenties, there were two women who intensely disliked me from day one. The CEO brought me into his circle of confidantes or, as the staff called us, his "entourage." I was a ripe target due to my age, and the fact that I was going through a divorce conveyed itself as a sore spot projecting from my forehead for all to see; but mostly, since I was invited into the CEO's inner circle without hesitation, these women were anything but kind and welcoming.

The CEO formed an instant affinity towards me that was obvious to everyone but me. The position offered to me was important—corporate communications director. These two women scrutinized everything about me, from how I dressed to my vocabulary. They tried to discredit me by calling me names and blatantly whispering to each other as they stared at me. I tried hard to win them over, as I always did with those who appeared distant or distrustful, to no avail. So, I reverted into my cavern of darkness, internalizing their unfair criticism.

As time went by and I was successful in the position, the women accepted that I was there to stay and backed off. As I had done before in my life, I proved to others that I was smart and competent. What I hadn't learned, however, was that the success I achieved in business was not the remedy for my internal low self-worth. I could be cheery and collegial with those women, but I could never let down my guard for even a moment or they might discover my Achilles heel.

I continued to need a remedy that I had not yet found, even as I advanced in my career and dazzled others with the appearance of confidence and polish. I hid inside myself, wrestling with the lonely struggle of low self-value.

Even at that stage of callowness about what I had to do to feel better about myself, I knew that no one could "fix" my inner turmoil but me. The work of developing self-worth as a powerful positive force has to come from you because only you can release the toxic garbage inside of you: the insecurities, defenses, fears, anger, any emotion or thought that is preventing you from living freely. Spouses, parents, friends, and counselors can all be wonderfully supportive, but we each have to walk our own path.

Yes, there is a path to self-worth. You will learn how to tune in to your intuitive, higher consciousness. You will discover how to talk to your self and how to listen to yourself.

If you don't know what you think and how you feel, how can you change?

Sustainable change can only occur through a deep connection to your Soul Self, the energy that is you. You will learn, as did I, that the bloom of planting and tending the seeds of self-worth is self-love, which we carry into the world to help heal what we can with kindness and compassion.

This transformative process of change will feel strange and challenging in the beginning—because it is. But as you move forward through the initial phases, you will experience wonderful sensations. A heaviness will leave your mind and body, replaced by feelings of calm and lightness. As this takes place, you will become increasingly eager and willing to immerse yourself in the process.

Remember, you did not ask for the low self-worth that plagues you. You probably did not even know there was a name for what you have been feeling. But now that you do know, take my hand, or follow my lead.

Let there be no more criticism piled on top of everything you have already stored up in a secret corner of your brain. All will be well. You are not alone. When you are ready to change internally, to connect with your Soul Self and build the self-worth you truly deserve, you will do it.

Instead of harsh criticism, neglect, ridicule, or expectations of perfection—which leads to low self-worth—parents, teachers, and others who care for children must listen to them, speak respectfully, give them appropriate attention and affection, communicate openly and consistently, recognize their accomplishments, and accept their mistakes. Positive self-worth will enable you to know that YOU MATTER.

Transformation Tenets

◊ Your sense of self developed during your childhood as well as traumas later in life.

◊ No single human being is responsible for their low self-worth.

◊ Your self-worth emanates from a deeper part of you, your innermost core being, your Soul Self.

◊ Sustainable change can only occur through a connection to your Soul Self.

A Human Mosaic Vignette

Rose's Reconstructed Heart

My heart went out to Rose when she shared her story of heartbreak with me. Her indigo blue eyes hid behind wispy, wavy, blond hair. She greeted me with a warm embrace, as though we had known one another prior to this meeting. I felt sad knowing that a person experiencing a betrayal inevitably suffers a plunge in self-worth. Rose had gone into her marriage with confidence, which may have given her a foundation on which to build a quicker recovery than the one she endured—if she had only had the tools to help her.

"I was raised to believe the person you marry will be your partner through life," Rose reflected about her life circumstances that nearly killed her. "I just assumed, in my innocent way, that the man I had known since I was very young was the one I would share my entire life with. My husband and I grew up together. Our parents were close friends. From my point of view, this marriage was our destiny. So, we married and had a daughter when I was twenty-three. My life was exactly what I had hoped for in every conceivable way," Rose stated.

Without warning, after their daughter's birth, Rose's husband told her he wanted a divorce. "I was completely dumbfounded, because we seldom fought. I believed we had a loving, wonderful relationship. He said to me, 'Before we end up hating each other we need to divorce.'" Rose was devastated.

"At the time that he sprang this on me, everything went black.

Although I had never done anything like this in my life, I started banging my head as hard as I could against the wall, and I felt absolutely nothing. Instinctively, I must have thought that physical pain would be a relief from the emotional anguish that was too much to bear. My body went into survival mode, as the gut-wrenching pain was intolerable." Much later, Rose recalled their conversation. For four years, her husband was having an affair with another woman. "I was overwhelmed with shock, disbelief, and grief when he revealed that he told that woman he loved her. *How could I have not noticed any difference in his behavior or in our relationship?*" Rose's voice was strained.

Rose immediately moved in with her parents. She was unable to function on her own or care for her daughter. "I was so broken. I felt like a total failure," Rose confessed. Blunted by her grief, the only thing Rose was capable of doing was crying. She rarely left her parents' home for two years. "It was excruciating. I believed I would never smile again. Occasionally I would fake a smile, but all I felt I on the inside was pain."

Rose believed her life had come to a fragile place. "This was the first time in my life that I dealt with any sort of depression. It almost took my life. Before the betrayal, the thought of suicide was foreign to me. But, suffering to such an extent made me understand what it felt to be so low, hopeless, and unable to do anything. I considered suicide. Thank goodness, I never attempted it," Rose confessed.

It took her five years to be able to function partway, and another fifteen years to start to feel whole, to feel part of the world again. She added that it took her twenty years to heal, however, she told me that she was still impacted by what happened. Rose shared this with me to convince anyone who has suffered trauma to seek help. "I still feel scarred by the whole thing, but now I'm okay. I learned how to be okay. "

Although Rose's recovery was a long road, she advises others not to give up their heart and soul, their entire life, to someone who never deserved it. "You need to do whatever you possibly can to take your life back. Don't let someone who betrayed you destroy you. I'm terribly sad looking back on how those thoughts and the awful grieving stole so many years of my life," Rose told me in a tearful voice.

"If I had believed in myself and understood that my ex-husband's betrayal was his cross to bear, not mine, I would have saved myself many years of living with tremendous pain." Rose urges others to learn how to be strong internally. "If I had believed that my life had meaning outside of my husband, I would have recovered faster. The key to getting through and beyond terrible pain is to have a strong inner core of faith and strength, knowing that you are worthy of love, despite how someone treats you. So, that when something happens in life that breaks your heart, you will know that with time, you will survive and heal."

Rose added, "With a strong sense of who you are, with self-worth and self-love, you have an inner resolve—a commitment to yourself—that you can transcend whatever challenges come into your life. I suffered far too long, thinking my life had no value. Do whatever you can to create a healthy foundation for your life. It's never too late to learn how to trust and love yourself."

Rose grew stronger and healthier by understanding that she had an identity that was not attached to other people, that stood on its own and wasn't dependent on being propped up by someone or something. She learned to find meaning in her soul's evolution that was derived from inner faith and wisdom.

Self-Trust

"As soon as you trust yourself, you will know how to live."
Goethe

All of the times during my life when trust was a piece of meaningless paper, torn into small fragments that I knew for a fact would never be taped together, the broken promises and continual lies, made me suspicious of everyone. Subconsciously, I created a safety deposit box in my brain called: Trust is a Farce. Never Trust Anyone. The key to the box was lost when I was three years old.

If you have experienced relationships with untrustworthy people, you know how injurious it is to your soul. What happens when you live through incidents during your childhood — or later in life — that shatter your relationship with trust, it becomes exceedingly difficult for you to possess self-trust. A vicious circle is formed in your brain…you cannot trust yourself, therefore, you certainly cannot trust others.

It is impossible to build self-worth without self-trust and self-love. If you have low self-worth, you are also lacking in self-trust and self-love. You were either denied something essential in your early upbringing, or you learned not to trust or love yourself in response to your experiences.

This does not mean that you cannot build your self-worth until you have learned to trust and love yourself. This process will happen concurrently, almost magically, as you work on building self-worth. But it must happen. These are the cornerstones of the foundation of self-worth. And when you are committing to transformative change, there is no cutting corners.

Let's look at self-trust first as it is the weightier of the two, as you will see.

In order to trust others, you must first trust yourself. Growing up in Santiago, Chile, there were many tumultuous events, including burglaries, earthquakes, as mentioned earlier, screaming and crashing that echoed off the stone walls as a result of my father's many betrayals of my mother, and my injuries when left with the maids (I haven't mentioned the time my finger got slammed in an iron gate when I was going for a walk with Elena. Held together by a mere ligament, my ring finger was gone, or so I believed as a little girl whose mother was crying hard as she held my finger together in a blood-soaked towel. Off we sped, on another mad dash to the emergency room. I still have a visible bump protruding from my right finger where the E.R. doctor sewed it together, sloppily I might add. But, at least I didn't lose my finger.)

My parents adored me, but parents played a very different role in their children's lives back then. They weren't involved the way I am with my kids, nor as intimately connected. My parents didn't realize that their issues had a tremendous impact upon me. My father's lies and mother's nervous breakdowns during which she was unavailable for months affected my ability to trust those closest to me, those who were responsible for me at that time of life. I had no role models of trustworthy behavior: a father who was a loving husband and reliably honest or a mother who was present and secure in her own identity.

Going away to a boarding school in Connecticut when I turned sixteen, I couldn't wait to be away from my parents' turbulent marriage. Yet there was a paranoia that clung to me, making me a target. I had my figurative protective armor on, but in unguarded moments, I found I was always thinking Someone is going to hurt me … I know someone is about to hurt me. It was a forgone conclusion that I was going to be rejected, lied to, or ridiculed. After boarding school, I was fortunate to have four wonderful years at Northwestern University, during which I received a great education and met terrific people from all over the globe, that is, with the exception of one guy...a person who felt the need to secrete his venom on me. On a miserable Chicago evening during a massive snowstorm, this person decided to slash all four of my brand-new snow tires, right before my final exam the following morning. Nice guy. Despite a few challenges, it was a good time in my life.

When I reached my mid-thirties, I noticed a recurring pattern in my relationships, both personally and professionally. It was as if I were a magnet for negative and critical people. This experience followed me from job to job and friendship to friendship. I couldn't understand at the time why others thought they could walk all over me. So, I thought of those who abused my intelligent and friendly overtures as the enemy. It was their fault.

It is much easier to blame others for your plight, to outsource the problems to another person rather than assume responsibility, by retaining them in your mental office space to manage yourself. When someone is rude or critical, you do not have to interpret their jabs as truth. And, to some degree, you might be projecting a persona that draws these sorts to you. This is not the easy way out, however, it is a way to better understand your situation.

After some focused time in self-reflection, I realized that people with low self-worth attract others with the same issues. Internally, I'd always been exceedingly hard on myself, so when people were critical of me, it seemed like an affirmation of what I told myself. Although outwardly successful, because I yearned for acceptance and approval from others, I had tried to befriend people who were unkind and not worthy of my time and attention.

Lack of self-trust weighs heavily on your relationships and factors into everything you do in life. Fear of failure, the need to be accepted and admired, second-guessing yourself, paranoia, and mistrust of others all stem from lack of self-trust.

Living without self-trust also causes you to judge everyone in your life. Even before you've had the chance to know someone, you are on guard for signs of betrayal or dishonesty. Distrust creates barriers between yourself and other people. How can you have an open and enriching relationship with someone when you don't trust them, perhaps through no fault of theirs?

I was desperate for acceptance from others; instead of focusing on developing my own self-trust, I worked vigorously to help others with their trust issues. It was the classic insane situation of doing the same thing over and over and expecting different results. I had to change. Before I could attract people I could trust, I had to learn to trust myself. I learned to do this at the same time I was discovering that my internal torment came from my lack of self-worth and self-love.

How We Develop Trust

According to Erik Erikson, the renowned psychologist and psychoanalyst who founded the theory of Psychosocial Development, an infant learns about trust within the first eighteen months of life. Erikson called this stage Trust versus Mistrust. He believed it was the most important period in a person's life because it shapes our view of the world, as well as our personalities. Trust is the fundamental building block of our development according to Erikson's theory, as it gives us hope, or what I refer to as comfort in believing that others will be there to take care of us. I have had a complicated relationship with trust since my early life in Santiago. Several traumatic episodes deepened my fear that I could not trust others. Living without a safety net creates a torrent of issues that bleed into every area of a child's life.

If an infant's needs are met—if fed when hungry, picked up when crying, if dirty diapers are changed, if cuddled and protected—the infant learns to trust and develops a bond with its caregiver. If an infant is left alone for hours to cry and cry, its brain's cortisol levels rise, creating a host of potential problems such as lowered immunity, anxiety, depression, and the beginning of low self-worth due to a lack of trust. Learning to trust at this early developmental stage of life is even more important than sensing love because an infant is completely helpless and dependent on others to survive.

If our youngest humans are not nurtured and loved, they will move farther and farther away from their innate sense of self. Exposure to negative stimuli has an immense influence on shaping personality. Adult expectations and cultural beliefs imposed on children further erode who we are at birth, even with the best intentions. We are taught that we should fit in, even in situations that make us uncomfortable and anxious. We are complimented when we perform well and are encouraged to work hard to accomplish goals and be successful. Children absorb their parents' disappointment, and worse, disrespect, if their expectations are not met. These messages cause us to scrutinize ourselves, evaluate our worth by our external achievements, and we inwardly chastise ourselves when we do not meet "standards" pre-determined for us. Our self-perception, once rooted in our Soul Self, is now further distanced by the judgment imposed upon us.

Revered poet, philosopher, and leader of the transcendentalist movement in the 19th century, Ralph Waldo Emerson (1803-1882), has had great influence on my thoughts and writing, and I have often relied on his sage words as a moral compass. His prose has the power to stir even the most hardened souls: "To be yourself in a world that is constantly trying to make you something else is the greatest accomplishment." Emerson's enlightened understanding of human nature is revealed through his simple yet profound words that awaken and inspire us to have trust in ourselves, to have faith in who we are as individuals, rather than be molded by societal mores.

It is a fact that our environment has the greatest impact on how we view ourselves. When we have been programmed by our parents, siblings, role models, coaches, and teachers to think and behave a certain way, we feel compelled to adhere to their beliefs. What begins as fertile, pristine ground in our young minds soon becomes populated by directives from our "authority" figures. Indeed, it is their role to teach us values, beliefs, and skills, however, these do not help us develop self-trust.

Were any of us fortunate enough to be raised by parents or role models who shared their wisdom about self-trust? My parents loved me deeply, but the life-lessons that I needed to be able to trust others, to feel comfortable in my innermost being, and to possess self-trust were not a part of my home education repertoire . When you are immersed in the tumult of events that reflect glaring deceit—watching your mother incapacitated by sorrow and booze, being bullied by girls with no reprieve—learning to trust oneself was not on the horizon for me. I carried my own inner distrust through my life until I understood, after traversing some jagged terrain that was deeply painful, that what precedes trusting others is learning to trust oneself.

Even if we have been adored and loved as children, there are many other ways we may lose our ability to trust. Boys and girls, women and men, can be sexually molested and assaulted at any age. Any one of us can be attacked or robbed and lose trust that we can be safe in the world. Just reading or listening to the news can impact sensitive souls who feel we can no longer trust our leaders, whether political, religious, or members of our local community.

Perhaps you were a trusting individual most of your life. Then someone you deeply love lies to you. Suddenly, the person you thought you trusted wholeheartedly is not trustworthy. In fact, they lied to you repeatedly. Betrayal at any age or stage of life can rock you to your core. It can drain you of your energy, your optimism, your power—and of your trust in yourself.

When you lose the ability to trust yourself, your sense of self-worth automatically plummets. Without the ability to have faith in our inner self, we cannot develop healthy self-worth. If we do not have the trust connection, we have to build that at the same time we build our self-worth. Self-trust truly is the basis for learning to value who you are and believe in yourself.

How Can We Learn Self-Trust?

Another quote that I have held closely to my heart, one that has aided me in my mission to heal myself is: "Self-trust is the essence of heroism." Ralph Waldo Emerson, American poet, essayist, lecturer, philosopher. Both pithy and profound, in just a few words, Emerson conveys a valuable truth—that trust in oneself enables a person to live with unshakeable steadfastness, perseverance, boldness, and a fortitude that never waivers. Believing in yourself, having inner faith in a world that is unpredictable and challenging, permits you to be the leader of your life. You do not depend upon others to feel adequate or at peace. You are your own hero.

> If you have not lived with self-trust,
> how is it possible to be your own hero?

Without a construct from which to work, how can a person learn to trust themselves? In the absence of role models, we learn self-trust by being aware of our thoughts, listening to what they are telling us and pausing to understand them, by being compassionate with ourselves, acting as though our beliefs, our life, matters. We do what we say we will do, behave with integrity, and stand by our word. We learn to honor ourselves by respecting our emotions, and as we do, we strengthen our relationship with our innermost Soul Self. This requires both courage and an understanding of who you are.

Learning to listen more closely and attentively to your thoughts is the first step to building self-trust. Unless you know what it is you are thinking, it is impossible to change. When you are fully aware and engaged with your thoughts, you have the chance to absorb them with clarity. This is the time to question them rather than move on. Where did these thoughts originate? What triggered the thoughts? Having a curiosity about what you are thinking and feeling enables you to better understand yourself. Why am I feeling fearful right now? Why do I constantly question my actions?

Respect and honor your thoughts and emotions rather than blocking them. Let them flow in and out of you, knowing that you are fully aware and mindful of them. Acting without thinking will perpetuate your lack of trust. Thrusting them into your internal lockbox for safekeeping will only permit them to linger. *Listen and learn* is an adage for a valid reason. Use it on yourself. With time and practice, this will become more natural to you.

Defining your values and beliefs is an important element of building self-trust. If you don't trust yourself to act in your own best interest, ask yourself why. When one lives in accordance with their moral code of conduct and their belief system, they feel good about themselves. Consider the issues that are causing you to mistreat yourself or make decisions that you regret. When a person lies, guilt, shame, and other negative emotions rise within them. They don't trust themselves to tell the truth, and, therefore, be trusted by others.

Be resolute in your commitment to live with honesty and integrity. Being truthful is one of the most effective ways to build self-trust. When you say what you mean and mean what you say, you are empowering yourself. You are dignifying who you are by being reliable and responsible. Anything short of this will perpetuate your lack of self-trust.

Each step you take by choosing to do something and not worrying about the outcome will help you build self-trust. If you behave according to your values and core beliefs, then each moment of each day you will have the opportunity to rely on your own intuitive thoughts and not fear what might happen. Allow your intuition to guide you. Give yourself the confidence to trust your decisions and know that, even if they didn't lead to where you had hoped, you will be okay knowing you are building self-trust.

Self-trust is exceptionally meaningful in your work to build self-worth as it is the foundation for every thought, every emotion, and every action you take. It impacts how you view others and how they respond to you. It plays a heavy role in all your relationships, and, particularly in your ability to feel in harmony with those in your life. The concept of self-trust was never discussed during my developmental years, and I did not know how heavily the absence of self-trust weighed on the quality of my interactions. I lived with dark sunglasses on at all times, dimming my own beliefs about myself and hiding from others. All the while, I knew that my inner faith and wisdom were inside of me, I only had to find a way to connect with it.

When I began to build my inner trust, I went back to my beloved Carl Rogers, who believed that trust was one of the fundamental attributes to living as a fully functioning, self-actualized human being. I asked myself, what would that look like to me? How would my life be different, perhaps better, and certainly more pleasant, if I were able to trust myself?

I had spent years excavating the roots of my distrust, which I will share further with you when we are ready to establish the routine of Self-Reflection. You already know that I had been injured by my early role models and what I observed was anything but trust, including my parents and authority figures like the maids in Chile, and my teacher in Rye, New York. I was further led astray from confidence in myself by being bullied by girls my age, and later by women with whom I worked and male bosses who sexually harassed me without a conscience—with no shred of guilt or shame. As a result of my childhood experiences, when I was an adult, if I learned that someone had been talking about me, I would immediately jump to the conclusion that it was critical. This was not delusional on my part, as I had endured a lot of moments in my life during which I was unfairly scrutinized. Rather than deal with it head on, I internalized the pain of rejection and condemnation. This prevented me from enjoying my successes and deepening my relationships.

I decided my strategy to develop self-trust would have to be the opposite of my normal reaction. Instead of internalizing the pain of rejection and condemnation, sometimes before it had even happened, I decided to externalize the pain.

I would pay attention to everything I was feeling as soon as I sensed it moving within me. Each time I had that old feeling that someone is going to hurt me, I would observe the situation I was in and who I was with. I would no longer force thoughts inside me. I would listen to them. Write them down. Describe any transformation in my mood. This was hard at first. It was painful. But each time I did this, the pain was less severe.

Within a matter of days, I was able to see patterns in my thinking that were directly in response to everyday issues in my environment. It was remarkable to note that when I made the conscious choice to be aware of my feelings, thoughts, and sensations, I realized how much effort I had put into suppressing my private pain.

Our physical bodies function largely autonomously. Our brain works exceedingly faster than our bodies, which enables our hands, legs, and feet to function with little effort, that is, unless we are learning a new form of exercise such as kickboxing, for example, then we need to pay closer attention to guiding our bodies to move in the right direction. Think about when you have a physical wound how your attention is drawn to that area of pain. When you slice your finger while cutting an apple, suddenly you become highly cognizant of the throbbing pain in that finger. It becomes a focus of your attention. To avoid aggravating the wound, you handle your finger gingerly. And, when you accidentally knock it against something, your awareness reverts to the cut. You are consciously aware of that finger. Because the pain is outside of you, it is easier to identify. You know it is there because you feel it and you see it. Becoming aware and focusing on your internal thoughts is not as simple since your thoughts and emotions are not visible, and, therefore, easier to hide, manipulate, or force away. But just as the cut on your finger heals with proper care and time, each of us has the ability to heal by learning how to be aware of our inner thoughts and think about the message they are sending us.

When you practice listening to your thoughts, rather than blocking them, a remarkable thing happens: you learn not to fear them. The less you attempt to manipulate them, by forcing them away, the more familiar you will become with messages that reoccur. This is a significant exercise that leads to self-understanding and to building self-trust. In a short period of time, you will become increasingly comfortable allowing your thoughts to rise to the surface, giving them freedom to express themselves, and allowing them to pass through and out of you.

I understood that I had to acknowledge the issues crowding my brain and clouding my vision if I wanted to change. Rather than blocking them, as I would have in my past, I began accepting them, allowing them to flow inside—and then outside—of me. With increased awareness of these thoughts, I formed an open mindset that permitted them to pass through me, unrestrained, and let them move out of me. It became easier to do with time and repetition. This was—no exaggeration—a life-changing process that not only enabled me to develop trust in myself but taught me simultaneously to trust others because I no longer had anything to fear.

What I did was to honor my thoughts and emotions, rather than shove them away or beat myself up about the fact that I still, after all these years, felt this way. Instead of feeling insecure about them—and loathing them—I acknowledged them openly and honestly. I found I could not only observe the thoughts, but I could catch them one at a time before they fell and changed my mood. I came to terms with the fact that they had distorted my view of myself and my life. My internal lack of trust diminished. I felt stronger and more peaceful. I would have done just about anything to achieve this state of being, as I knew how vastly it affected my entire existence.

I also pledged to myself that I would no longer live without boundaries, as this was totally emblematic of my lack of self-trust. I could never seem to establish boundaries for myself, not even with my very closest friend. No more. The lack of inherent self-trust made me feel as though I had to accept anything someone said or did to me, because somehow, I deserved to be mistreated. Establishing boundaries, setting limits to which I would involve myself with others, was one of the most liberating aspects of building self-trust and self-worth. I would decide for myself how much time to allot to certain "needy" people, rather than be run over by their demands. And, I would no longer stand for any abusive behavior or conversations.

In addition, building my self-trust required that I abandon my tendency to make excuses to myself to lessen my inner guilt and shame about past mistakes. I scrapped my defenses and replaced them with the truth. I accepted my past with grace, so that I could be in alignment with my soul.

Until we accept our past, our thoughts will be held up by the roadblock entrenched in our brain, one that prohibits us from fully experiencing the beauty of life. Learning self-trust removes this roadblock and permits joy to enter where there was once distrust and self-doubt.

Along the path to build self-trust, I continually reminded myself that I did not have to be my past, I did not have to continue to relive that pain. Instead, I chose to design my future in the way that would open my mind, heart, and soul to the brilliance of being alive.

Self-Trust Tips

Pay attention to what you are feeling.
Honor your thoughts and emotions by letting them flow.
Write down what you are thinking and feeling.
Externalize rather than internalize.
Notice patterns related to individuals or situations.
Catch the thought before it falls.
Pause, reorient, and move forward.

Note: If you are presently in a relationship with someone whom you cannot trust due to their dishonesty, you must begin to distance yourself from them. I know this is not easy, especially when it is a spouse or sibling, a close friend or a colleague. Continuing to subject yourself to a relationship with someone you feel is not open and honest will inhibit your ability to build self-trust, self-love, and self-worth. I am not suggesting that you excise them from your life, just for the time during which you are focusing on developing self-trust. Once you feel confident and secure, no matter what others are saying or doing, it will be safe for you to resume exposure.

I have always loved this quote by Eleanor Roosevelt, "No one can make you feel inferior without your consent." Such empowering words crafted by an extraordinary woman! Only until I learned self-trust was I able to harness the meaning of this quote and apply it to my life. If you feel at peace with yourself, you will not permit others to make you feel otherwise. When you learn to trust yourself, what other people say and do will not change how you feel about yourself. You not only know that you always have the choice, the freedom, to respond to someone as you wish, you can feel that it is true because you learned how to turn distrust into self-trust. The more you build inner trust, the easier this becomes.

I promise you, from someone who walked this path repeatedly, when you learn to trust yourself, everything that you once considered a threat becomes an opportunity to strengthen your resolve to be strong and comfortable within yourself. It was truly liberating to realize that whether I made the right choice or the wrong choice in any situation, it did not diminish me as a human being. I was in pursuit of self-worth and nothing could stop me.

As you begin to trust yourself, your decisions, and the people in your life, you will gain a real sense of freedom. You have unchained yourself from the handcuffs and are free to experience life as it is, in any form.

> Self-trust is a bridge to self-worth,
> which is a bridge to self-love.

Transformation Tenets

⬧ Self-trust is the foundation for every thought, emotion, and action, and impacts every relationship.

⬧ Self-trust develops through listening to your thoughts, honoring them, becoming self-aware, having self-compassion, acting on your values and beliefs, and behaving with integrity.

⬧ Setting boundaries is key to investing time in yourself.

⬧ Listen to your intuition, or gut-check response as you build self-trust.

Connecting with Your Intuition

"Intuition will tell the thinking mind where to look next."
Jonas Salk, discoverer of the Polio vaccine

Through our early developmental years as we move away from our Soul Self due to parental and cultural expectations, we lose touch with our intuition, which is a facet of our soul's energy. Driven by external rewards such as acceptance and approval from others, we conform to societal standards. Our decisions and actions become based on what we feel we ought to be doing to be successful in the world. In the process, we lose touch with our own beliefs, values, and desires. We lose connection with who we really are.

One of the most obvious signs that I had lost touch with my intuition was that my gut-check response that we all have when facing potential danger was out of whack. It is our gut that signals to us before anything else what feels right and what doesn't. The problem was that I had internalized so many negative messages about myself that my gut response was going off all the time. My brain had overridden my intuitive voice. Outwardly I performed fine, but inside whistles and sirens were going off.

With many people, it's the opposite when they have lost touch with their intuition. They have no gut response. Their learned patterns of thinking have overridden their internal gut feel. Based on research on the brain, I can guarantee you that the body knows when you can trust someone or something and when you can't. Humans have been wired for

that since we began walking on two legs. It is the fight or
and is our survival reaction to fear.

If you use all your senses to check in with your body
bottom, you will feel heat or sweat coming from some area   ~y
when you are fearful, even if you don't consciously feel the fear. Similar
to a gut-check, this is a sign that you may be in a risky situation or
with a person who may not be telling the truth. The Office of Naval
Research has been funding a four-year research program to explore
the phenomena it calls premonition or intuition, which they assure the
public is not based on superstition. We do have a "sixth sense" that warns
us of danger. Our brain and our body are constantly working on our
behalf. We only need to relearn to listen, as we did when we were young,
to our intuitive voice, our gut response, as it is our deep connection to
our innermost core self.

Swiss psychiatrist Carl Jung (1875-1961) studied intuition in
relationship to personality. His writings pointed out that people with
a high intuitive sense let their own thoughts and beliefs direct their
experiences, rather than allow preconceived ideas and opinions of others
to drive their decisions. One component of Jung's theory about intuition
is that it enables a person to access their inner, unconscious self and
have an awareness of that gut feeling when it is triggered: "Intuition
is perception via the unconscious that brings forth ideas, images, new
possibilities and ways out of blocked situations."

Jung's theory about intuition is that it serves an important role in
our lives. "Intuition gives outlook and insight; it revels in the garden of
magical possibilities as if they were real." During the process of learning
to accept, trust, and love yourself, make room for your intuition as an
important guide in your life, the unconscious part of you that is there to
help lead you in the right direction. When your gut speaks to you, listen
to what it has to say.

Self-Love

Mother Teresa, Saint Teresa of Calcutta, was an extraordinary human being. Her life can be embodied in one word: LOVE. Called "The Light of Love," Mother Teresa's devoutly compassionate and luminous spirit as a tireless missionary was focused on humanitarian efforts to serve the poorest of the poor. Her deeds exemplified the living personification of a saint here on earth. Her faith was the foundation of her life. Yet her daily inspiration stemmed from her life's mission—to spread love. Throughout her life, she was a source of hope and inspiration unlike any other.

The most sacred connection we have as human beings is to love one another. Everything else we experience in life is minimal relative to the magnitude of love. No matter who you are or what you've endured during your life, every human being seeks the divine power of love. Nothing else compares to it. I believe love is our purpose in life.

My parents were wonderful, but they had busy lives, as parents do. I wasn't raised in an atmosphere in which the subject of self-love was a topic of discussion. Neither of my parents ever said to me when I was young, "Annie, how do you feel about yourself as a human being?" "Do you love yourself?" "Do you feel your life matters?" It's not that they didn't care about my internal emotions, it's just that their focus was on more immediate matters. The focus of most parents was on physical wellbeing versus mental and emotional. They did the best they could, given what they knew.

Our parents or guardians—if we were fortunate enough to have them—weren't schooled in the *"how to raise a child with self-worth,"* training program. For one thing, of course, there is no such program, which I hope to remedy. Those responsible for us were entrusted with tremendous power over our mental, emotional, physical, and spiritual health. Yet knowledge and experience about parenting has never been a prerequisite for raising a child.

Absurd, isn't it? You've got to get a license to drive a car but becoming a parent requires no education or credentials, nor understanding of values, morals, or belief systems. There is no mandatory process of evaluation to determine whether a person has the capacity to care for a child. Although it's been this way since the beginning of procreation, wouldn't you agree that it would be wise for parents-to-be to learn in advance how to raise a child with self-worth? It's no surprise that there is such a prevalence of low self-worth among our population, and that it spans all socio-economic, cultural, ethnic, religious, gender, or sexual preferences.

The Development of Our Sense of Self

By the time we are 18 to 24 months old, emerging language skills help us grasp the concept of self. By the ages of three and four, children see themselves as unique and separate human beings, are fairly self-sufficient, and have a self-image that includes their physical attributes, names, ages, genders, social affiliations, possessions, and abilities. A young child's self-image is forming rapidly as they interact with others and receive feedback about their behavior.

By the age of five, when preschoolers officially start attending our school system, children are aware of how they are viewed by others. It is a challenge to enter a bigger "pond" where there are more fish that can swim fast. Kindergartners are transitioning from the "me" phase to the "us" phase. If their feelings of self-worth are not strong, they will have trouble speaking up when their needs are not being met. Feeling ignored can lead to internalizing emotions, potentially leading to devaluation of the self.

The education we hope our children receive and the one they get is dependent on many factors. What school a child attends is often as random as buying a lottery ticket. We can't guarantee compassionate, enlightened teachers who want nothing more than to open a child's mind to learning and personal growth as well. We also cannot expect teachers to have the capacity to mold a child's sense of self, but great teachers certainly have an impact.

The missing element in young lives is learning how to love ourselves, especially if we never experienced unconditional love. Even those of you who have been in a loving and nurturing environment do not necessarily learn about the magnitude of self-love.

It is of particular significance today for children to build self-love as they grow up in a world that is not safe the way it was when I grew up.

For many of you, living without self-love is all you have known, having existed with a vacant, lonely space inside of you that nothing seems to fill. Lack of self-love is more common today than ever before. Life used to be simpler, our expectations less and fewer, and there was no instantaneous form of communication other than the telephone.

Today, with easy access to social media, bullies, terrorists, bigots, and other destructive persons or groups, there is a widespread audience that is easy to reach.

This has promulgated a strain of viciousness that has impacted thousands of young people, teenagers, even those we think might be accustomed to the spotlight, therefore, desensitized to criticism—actors, singers, artists. No one is immune to criticism and unwarranted cruelty. Many celebrities have shut down their accounts due to denigrating comments they have received from people they do not know.

The most disturbing aspect of the social media ranting is that people, especially children, teenagers, and young adults, hear something malicious about themselves, and rather than ignore it, they internalize the comments and, in time, believe that these vicious statements are true. They take the comments as a reflection of what is wrong or lacking about them. Why? Because even those of us who have self-worth can still be sensitive to what others say about us. It is human nature to care, to care about yourself and others.

From the beginning of the social media revolution, I have hoped that there would be some type of screening process to filter and remove negative comments from being sent or appearing publicly. Would this contradict the First Amendment to the U.S. Constitution's freedom of speech clause? Yes, perhaps it would, however, the upside is reduced conflict, anger, hatred, bullying, and other terrible byproducts that are the downside of immediate outreach and contact with others. Prohibiting critical or negative words from being broadcasted anonymously would also serve to engender positive, uplifting communication that would strengthen our country rather than weaken it.

You Deserve to Love Yourself

"Not I, nor anyone else can travel that road for you. You must travel it by yourself. It is not far. It is within reach. Perhaps you have been on it since you were born, and did not know. Perhaps it is everywhere—on water and land."
—Walt Whitman, "Leaves of Grass"

When the term self-love became popularized in the 1960s by the hippie generation, it was in response to the devastation caused by the wars and other detrimental environmental factors. Hippies were all about love and peace—which is truly the salve we need in our world today. Just a bit of love goes a very long way towards healing. And, peace…Only a mindset of peace and unity will help to repair the broken pieces of our fractured world.

Self-love was an anomaly to me. I wondered as an adult if I could ever learn to wholly love the person I had spent decades castigating for my "performance" on the outside, which was how I judged my worth. I know now that I can, that we can, learn to love and care for ourselves as tenderly as any devoted and enlightened parent. The development of our sense of self never stops. It may pause when we are stuck, but due to the brain's ability to create new neural pathways that will support our growth, we can choose to move through any impediments to fully love and appreciate who we are inside.

I knew I loved my husband, children, mother, brothers, dearest friends. I love them all, unconditionally. There are aspects about each of them that I might not like at times. I don't always agree or approve of their choices. But, that doesn't lessen my love for them. And, it shouldn't be any different for the way I feel about myself. I am going to make mistakes and, even fall short of a goal. But I will always treat myself with the reverence and love that I deserve.

Through the process of building my self-worth, I began to understand that I could love myself unconditionally when two things happened. I had to STOP being hard on myself and revisiting all the negative messages and memories that so dominated my thinking. And I had to ACCEPT myself for who I am. Self-love is a product of planting the seeds of self-trust and walking the path of building self-worth.

Once you begin the journey to self-worth, you have a platform to stand on from which you can see clearly that your life matters. We all make mistakes but learning about self-worth gives us the tools to recover, restore, and reinvigorate each time with more stamina and resilience.

What is love? Love is more than a feeling of deep affection or desire. Love is an action. I have read many definitions of love, but most are about romantic love, parental love, love of God or a Higher Power. Here are some of definitions of love that can apply to self-love.

To love yourself means taking responsibility when you are wrong; not blaming others for your problems; working to make things right; allowing the journey to be the teacher; not taking things personally.

To love is not to feel the absence of fear, but to make friends with fear. Once you accept the full spectrum of who you are, you realize fear, doubt, uncertainty, jealousy, irritation, and frustration, are all facets of a complete human being. We do not have to shroud them in secrecy or barricade ourselves from negative feelings. We only have to approach these feelings with curiosity, wonder what is causing them, accept them as the truth for this moment, and move on without judgment.

Love requires attention. It is not selfish to make time for yourself. Whether you set aside time to reflect, read, sleep late in the morning, to ignore washing dishes until the next day because there is a movie you are longing to see, or simply not answering your phone because you don't feel like talking while you are taking a bubble bath and reading a magazine—do something for yourself and only you. Nurturing yourself is an integral characteristic of self-love. It is soothing, relaxing, uplifting, energizing, soulfully enriching, and a time to feel peacefully in sync with your true inner self.

Love understands. Sometimes you are going to fall back into old habits of negativity. This happens to all of us. Change is not linear. There are twists and turns around curves we didn't expect, peaks and valleys that require greater effort on our part. The trail to transformation can be challenging at times. You might find that you are having a tough day and decide to stop trying to feel better by convincing yourself you are fine with tormenting yourself. It has worked so far, after all. You are still here. Love understands there will be moments or days like that. And because it understands, it stays with you until you can say I love you to yourself again.

Love raises the vibration of your energy and attracts others to you who have a similar energy or vibration.

Love makes you want to share your spiritual light and optimism with others through thoughtful and kind words and actions.

Self-love is simply the origin of all the good things you want to feel inside you. It provides contentment, joy, the courage to do what is right, a measure of freedom from anxiety and depression. With self-love, you can transcend and survive anything.

Loving yourself is central to your existence. When a person values and respects who they are as a human being, they have the capacity to be open to the world as a fully self-actualized human being, to echo Carl Rogers.

> The world needs the powerful, positive energy you generate when you believe in and practice self-love.

Transformation Tenets

◇ Self-love develops by paying attention to how you are feeling, and by fully accepting yourself just as you are.

◇ Self-love involves taking responsibility for your thoughts and behavior, not blaming others for your issues, and not taking things that happen personally.

◇ Self-love enables you to be open to and accept fear, knowing fully that those emotions will pass.

◇ Self-love is concern and care for yourself, which means being compassionate and understanding, especially when things don't go the way you planned; self-love radiates outwardly to everyone and everything.

How Do We Evaluate Our Self-Worth?

"To know thyself is the beginning of wisdom."

—Socrates

One would think that by the time you're an adult, having lived through decades of life experiences, you'd have a keen sense of self-awareness and self-understanding. This is not the case, however, as far too many of us allow external issues to dictate our course from day to day, week to week, month to month, and soon years have elapsed while we still live with the same issues of self-doubt, fear, anger, insecurity. We know that something does not feel right, but we don't take the time to figure out what it might be and to find a way to change what isn't working. We fear that when we do take a moment for introspection, we may not know how to deal with what we find.

Many people say they don't want to face their innermost self to deal with their internal fears. Others pretend not to care, or they block out their thoughts. "I am who I am and that's just the way it's going to be," said my friend John, even though his frustration with seemingly trivial things belied how he truly felt. To step back and look at yourself without blinders is not easy.

Those of us who are introspective are more likely to be aware of our emotions and thoughts. But even so, life has a way of intruding on our connection with ourselves. We lead hectic lives that fill our days with never-ending tasks, ones that consume us mentally and physically, and drain us emotionally. We squeeze in time to exercise, maybe; to sleep, hopefully; to eat, not always nutritionally; and to spend time with family and friends. At the same time, we push ourselves to study, work, work harder and longer, make sacrifices on a daily basis, and, least of all, focus on ourselves. With the daily grind of life, we put off addressing our innermost thoughts, especially those that are troubling.

There are hundreds of approaches available for health and wellness, many books and articles on feeling strong and living your best life. The fact is that if you don't know how to apply the guidance, and don't have the ability to lean inwardly, to learn how to trust and believe in yourself, these external methods or fads will only yield transitory benefit. Applying techniques to repair your external self can be helpful for a limited period of time, but holistic transformation—mind, body, and spirit—can only occur by focusing on building your inner core being.

Ask yourself these questions:

- How do I feel about myself as a human being?
- Do I know who I am on the inside, in my core being?
- Are my outer actions in tune with what I think and feel inside?
- Have I been programmed to view myself merely by my accomplishments or failures?
- Do I feel constantly judged by others?
- Do I second guess myself and doubt my decisions?
- Am I filled with insecurities that I can't seem to shake?
- Do I behave in ways that I know aren't healthy, yet I continue to do so anyway?

Most people don't know what to say to the first question unless they truly do have a healthy sense of their self-worth. Many will answer NO to the next question because they haven't taken the time to consider who they are; and in fact, may think it's a waste of time. The third question often stumps people as it requires thought and evaluation. But too many people answer YES to the rest of the questions.

Do we evaluate who we are by our accomplishments? By the way people treat us at any given point during the day? How much we weigh? How much we earn? Our society promotes high-achievers, and, therefore, the majority of people I know and interact with rate themselves on a scale of successes versus failures. This stringent self-measurement tool has been used by our parents, teachers, bosses, friends, for centuries as the way to judge a person's worth. We look at external issues as a barometer of good and bad—and herein lies the root of low self-worth.

> Self-worth cannot be based on who you know, what you do, how much money you have, what you have achieved, or how you look. It can only be based on who you are.

Transformation Tenets

- ◇ No matter what external accomplishments or failures we pay attention to and identify with, none will address our internal tension.
- ◇ Holistic transformation, a process that engages us mentally, emotionally, physically, and spiritually, can occur only when we work to develop our inner core self.
- ◇ Develop your list of questions that reveal answers that relate to significant areas that obstruct your ability to be comfortable with who you are.
- ◇ External barometers or standards are false indicators for how you feel about yourself; focus inwardly to discover the true essence of who you are.

A Human Mosaic Vignette

Leslie's Search for Love and Acceptance

Leslie and I met at a party when I was in my mid-twenties. It took me a few minutes to "break the ice" with her as she was not willing to offer much in the way of conversation other than a "Yes" and "No" to my questions. I was intrigued by her silent, distant demeanor, which belied something deeper, something that she was restraining with all her might. At least, that is how she came across to me. I didn't see Leslie for many years after that, however, when she ran into the host of the party where we had met, she heard I was writing a book about self-worth and decided to call me.

With labored breath, Leslie told me she wanted to hear about the book. After an hour of conversation, she mentioned that she had been going through a dreadful time. Soon afterwards, we spoke about what she had endured, after which she asked me to help her. She was prepared to release a lifetime of loneliness and suffering with the hope that she could change the direction of her life and possibly help someone else who felt similarly.

"Approval and recognition have always been the deciding factors in my life," Leslie began letting her thoughts flow without restraint. "My parents' only focus was on working so that they could sustain our household. I was, for the most part, completely overlooked, ignored, and made to feel as if my life was a heavy, annoying obligation," Leslie looked at me with no emotion whatsoever. "My father was always silent, but he carried his anger in a tightly contained glass jar that remained sealed until the pressure exploded and the glass violently shattered. I was smart enough to know that I should stay as far out of his hair as possible," Leslie said. She was a smart little girl who learned early in her life to take care of herself since no one else would.

"My mother was not a factor in my life. She was completely subservient to my father and was consumed by him to the extent that I was paid no attention. My father was the source of our fears, our insecurities, our inability to express ourselves at all. He took out his inadequacies and frustration on his children. I was often beaten with a belt that left large, dark bruises on my body and scars on my psyche. It was all I knew," Leslie went on to say that her mother would not defend her because she was afraid that he would turn his violent rage on her.

"I silently searched for love and acceptance anywhere outside of my house; my yearning for kindness and attention was the only thing that kept me going. At the age of sixteen, I attached myself to an older guy who seemed to like me a bit. I got pregnant and thought that I might have found my salvation. If nothing else, I would finally find out what unconditional love was." Leslie had her baby and moved out of her parents' house into a small apartment. She got a job at a drugstore and raised her baby by herself.

"I loved my daughter but being blessed with motherhood and the miracle of a healthy, beautiful child did not change how I felt about myself. I had no worth. I was searching for someone to acknowledge my worth and kept coming up empty. In my never-ending hunt for someone or something to cling onto, I got involved in drug trafficking and led a dangerous lifestyle with too many sexual partners to count." Leslie said that between the crazy lifestyle and raising her daughter, she was living on the very edge every single day. It was a matter of survival.

Smart and resourceful, as Leslie aged, she pulled away from that lifestyle and developed her technical and administrative skills. She was able to get prestigious positions with several major, international corporations, as well as start her own small ventures. "On my own, with no education, I went from zero to a net worth of one million dollars. I taught myself everything, and I developed a never-quit work ethic." Yet, despite how Leslie turned her life around, she was still suffering.

At the age of sixty, Leslie was diagnosed with cancer. She had always prided herself on being self-sufficient, able to fix anything, and this time, she could not repair this problem that had cropped up without warning, the most complex and frightening one she had ever faced. "I have never relied on anyone for help or support. But when cancer reared its ugly head, I fell apart. I needed support." After a double mastectomy, Leslie had reconstructive surgery that was botched up twice. It left her with disfigured breasts that were immensely painful and constricted her mobility. She melted into a river of self-doubt and anguish.

When Leslie and I reconnected, it was right after her diagnosis. We started speaking regularly. After she recovered from her mastectomy, she endured the two reconstructive surgeries that failed. She crashed. Sobbing over the phone, she could barely speak. "I need to figure this out. I have to have a plan. I need something to look forward to. I cannot see beyond right now, this very moment." Leslie asked me to work with her on a program that would help pull her out of her deep despair. "My entire spirit was in the garbage. I thought I was ugly, I knew that I was scarred for life, and believed that no one would ever hold me, care for me, be attracted to me, or love me again." She was alone, weak, and depressed. Although Leslie lives in another state, we had face-time often and met in person when we could.

My first recommendation was for Leslie to seek counseling, which she had already checked off her ever-present task list, one that she had kept since she was a young girl. She had also been to physical therapy to help with the aches and pains. Since Leslie is a vegetarian and has always recognized food as fuel for the body, I only suggested she step up her intake of carbohydrates and protein, as well as water. She could not exercise due to her recovery from several surgeries, therefore, we started with deep breathing exercises, then moved to meditation and stretching exercises. These small but valuable steps reduced her stress in five days.

Within a short span of time, we discussed the significance of understanding how the brain changes as it learns new information. Leslie learned that she had within her the ability to alter patterns of thought by adopting new activities that would include what we had already started, in concert with practices to diffuse negative thoughts by releasing them and making room for new thoughts to enter.

In the subsequent weeks, I asked Leslie to create routines for herself that included the following practices: Gain Perspective, Generate Positive Self-Talk, and Coping Strategies, which she incorporated into her daily life one at a time, when she was ready. This was a challenge for Leslie, a person who has always thrived on them, but it was far different from any she had tackled thus far in her life. Leslie was always focused on solving other people's problems. This was tough for her, because she had never before "lost control" as she stated, but was eager to pull out and away from the self-defeating place in which she was stuck.

Leslie and I worked closely together, speaking several times per week. With the power of Perspective and other Practices, combined with her desire to feel stronger and healthier, Leslie grew out of the morose condition in which she had been suspended for nearly ten months, and began to slowly heal and recover. Her commitment to improve was remarkable, and I knew after a few months of working with her that she was determined to maintain her efforts to rehabilitate her body, mind, and spirit.

"It took years to realize that my life is not the responsibility of someone else. Not my parents, friends, daughter, or men. I was terrified of never finding my own sense of value." Leslie realized she was basing her worth on what she looked like, and in her mid-sixties, she came to terms with the fact that she would never feel worthy if she looked for it outside of herself. "I knew that life would not hand me the instructions on how to value who I am, it had to come from me." After a long period of grieving, during which Leslie reflected on her life, she was able to see how desperately she had sought approval from others, craving love in any form she could get, because she never received any from her parents while growing up. "But it wasn't out there. I had to discover it inside of me. No, I had to develop it for myself. No one could do it for me. I am still working on myself, however, now I have a sense of calm that I never had in my entire life. I know that my life is valuable just as much as anyone else's. It is up to me to believe in who I am and fill my own heart with love."

Building Self-Worth

"What I am looking for is not out there; it is in me."
Helen Keller

After years of living life in a reactionary state, basing how I felt about myself on how others treated me, I came to a profound realization. I would never find any sort of fulfillment, contentedness, or inner peace by searching for it outside of myself. The delusion that some mystical person or grand opportunity would make me feel worthy had been a farce for my entire life.

It is easy to understand how I became outwardly driven, since from the time I was born everything outside of me ruled my thoughts. I had little space of my own to think without disruption and no knowledge about building my inner realm of self-worth. My mother's total happiness was predicated on my father and his behavior. As we moved from country to country, the only way I knew to be was to fill my inner discontent with external stimulation. This served as a short-term remedy, but then the same feelings would rise within me. I wore thin of constantly beating down my emotions and knew that the only way to live the life I dreamed was to change my thinking.

So, I arrived at the intersection of my life, the defining moment. I felt compelled to make a life-altering decision about myself in order to move forward. I knew with greater clarity than I'd ever had before that I no longer wanted to feel as I'd been feeling.

That said, I didn't have a precise roadmap in front of me. I wasn't sure what would or could happen. I only knew that I had reached the point of no return. All I wanted was to feel at peace with who I was and not continue to battle the issues that had beaten me down my entire life. By the time this moment arrived, I had suffered through the loss of eleven close family members and friends in a matter of seven years. I knew with more assurance than ever before that healing myself and creating new thoughts could not be as hard as dealing with all those sad losses.

What would I do? Which way would I go? How far was I willing to pursue the issues that I'd buried in the steel vault in my brain?

When one suffers from low self-worth, he or she also lacks a sense of spiritual connection within, with others, and with something beyond the routines of daily life. At this time of new beginnings, I learned that building a spiritual connection is part of building self-worth. My feelings of unworthiness were not going anywhere without a belief in something sublime.

This did not mean that I attached myself to a particular religion. Spirituality has numerous definitions, but I believe it can be whatever you wish it to be, as long as it brings you light, joy, healing, and love. My spirituality is an energy that resonates within me, around me, and is the infinite wisdom that abounds in the universe. Spirituality transcends any ties to material things, hostility, bigotry, bullying, and intolerance. It lifts one out of the role of being a victim or a perpetrator, which is often a cycle.

Many struggle with their religious or spiritual beliefs, largely due to the fact that they cannot empirically prove the soul or spirit exists. If you cannot touch, smell, or see it, how can it be real?

All you have to do is take a philosophy class and you'll soon realize that what is real is purely subjective. Is your imagination real? Your dreams? Have you experienced Deja vu? How real does it feel when you go someplace new, yet you know you've been there before? That familiarity that you've done something that you're certain you've never done cannot be scientifically proven, yet you feel absolutely certain that it took place. Scientists explain this as a neurological anomaly that is caused by an electrical discharge in the brain that creates this sensation.

Even those of you who are not spiritual or religious, valuing who you are in your innermost core self and accepting yourself under any circumstance, requires that you focus your attention on the invisible you, that Soul Self that no one but you can know deeply. It involves taking the steps to know who you are apart from your worldly experiences. For me, this meant believing that who I truly was internally was the source of my existence and was not attached to my corporeal being. My internal source of life and energy had to be tapped into in order to build my own self-worth. And, I was the only one capable of doing so.

There are instances in everyone's life that cause us to question reality versus spirituality. Have you ever experienced a sensation of being touched on your back or arm while feeling upset or needing support? Several times during the course of my life I've felt this warm sensation rise from my hand up my arm that caused a physical effect called cutis anserina or horripilation, known as goose bumps. The first time it happened to me was when I was extremely low, missing my father so much that the fierce pain in my heart felt as though a knife was slicing through each coronary artery. As I sat there mourning, I suddenly felt warm air blow across my arm. What caught my attention was that it was only on one arm. Typically, if I'm warm or cold, the physical effect is throughout my body, but in these instances, the sensation was only on my right arm. Peculiar as it was, I knew it was my dad's energy lovingly stroking me to a state of tranquility.

I like to think of spirituality's role in self-worth as similar to the fundamentals of Traditional Chinese Medicine. If you've ever had acupuncture, you've experienced the use of energy, or Qi, to heal pain or illness, including mental and emotional disorders. Correctly placing needles on the body's meridians—pathways along the body where energy flows—is a practice that allows energy that is blocked in a person's body to flow freely again to restore health. The Chinese practice of acupuncture has worked for 2,500 years. Today it is at long last being adopted by some Western medical practitioners as a holistic health practice.

The existence of a soul is something that has been debated for hundreds of years and more recently studied by scientists, who locate the soul in the brain. My belief is simple: the soul is you. It resides inside you, but also radiates out of you. It is in the energy in your cells and the energy in your imagination. To connect with your soul does not require a medium or a priest. Your soul is your intuitive, pure self, the center of your being, the energy that is who you really are without wounds, defense mechanisms, or misconstrued thoughts about who you should be. The You that is eternal, that will always live, is Your Soul Self.

The way to know your soul is to clear away the debris that often blocks access in those with low self-worth This is why we must eventually look at our worst fears and most negative thoughts about ourselves. That all has to shift so we can move the rock from in front of the cave where our soul has retreated. Many of us lost connection to our soul as we moved away from our core being due to the consequences of low self-worth.

I felt relief and also elation that I came to the point where I was ready to look inside rather than hope that something outside of me would take away my pain. The adventure of self-discovery has been invigorating: the realization that something was wrong, the identification of my low self-worth, the search for how to build healthy self-worth, the reconnection with my soul, self-trust, self-love, and so much more you will also experience as you move along the path to self-transformation. Before the actual process begins, it is important to have this background of knowledge to understand what it will mean to you and your life when you reconnect with your innermost Soul Self.

Once we connect with soul, unblock our energy and let it flow where it is needed for vitality and health, we are generating healthy self-worth. You can almost hear it humming as it gathers strength. When we allow the issues that have created our internal tension to flow out of us, we are cleansing ourselves mentally, physically, and spiritually. It's a Soul

Detox. A Soul Detox is a cathartic release of toxic energy that permits new positive energy to enter and replenish us. This is not an instantaneous, quick-detox, as one might expect with a food cleanse or a sugar detox. This takes time, as all the negative energy that has caused our low self-worth cannot be released overnight. You will recognize signs of detoxification when you feel you have more energy, see yourself with greater clarity, and make constructive choices that lead you down the path to a positive sense of self. We will walk through the process of a Soul Detox, which is a cumulative, energizing and renewing state that one attains after spending time on the practices.

As we build our self-worth, we will begin to shed insecurities, let go of anger and resentment, jealousy, self-doubt, and distrust. We will throw out what is not working. We will take inventory and toss or repurpose what is negative and causes us angst. We will sweep the scary cobwebs from the corners and brighten and redecorate our interior space with positive affirmations and messages to ourselves that only we can see and feel. And, we will permit new, beautiful, vibrant thoughts to replace the negative ones.

It takes some time and focus to make a new space, a new dashboard for all our daily operations and interactions. Our past intrudes on our present, often contaminating our thoughts and behavior with old feelings of unworthiness through our own or others' criticisms or impossible standards (impossible because they are no longer what you aspire to). Clearing out the archaic and obsolete thoughts—those you want to expel as they no longer have power over you—will enable you to arrive in a new space of living, in which you can enjoy the blessings that surround you, live in the moment by being open and attentive to your life, and relish the beauty of every single day. This is what self-worth brings to you and your life.

Always know in your heart and mind that building healthy self-worth is doable, no matter how low you have felt. I have no question in my mind that you are an amazing person and deserve to feel great about yourself; it is only a matter of **you** believing that you're amazing.

Part One: What Is Self-Worth and Why Is It so Important?

As you read earlier, my mental state of see-sawing up and down, depending on what was happening at the time, caused me immense anxiety. The fact that I allowed others to erode years of my life away saddens me, yet it also motivated me to strive to create a sacred haven inside of me that was transformative in every facet of my life.

This tranquility may best be described as an enlightened state that reveals to you your life's purpose. You will feel renewed and connected to the energy around you and to others. Your relationships will be enriched as you are able to trust yourself and also trust others. You will know what it means to feel free of critical voices that sabotaged your days and disrupted your nights. And, you will fully understand and experience what it means to feel at peace.

I will walk you through the steps as we move through the chapters in this book. Building self-worth takes time, but bit by bit, step by step, you will begin to feel the internal conflict diminish, the weight of your burdens lighten. We will build powerful self-worth that is founded upon learning how to respect and honor yourself, how to let go of distrust and self-doubt, and how to develop an inner state of being that is based on self-love. Although this is a program of practical steps, you will experience a spiritual evolution as you develop your self-worth and feel gratitude for the beauty that is within you.

> Self-worth is based on one premise: that you look within to reconnect with your Soul Self

Transformation Tenets

◇ A spiritual connection, one that transcends anything material, is crucial to the process of change.

◇ Even people who are not spiritual know that inside of them is their Soul Self, an energy they sense, feel, and that is their source of loving energy and wisdom.

◇ When you commit to a Soul Detox, you are releasing toxic thoughts and unblocking the energy inside of you and letting it flow naturally to the areas that need healing and light.

◇ You are the corporeal or living expression of your soul, the energy that comprises your cells and your existence.

Be the Leader of Your Life

Before you begin the process of building your self-worth, take the phrase *I am the Leader of my Life* and put it on a large poster board to hang in your personal space, the place most sacred to you. Add the line: I will live in alignment with my soul. These two important pledges will serve as a constant reminder to you that you are on a positive mission to guide your thoughts and actions in accordance with your true inner being.

Part Two

Committing to Transformative Change

Low Self-Worth
and the Fear of Change

"Fear makes the wolf bigger than he is."
German proverb

My mother remained married to my father despite the suffering she endured from his affairs with other women, his lying and manipulations, and the denials that literally drove her crazy. She was an extremely fragile person when they met, having lived through a tumultuous and hostile childhood, and suffered low self-worth. When she married my father, a handsome, highly intelligent, athletic and powerful man, she thought she had found her place in the world and that she was safe at last. It wasn't long after they were married, however, that my dad began having affairs. As much as I adored him, my father's continual betrayals nearly killed my mother.

Today, my mom and I are extremely close friends. She has outlived my father, which is perhaps poetic justice. But why couldn't she take herself out of a marriage that was so clearly toxic and dangerous to her health, even given societal expectations at that time?

As she has discussed many times with me, my father had great jobs, made lots of money, and took care of my mother in every way—other than being loyal, respectful, trustworthy, kind, and loving. To a person with low self-worth the outer trappings of success—beautiful home, fashionable clothes, the ability to travel—appear more important than values like loyalty, respect, trust, kindness, and love. Because we don't love ourselves, we turn toward the material, or external things for comfort.

It was easier for my mother to stay in an abusive marriage than to get a divorce because she was terrified of change. The unknown, which was frightening to her, although it might have been beautiful and exciting and far more rewarding, was a black hole she might drop into and disappear, instead of a portal to light. Fear stunts. Fear of changing oneself cripples one's life.

This is the case for millions of people who settle for the "comfort" of living with what they know, as opposed to taking a leap of faith. For so many, their perceived comfort is actually damaging and uncomfortable, yet the fear of what they don't know supersedes the reality of what they know and have to face. This is neither healthy nor wise. Without accepting that change is a natural part of life, intrinsic to the human state, there will be no improvement.

Early humans were programed for fight or flight. As we have become lazier and weaker due to the lack of wild animals eyeballing us as prey, and the ease of shopping at the grocery store instead of hunting our own food, many of us choose flight—not in a literal sense as in fleeing for our lives. But we choose to go inside ourselves and hide in a little corner of our mind festooned with messages like I am worthless. I'll never be able to lose my fear of rejection. I've had so many cups of tea there, and a few martinis, comforting myself by saying I will show everyone that I am successful. And I did and do. I am good at an amazing number of things. No one who knows me would say I'm a deadbeat. But until I put the effort into figuring out how I could change what I believed about myself, that's who I was to me.

I refer to this state as living at the intersection of Nowhere and Nothing. Nowhere as I was always on the precipice, in a state of suspension, waiting and watching, being an observer of my life. The Nothing came from the fact that growth and transformation do not happen when you're stuck at this intersection of your life. I understood that nothing would change unless I did something about it. You are bound to this spot out of fear or inertia, even though there is a way out.

I'm not downplaying the challenges in your life. I have interviewed people whose situations were confounding regarding change. Sometimes there are legitimate factors to take into account before leaping, for instance, if your job is terrible but you are supporting a family, you must be strategic. Caregivers who are responsible for the life of an elderly person who verbally abuses them often feel trapped by responsibility. But there is always a way forward. There are modifications and adjustments that can be made at any point. Perhaps you can't quit a job that perpetuates your low worth; but you can begin taking steps to facilitate a transition. If there is no one else to take care of your problematic relative, how about respite care that would allow you to spend more time in nature connecting with your Soul Self? Sometimes once we begin the effort to change, making a whole-hearted commitment to changing follows.

You can't change your past, but you can change your future by transforming your thoughts and emotions, which dictate attitude and drive behavior, reactions, and responses. Change is about innovation, modification, revision, resolution, transition, and transformation. All Good! You do not have to be stuck in negative patterns suffering from low self-worth.

> Inside each of us—even the bitter, negative person—lives the note of hope that is our soul's sustaining song.

Transformation Tenets

◊ Fear is a common saboteur of change.

◊ Every human being has the choice to move beyond discomfort to discover a healthier, more fulfilling life.

◊ The past is over. Become an active participant in your life by focusing on creating a present and future that is nourishing and joyful.

◊ Everyone needs change to keep their brain active and to build new neural pathways.

A Human Mosaic Vignette

From Psychotic to CEO

A man I interviewed many years ago called me one day and mentioned that there was someone I needed to talk to for my book. He said, "You won't believe this guy's story, it is the pinnacle of what you would define as monumental life transformation." A few weeks later, I was sitting in the lobby of a nationally renowned drug and alcohol treatment facility waiting to meet this person. Seated across from me was a young, handsome, well-dressed preppy-looking-type wearing a blue and white striped button down shirt. There was an over-stuffed green garbage bag next to him which he held onto with his pale hand. He appeared to be waiting for someone or something important as he drummed his other hand against the wooden arm of the chair. Suddenly, a tall, muscular man walked up to him and preppy stood up immediately to greet him as they hugged one another tightly. "Hey, man, please call me as soon as you get access to a phone and let me know if you are okay," he said to preppy. Preppy teared up and told him he definitely would stay in touch.

Since I was sitting only a few feet away, I heard their brief, emotional exchange. Emotion rose within me, emanating from the compassion I felt for the two friends as they parted. I looked directly at preppy and, in my typically unabashed way, asked him why he was at the facility. Preppy looked at me directly in the eyes and told me he was there for heroin addiction. This was his eighth time in rehab, and by far, was the best it was life-changing, and believed that this time,

ıgh to make it.

.e CEO of the facility, permitted me to interview

s. He was as raw and candid with me about his life

er known. After our day together, I truly grasped how

ıc.   ings are. His purpose in sharing his story is to provide

inspiration .   ners who are suffering from low self-worth, to let them

know that they can change and improve their lives if they commit and invest time in themselves. Todd made it a point to tell me during our visit and subsequent interviews that if his challenges and transformation help at least one person decide to change their life—*to save their life*—through building self-worth, then his story would have meaning and value.

Todd is living proof that even after near-death, anyone can change when they choose to make the commitment to themselves. The fact that he is alive today to be able to share his story of survival is extraordinary.

The memorable day I spent with Todd had a revolutionary impact on my understanding of the human brain and its capacity to recover from severe trauma, then restore and rebuild damaged areas. Through neuroplasticity, we know that our brain can form new pathways and transmit messages around areas that may have been damaged by drug and alcohol abuse. In Todd's case, you will hear how truly powerful our brain is in following our lead.

A prince of a man—gracious, humble, smart, generous—Todd was mind-blowing in his honesty with respect to his tenuous travail to near death. Miraculously, Todd survived years of self-destructive behavior. "My parents loved me, however, from what I remember my father was gone a lot due to the demands of being a physician. When he was home, he was really tough on me. He ruled with an iron fist anytime I didn't do exactly what I was supposed to," remarked Todd. "I felt nothing was ever good enough for my dad, and the relentless approach he took to point out those errors made things really hard." In Todd's young mind, reconciling the disparaging comments and aggressiveness he endured was complicated; it was difficult for Todd to feel safe, particularly with his emotions.

The downward spiral began when Todd was in elementary school. "I remember it felt like there were only two people in the entire town with red hair, myself and my sister. While she was told how beautiful her hair was, I was made fun of for mine. I hated having red hair. I was angry at my parents, myself, but mostly at God, and that is when I began acting out against the world." His red hair was the focus of incessant jokes and jabs. With time, the taunts and bullying beat him down to such a low point that it obliterated whatever self-worth he may have had—if any. "I even shaved my head to try to hide the natural color of my hair, to try to fit in."

Todd believed the only escape from the internal anguish he suffered was to rebel against society. His first experience was drinking moonshine when he was only six years old, calling it "funny juice" because he observed how humorous it made his best friend's father after he had a few drinks of the stuff. The liquor enabled Todd to momentarily suspend his insecurity, making him feel a sense of power. As he grew older, his drinking became heavier and more frequent, and he began taking drugs. By the time he was in his teens, he rebuked everyone in his town, and immersed himself in a lascivious lifestyle—one filled with violence, drugs, booze, and crime. For years, Todd lived this way, evading the law and destroying his mind and body to block his low self-opinion.

When he reached the threshold of his addiction, Todd took things to an extreme. "I reached a point where I could not function on a day-to-day basis without at least a 250-milligram dose of Methadone, a potent opioid much like morphine, and this was at the low-end dose for me. I often would take 350-400 milligrams to be able to feel normal. On top of that, I also wanted to get high, so I would smoke crack followed by five to ten Xanax pills. I couldn't believe my ability to tolerate so many toxic substances and still stand on my feet. Heck, I couldn't believe it took that many toxic substances to actually get me to stand on my feet." But, after a few days of over-the-top binging and a run in with law enforcement, Todd found himself in the most desperate situation of his life. His body and mind had reached its limit, and both begin to collapse. "As I was escorted into the Fayette County Detention Center in Lexington, Kentucky, I realized the hell I was getting ready to experience. I had just smoked about two ounces of crack in a forty-eight-hour period and had no Methadone left. I was in trouble, and I knew it."

As he lay at the bottom of a deep black hole — the hole in his mind that he had been living in for most of his life — Todd asked himself why he had to continue to suffer with this affliction? Why wouldn't God just allow him to die? And with that last thought, Todd slipped into a state of delusion, hallucination, and physical deterioration. The withdrawal from the large amount of cocaine, Methadone, and Xanax caused Todd to begin to decompensate mentally, and he lapsed into a state of psychosis in which he lost complete connection with reality.

Hovering between life and death, Todd was removed from incarceration through actions taken by an attorney his parents hired. They transported him to a small treatment program located in Georgia where Todd was given the opportunity to begin to heal. As he slowly came out of his psychotic state, Todd realized the choice he had to make. "I took the hardest road possible. I went cold turkey off everything. It was three months of torture. Getting past the psychosis from the cocaine withdrawal was one thing but coming off 300 milligrams a day of taking Methadone habitually for many years was unbearable agony. The sad part was that the physical pain was child's play compared to the emotional anguish I suffered."

Todd desperately wanted to believe that he was a good person, that he had worth as a human being. Through all his agony, he finally understood that the only way to improve his life was to learn to value himself, to build self-respect, and to live a meaningful life. With faith and resolve as his pillars, Todd knew in his heart that he had to change. He was willing to do whatever it took not only to survive, but to transform for good.

Part Two: Committing to Transformative Change

For the first time in his life, Todd focused inwardly. He worked on developing what he termed his "inner wealth," during which he concentrated on building internal strength as his foundation. He knew that nothing material in the world could be more important than valuing who he was as a person, and he recognized the importance of having a relationship with a power greater than himself. At the end of our conversation, Todd shared the values he chose to support his effort to push past the pain: Honesty, Courage, Faith, and Selflessness. These four words have served as his guidepost in directing Todd towards what matters most in life.

From the riveting interviews with Todd, I learned much more than I anticipated. With an open mind and heart going into our meeting, I exited with humility, awe, and infinite respect for how he transformed himself. I had no idea that I would be meeting with a former drug dealer, criminal, and addict. However, more importantly, a person who had the strength to move from a position of excruciating pain and suffering, to now living with hope, optimism, and at long last, peace.

Todd's survival from near-death and courageous transformation exemplifies the inherent power within each of us to effectuate personal change when we focus on our inner selves in order to develop a powerful force of stability and peace. Whatever your belief system, when you make the decision to commit to change, make it your personal pledge to yourself, and you too may develop a story such as the one Todd shared with me, one that he called, "From Psychotic to CEO".

Making the Choice to Change

"A human being is a deciding being."
Viktor Frankl, Austrian neurologist, psychiatrist, and Holocaust
survivor; inventor of logotherapy, part of existential analysis

At school in Bonn, we learned about Viktor Frankl, a concentration camp survivor. Of particular intrigue was his extraordinary inner strength, towering courage, and humanistic wisdom. A brilliant psychiatrist and neurologist, Frankl was taken prisoner by the Nazis during Hitler's horrific rule. His survival is a case study of the profound power of the human brain.

Frankl's background gave him an acute understanding of the magnificent human brain, which was what helped him cling to life in the face of being dehumanized and exposed to the horrendous stress of life in Auschwitz and other camps. He conditioned his brain to separate himself from his environment, even under the most brutal and barbaric of conditions, by relying upon his ability to exercise the most fundamental freedom in life: "The ability to determine one's own attitude and spiritual well-being." No sadistic Nazi SS guard was able to take that away from him or control Frankl's Soul Self. When he saw that it was those who had nothing to live for who died fastest in the concentration camp, he willed himself to think of his wife. In doing so, he realized, "The salvation of man is through love and in love. I understood how a man who has nothing left in this world still may know bliss, be it only for a brief moment, in the contemplation of his beloved."

Part Two: Committing to Transformative Change

His capacity to survive the atrocities that were inflicted upon him underscores the mind over matter philosophy—that even in the most dehumanizing, destructive situation imaginable, one can will themselves to transcend suffering and find meaning in life.

Your brain, the most powerful tool in the universe, is at your service twenty-four hours a day. It will help you to not only survive unthinkable circumstances, but to regain your footing and transcend that experience.

No change is sustainable, however, unless it is internal and intentional, as was Frankl's, who chose to change to save his life. On a day to day basis, people want symptomatic relief for their suffering, but they don't really want to change. Moreover, changing something about yourself because you think you should, or because others want you to, does not provide authentic motivation; even if there is movement and effort toward change, if it's not internally driven, it is unsustainable.

I know too well the consequences of giving away my power to make choices, as I've lived much of my life allowing other people and events to direct my decisions rather than taking the lead myself. I didn't have a firm grasp on who I was in my innermost self. I didn't spend time doing a self-inventory of what I wanted for my life, but moved toward the nearest, most appealing target. I wasn't what you'd call a "drifter," yet I landed positions with companies without researching them thoroughly or identifying for myself what would suit me and my future.

It was the same with dating, marriage, dating again…I dated athletes, attorneys, salespeople, a guy from New Zealand who might have liked men more than me, corporate executives, politicians, smart, dumb, sophisticated, a country cowboy, a black belt in karate—the only commonality among the types was they had to be single and male. I was on a man-marathon to fill the void inside of me. I truly believed that I could find the answer to my restlessness by being in a passionate, intense relationship. What I found instead was men that were handsome but dumb, intelligent but selfish, intriguing yet unreliable, and the guy from

New Zealand…well, let's just say that our romance is a bizarre story for another book. And the search went on, and on, and on…

Until I finally got "it," meaning the lightbulb moment; the revelatory thought that my life was mine to manage. I wouldn't find it out there, in the vast sea of men, jobs, or money. Instead of following the leader, I became the leader. When I changed, everything changed. As I began the process to build my self-worth, the knowledge that I ALWAYS had a choice about how I wanted to feel every single second of the day was my anchor.

> Choice is the gift of human consciousness.

Transformation Tenets

◊ The mind is mightier than the flesh.

◊ Change is only sustainable when it is intentional and stems from within.

◊ Your brain is at your service, every single moment of every day.

◊ Lead your life—because, by the way—it is YOUR LIFE, by choosing to change how you feel about yourself.

Part Two: Committing to Transformative Change

The Commitment to Change

"The only thing that is constant is change."

— Heraclitus, pre-Socratic Greek philosopher

Change is an inescapable, fundamental tenet of life. Change is filled with the constant motion of matter and energy. Our physical form may be finite, deteriorating as the elements of our body break down, but the collection of atoms that is us will always be around; we simply change form, our energy continuing to echo throughout space until the end of time.

A profound and meaningful discovery I made before writing this book was learning that our amazing brains have the ability to help us change through a process called neuroplasticity, or brain plasticity. Neuroplasticity is a term I ask you to become intimately familiar with during the process of building self-worth as it allows our neurons to adjust their activities in response to new situations or changes in environment. It also affords us the ability to generate new neurons. When I learned about our brain's ability to form new neural connections at any age or stage of life, I felt as if I had solved the most complicated puzzle imaginable. It was glorious to know that no matter what someone has been through, they can physically evolve their brain and develop new thoughts and behavior.

This understanding itself felt as though I was seeing lightening for the first time! Why?

Because now I had empirical evidence that our brain likes to change, it thrives on learning, and it functions more effectively when we take on new challenges. *The fact is that the human brain needs to absorb new skills and information to preserve and protect itself from degenerating.*

And, on a side note, I had a ready response to everyone who has said to me, I can't change. I am too old to form new habits. Look at me ... do ya think I can help this old brain? The science of neuroplasticity is amazing as it enables us to transform ourselves anytime we wish. Further information will be discussed later in this section.

Change can and will happen, so you might as well choose to commit to the kind of change that will transform your life. But choosing to change is a personal pledge, not just another goal to add to your list. You are not resolving to start exercising on January 1st. You are committing to changing your life.

The decision to elevate your self-worth and live a more enriching life has to be made by you, not forced upon you by others. Trying to force change is as exhausting as Sisyphus pushing that rock up the mountain, only to have it tumble down as he got to the top. By definition, force means physical coercion. Psychological force means pressuring your mind to adopt new forms of behavior without the emotional component that is needed to provide the support.

It comes as no surprise that in most cases in which we force ourselves to achieve a tangible result, our old pattern of behavior typically comes screeching back. We all know people who tried to lose weight or stop drinking, only to find their old ways resurface. Either they don't have the right framework or support for change, or they have not fully committed.

Long-term, enduring change requires a commitment beyond desire and motivation. It is a deep, comprehensive understanding of what you want to achieve, a conviction to which you are resolutely devoted. This includes upfront evaluation and analysis, preparation, daily timelines, and goal attainment markers. Every meaningful challenge we pursue in life deserves this level of forethought and care.

We will do this together, so you have the strategy and tools to support your effort. Of course, flexibility is always a factor as life is not predictable, and circumstances arise that might interfere with your plan; however, knowing that you have a framework from which to work ensures you have a map to guide you.

In order to make this Olympian effort, you will need to practice what I refer to as intensive self-care. You will learn about treating yourself with respect, loyalty and honor, kindness and love. You will learn to trust yourself. You will honor your Soul Self. These are all the invaluable qualities that my mother never gained from her upbringing or marriage to my father. These are also the ones that I had to learn for myself.

You will not punish yourself for mistakes or poor performance of your commitment to this process. When one falters in their commitment to change internally, it is reflective of the way one feels about themselves at the core. Each of us is different, and no one approach works for everyone, but through trial and error, you can find a pathway to healing and thriving.

> Commitment is what turns a promise into reality, skepticism into integrity, weakness into strength.

Transformation Tenets

- ◊ Neuroplasticity is the science that proves our brain can learn new thoughts, skills, and behavior at any age or stage of life.
- ◊ When you commit to personal change, you are making a powerful pledge to yourself, a sacred vow.
- ◊ True commitment is rooted in resolute conviction that is based on analysis, preparation, and goal-setting.
- ◊ Intensive self-care involves honoring yourself through approaches to enhance yourself mentally, physically, and spiritually.

Recommitting to Change

"Our greatest weakness lies in giving up. The most certain way to succeed is always to try just one more time."
Thomas A. Edison

Now that you know with certainty that your brain enables you to learn new patterns of thought and behavior through the science of neuroplasticity, my hope is that you, dear reader, have a new and reinvigorated outlook about self-change, and, moreover, that you also know that you possess an *instrumental* role in the process of developing healthy self-worth. The only obstacle that stands in the way of your commitment to personal transformation is your mindset about the process. As we have discussed, change is not easy, but it is the most certain way to rewrite the script of your life.

Even after we have committed to personal change, there will be moments that throw you off, events that take precedence, or emotions that interfere—this is the nature of living as a human being in a world that is in constant motion. With the best of intentions, you establish a plan for yourself, and, then there is a bump in the road. Something triggers a thought or behavior and impacts your mood, and you fall back into your former patterns of behavior. This occurs because life does not stop to clear a smoothly paved road for us. We have to navigate around uneven terrain that causes us to trip, to traverse unexplored trails along which we lose our way. But, don't stop or give up your mission to heal yourself and gain inner strength and calm.

You are worth the effort to regroup and get back on your journey to develop positive self-worth.

I queried a large number of people from diverse backgrounds throughout the course of the last several years, asking why personal change is difficult and often unattainable. Although multiple factors were mentioned, the inability to maintain one's commitment was by far the most pervasive reason people were defeated. Some cited an event that took place which was outside of their control and sabotaged their effort. An emergency, an injury, or monetary restrictions were cited as justifiable causes. Other reasons for quitting were: I can't stick with it, it's too difficult, I'm too lazy, too old, it's such a long-term issue to resolve, I haven't had enough tangible results. A large number of individuals fail to reach their goals even when it impacts their health or marriage. One must understand that there will always be circumstances that challenge us along the path to building healthy self-worth, as life does not stop for our personal growth plan.

Alcoholics Anonymous has a saying, "Relapse is part of recovery." Because the chances of your self-worth recovery getting derailed are fairly high, there is a built-in back-up plan, a fail-safe measure, that you can use. ***Recommit.***

When we marry, we make a serious commitment to love and honor one another for the rest of our lives. We do not marry expecting to divorce. Yet more than 50 percent of couples do. What is important in marriage is not the original vow, it is recommitting to our relationship every day, or if not every day then at least when things get iffy. We all have some slips in our commitment, when we disappoint ourselves in thought or action. This is part of being human. Your commitment, or personal pledge, will involve some setbacks, but you will have within you the resolve to regroup and continue marching forward.

There are definitely consequences when we slip. For example, what if your goal is to be kinder to yourself in regard to the stringent expectations you have for orderliness? You know this is a perfectionist objective you assigned to yourself as a child in order to be loved, and one about which you have intentionally committed to lighten up. Your goal now is to be more patient and loving toward yourself, not to punish yourself with angry chores. This is important to your partner as well, because when you indulge in your perfectionism, you get angry at him because he has no problem with being more relaxed with respect to housekeeping.

As the house follows an organic evolution from 5-star hotel standards to the home of a normal family, you become more and more tense and finally start insulting your partner about being lazy and sloppy. In fact, equating extreme orderliness with love is your problem, not his. You have let down not only yourself but are taking down your supportive partner as well. It's not him you are mad at, it's yourself. You have broken trust with your commitment to change, heightening your negative emotions and triggering your low self-worth.

This collateral damage not only affects your partner's well-being, but your own heart rate and blood pressure; it depletes your energy level, causes headaches, muscle tension, sleeplessness, and stomach cramps. Your anger reduces your mental clarity and acuity, promoting distractibility and irritability. You feel regret, shame, guilt, inadequacy, frustration, depression, and fatigue. You have failed.

Except you haven't failed. Just as you can get back up after a fall, you can recommit to your change goals. After several of these episodes, you will develop trust in yourself that, with planning and prompts, you can do this.

Personal change is not a linear process. If you understand this salient point from the beginning, you will be gentler with yourself during the potential setbacks. You've made a pledge to yourself, pause, take time to breathe and refocus, and recommit to moving forward.

The key to enduring commitment is to recommit every day; if that fails, do it the next day because you are worth it.

Transformation Tenets

- ◇ There will be setbacks that pull you away from your objective, but you will rebound and recommit.
- ◇ Know that you can always regroup and return to your program for change with renewed zeal and focus.
- ◇ Remind yourself throughout the process of building self-worth that the only obstacle is your mindset.
- ◇ Being adaptable is part of developing self-worth.
- ◇ There is only one person you disappoint when you walk away from your commitment—yourself.

Intentional Change Theory

"Change is the end result of all true learning."
Leo Buscaglia, American author and motivational speaker, also
called "Dr. Love."

"Change, and in particular, intentional or desired change, has not been understood nor systematically studied," Professor Richard Boyatzis told me, hooking me immediately. Of all the interviews I conducted for this book, his was the most revelatory. A professor of Organizational Behavior at Case Western Reserve University, and widely regarded as an expert in the field of emotional intelligence, behavior change, and competence, his impressive background includes research on the human brain and how it is impacted by positive and negative events.

Richard had been trained to think that he could use his knowledge to guide people to reflect through their problems to find a resolution. After practicing psychotherapy for nine years, however, he was disenchanted with that technique. Spending hours upon hours with his clients cycling through the broad array of issues that held them hostage didn't seem to provide the help they needed. Fortunately, Richard had an epiphany: focusing on the negative—the problems—was having the opposite effect of clearing away troubling thoughts to make way for solutions; it was deepening the malaise, perpetuating despair.

Absolutely, I thought. I had been noticing that for more than nine years in my informal practice of trying to cure myself. I knew what the problems were—H-E-L-L-O—I had been living with them for my entire life—I just never found the solutions.

Part Two: Committing to Transformative Change

I believed I could think my way out of the anguish I felt when I was bullied in school, as well as other internalized traumas. But the longer you spend thinking about who, what, when, where, and how something happened in your life to cause your low self-worth, the more time and energy you expend in that negative zone. Our brain has been conditioned to want to retrace those hurtful experiences because it is the path of least resistance, having already worn a groove in our neural pathways.

You know how this feels—that it truly does not help you in anyway when you retrace angry thoughts or unsavory experiences. Holding onto distressing thoughts leads to a vicious circle inside of you that intensifies the more you fixate on them. The longer you allow sadness or anger to fester in your mind, the harder it is to let it go. Many of us choose to block our thoughts by forcing them away. But they lurk in our brain, waiting for the next chance to break through the blockade we have created. Our highly attentive brain reminds us of what we would prefer to ignore, or wish would evaporate into the atmosphere.

During my interviews with Richard, he shared findings that revealed a fascinating discovery. His research proved we cannot focus on the negative if we want to change our thoughts and behavior. This was incredulous to me, being someone who has always relied on my brain to think through problems and find a solution. Richard explained that when we dwell on negative thoughts, we are using the wrong part of our brain. By using fMRI (functional Magnetic Resonance Imaging), which measures brain activity by detecting changes through blood flow, Richard's studies demonstrated the changes in the brain that resulted from Positive Emotional Attractors (PEA) as opposed to Negative Emotional Attractors (NEA). What this means is that the most powerful way to change is not to intellectualize your problems away, to continue focusing on what is not working, rather it is to focus on something positive, something you wish for your life. This approach releases you from the clutches of negativity and frees your mind to be open to opportunities to positively evolve.

Arousing the Positive Emotional Attractors allows a psychophysiological of being open to new ideas and discoveries. Psychophysiology, or the science that is concerned with the interaction between mind and body, allows us to understand the correlation between how we think and feel, which is pivotal to catalyzing personal change. Arousing the Negative Emotional Attractors stops the sustainability of any change because you are not intrinsically motivated. Aha! This made sense. I thought about how much of my life I had spent in my brain looking backwards on what had troubled me, instead of being in the present and paving a new and exciting journey for myself. This mindset is precisely what prohibits so many people from achieving lasting transformation. They are focusing on the problem, not the dream. They are stuck in the negativity rather than being emotionally inspired.

The greatest source of motivation stems from positive energy, not negative. When athletes compete, their training is far more than just physical. Their mental training is what sets them apart and instills within them the inner power and determination. Mind over matter is a phrase that will always have meaning because our mind is an incredibly potent motivator. When we believe something, we are mentally and physically committed. Our bodies follow our brain's lead. Athletes are trained to possess steadfast confidence, to have positive, energizing internal language or self-talk, to overcome anxiety or frustration through mental discipline, to be highly motivated at all times, to have intense focus and commitment, and to envision their winning performance. This highly focused and positive mindset enables them to perform at their peak level.

Long before sports psychology was integral to athletic competition, the great Greek philosopher Plato (424BC to 347BC) stated: "Human behavior flows from three main sources: desire, emotion, and knowledge." In this particular order, desire fuels one's emotions, emotions then translate into thought and behavior. Plato understood these key drivers of human behavior were integral to long term sustainability.

Mental training is an invaluable component of numerous other professions. Musicians, ballet dancers, business executives, firefighters, surgeons, nurses, artists, architects, and many other professions rely on mental techniques to achieve their goals. Visualization, a process of envisioning what one wishes to achieve, is another form of mental training that has been a highly effective tool in coaching. When I have asked a client to envision how they wish to feel, for example, relative to where they are today, we create a vision statement and action steps that incite them towards achieving their dreams for their lives. When they become enthusiastic, their positive thoughts lead to engaged, focused, and energized movement towards their vision.

Richard's research demonstrates that using a Positive Emotional Attractor, which emphasizes compassion for an individual's hopes and dreams, enhances behavioral change; while using a Negative Emotional Attractor, focusing on externally defined criteria for success and the individual's weaknesses, does not lead to sustainable change. PEA engages the parasympathetic nervous system, showing more activity in areas of the brain associated with positive affect; NEA engages the sympathetic nervous system and parts of the brain associated with negative affect. This evidence-based research allows us to understand that developing a positive sense of self, learning to accept, honor, trust and love yourself involves a mindset that is not predicated on want or need or have to or must do. Intellectual demands such as need to do or should do, do not engage a person emotionally or spiritually. Sustainable change is not likely when you consider it a problem, a chore, something that has to be done.

I was stunned when Richard said the mistake that most people make when trying to change is they focus on the problem, which impacts the hormonal system, which then shuts someone down. "You have to engage your parasympathetic nervous system so that you change your hormonal flow," Richard pointed out. "Focus on context, not problem," he advised. "Context is your dreams. What you wish would happen." This interview turned my prior understanding of behavioral change on its head.

Think about how motivated you are when you are going on vacation. Your attitude is hopeful, your energy robust, you're eager to do whatever it takes to prepare for the adventure ahead. Chores and everyday tasks are handled with ease, and you heap intensity into your work in order to take care of pending projects prior to your departure. The happy vibes are dancing inside of you as you operate on all cylinders. The endorphins are in full effect. Naturally, this mindset is based on an experience about which you look forward and anticipate being pleasurable. But, this is the point. Human beings are prone to respond favorably towards what excites and invigorates, towards the things they love.

What an intriguing find: focusing on what you believe is wrong or bad about yourself only makes you feel worse. I had been pounding the incidents of childhood bullying into my brain, ensuring that those thoughts would never disappear, instead of releasing them, which would have saved me years of internal anguish. I learned from speaking with Richard that the release would happen naturally if I focused on how I would ideally love to feel about myself, thereby producing hormones that would open my mind and heart to change.

What Richard shared illuminated for me the reasons why traditional approaches to attitude and behavioral change have not been effective when it comes to building self-worth. Ongoing emphasis on past pain continues to strengthen those toxic thought neural pathways in our brain.

It makes perfect sense, doesn't it? The more you dwell on a problem, the larger the problem grows, to the extent that you may become overwhelmed by the recurring, weighty thought patterns. Readdressing what went wrong in your past brings it into your present, and the burden continues to occupy space inside of you.

With a monumental emphasis on the "AHA" moment, this was truly a profound point of awareness and understanding for me. It clarified the mountain of issues that I'd been trying to address, and why it had been such a steep climb to the top. I actually didn't have to continue to retrace my heavy footsteps. Instead, I could approach internal change from a new perspective. Recognize and acknowledge what happened in the past, work through a process to accept what happened, and move beyond it by creating the present and future as you dream it to be.

> Change your life by focusing on the context—who you want to be—rather than on the problem—the negative way you see yourself. Decide how you wish to feel and create the inner life you deserve, which will manifest in your outer life as your brain learns a new way of thinking.

Transformation Tenets

- ◇ Our brain is programmed to retrace trauma; when we focus on the negative—the problem—we perpetuate the issue and deepen the despair.
- ◇ Our greatest source of motivation comes from positive, inspiring thoughts and energizing ideas.
- ◇ Focusing on the PEA, Positive Emotional Attractors, facilitates self-change by arousing a psychophysiological condition, the mind-body connection, which enables you to be open to new ideas and discoveries.
- ◇ The path to self-transformation is not by dwelling on negative events, but by dreaming about the future.

The Ideal Self, the Real Self, and the Ought Self: Who Am I?

Richard Boyatzis' "Intentional Change Theory," which was borne from an earlier theory that he and Dave Kolb developed in 1967, centers on the notion that each one of us has three dimensions of who we are: the ideal self, the real self, and the ought self.

At birth, we enter the world as our real self, with no preconceived notions for who we should be or wish to be. Within a short period of time, the people who influence us in our environment—parents, grandparents, siblings, guardians, babysitters, teachers, coaches—fill our brain with statements that impact the wiring of our brain: 'Look at how your brother picks up his toys and puts them away. You need to learn from him.' 'You should clean up after yourself.' 'Eat all of your vegetables or you won't be healthy!' 'You have to be quiet in school because that is proper behavior.' 'Be nice to your cousin, even though she teases you.' 'Your friend Julie already knows how to spell, it's about time you did as well.' These are examples of statements that children hear and store in their brain at a very young age—what they ought to do and how they ought to think and behave.

The ideal self is our desired mindset, the way we wish to feel about ourselves, without the negative memories and self-punishing inner critic. It is the state of living with an open heart and mind, of being fully engaged in your life and living with joy and exuberance.

So, what do we do to create our ideal self? Here are some steps that will guide you to develop an awareness and understanding of what truly inspires you. How you wish and deserve to feel is a huge incentive to self-transformation. Give this a try and devote time to this exercise as it will uplift you in ways you never imagined.

Ideal Self

First, you need to imagine your ideal self, which is the emotional driver of intentional change. Who would you like to be? How would you like to be? Where would you like to be?

Envision your desired future. Think about your hopes and aspirations. Pay attention to what excites you. What is your passion, no matter how drastically different it is from what you are doing now? Write down all your dreams, whether attainable or not.

Now go ahead and invest in Hope: Imagine you can attain your desired future. Pretend to be an optimist instead of the skeptic you have been.

Then list aspects of your core identity: Strengths, character traits, areas of knowledge, important personal relationships, significantly positive work and personal experiences.

This is your personal vision for yourself. Just the way champion athletes see an image in their mind of themselves performing at their peak before and during competition, replay your personal vision of yourself over and over. Remind yourself of the concrete research that shows the power in focusing on a desired goal; plus, people who develop a deep emotional bond with their personal vision can more easily make a commitment to change.

The next step is to define your real self—the person you are right now in both private and public. For many of us, our self-image is some mixture of awareness of our own real self and the feedback we receive from others about who we are. To really consider changing yourself, you must have a sense of both what you value about yourself and want to keep, and what aspects of yourself you want to change. Where your ideal self and real self are not consistent can be thought of as gaps. This is about building on strengths, though, not about dwelling on weaknesses. The output of this second discovery is a personal balance sheet.

The third step is developing a Learning Agenda and Plan. How can you move forward with your personal vision? Write down short and long-term goals as a teacher would when writing a curriculum for her classroom. Then fill in under the goals what you need to learn and do to accomplish them. The brain can only handle a few developmental changes at a time, though, so make sure you are excited about what you choose to try first. Then you can add more goals, building on what you have accomplished. Remind yourself that without preparation and planning, sustainable change is left to randomness or chance.

Fourth, put your learning agenda and plan into place by Practicing Your Desired Changes. This will help you transition into new habits, whether developing a new skill or replacing an old negative belief with a positive one. Since you are experimenting with new behavior, it should be tried out somewhere you feel safe, not in a potentially hostile environment. After practicing something new, reflect on what happened and evaluate what might need to be tweaked.

Lastly, identify the relationships in your life that are important to you. Engage these individuals and groups in giving you feedback on your new behaviors. This will provide a context in which you can see your progress on your desired changes. Often, our relationships can be sources of support for our change as well as for feedback. They also can help us from slipping back into our former ways of behaving.

The ought self is our understanding of what others want us to be and do. This could also be called our "worrier" instead of "warrior" ideal self. When we are in the ought self, we spend more time in the past and on our problems. This engages the sympathetic nervous system, producing a self-perpetuating negative state where we close down and feel worse about ourselves.

> We are a complex composite of constructs that include who we are in our Soul Self, our innermost being, or our Real Self, our Ideal Self, who we wish to be, and our Ought Self, who we think we should be to be successful and loved. Our life offers us the opportunity to be who we dream as our Ideal Self.

Why You Can't Think
Your Problems Away

"I had therefore to remove knowledge,
in order to make room for belief."
Immanuel Kant, 19th-century German philosopher

I have a confession to make. When I first began writing this book I was focused on behavioral change. After several years of research, interviews, and a ton of writing, I reached a revelatory conclusion: human behavior is the symptomatic manifestation of how a person thinks and feels. The behavior is not the problem. What drives the behavior is the problem: one's inner sense of self. Who you believe you are is manifested in your behavioral patterns. I had invested a lot of time writing about how to change a person's behavior and had to reorient my work toward the invisible dimension of who we are—how one feels about one's self internally. Self-worth. This is what truly matters, our SELF is the nucleus of our lives, I thought to myself.

Now I can move forward.

In my case, there was no obscurity or equivocation as to what in my past was the source of my struggle with self-worth. On the contrary, all I had to do was open my black leather notebook and see the list that I had developed for myself before I even attempted to begin the process of working on myself. It was all right there. And, just the process of writing it down was a huge relief for me.

My meticulous memory had several different files that were kept intact, updated, and reorganized as experiences in my life further deepened my inner turmoil. So, for me, knowing just what happened was straightforward as opposed to many people who feel completely perplexed as to how they became such fractured, fragile souls. What baffled me, nonetheless, was how to separate who I was today from what happened to me in my past. I'd always thought of human beings as the composite of their genetics and environment, nature and nurture, and knew that to be accurate. But, to suffer throughout your life couldn't be what the universe intended for us, could it? Why are we here if we are meant to suffer?

What became vividly clear to me was this existential dilemma: we are all going to encounter rough times, some far graver than others. How do we survive and hope to thrive? Not everyone is as strong as Viktor Frankl, who willed himself to focus on something beautiful in the midst of hell. But there must be something we can do.

I've always been a solutions-oriented person. Okay, there's a problem. Let's figure out what to do to resolve it so that we can move beyond it. Problem-solving is a terrific way to deal with pragmatic or complex issues that crop up. But when it comes to painful emotions, no amount of technical, analytical, or intellectual aptitude will do. Sure, you can find a way to distract yourself from these recurring thoughts by focusing on something else, but they'll remain inside of you.

When it comes to self-worth and other developmental issues that pertain to our life experiences, there isn't a linear path to follow, or an if-then solution. Dealing with deep-seated emotions that have caused you years of anguish does not fall in line with seeking an answer to a problem or following specific instructions to achieve a desired result.

Understanding this caused me to retrace my steps in my thought process and in my writing. I had it all wrong. Well, not everything I'd worked on was off-base, nor did any of it have to be tossed, but my approach to change had to be re-invented. Logic was not the solution.

In our second interview, Richard Boyatzis expounded on why one can't think their issues away: "When you are intellectualizing a problem, you're using the wrong part of your brain."

This is what he meant by that, as stated in his article, "The Ideal Self as the Driver of Intentional Change." Arousal of a fear stimulates neural circuitry starting in the amygdala (the center of emotions in the brain), with dominant activity in the right versus the left prefrontal cortex. At the same time, it promotes activation of the sympathetic nervous system, creating a set of neural and endocrine processes that stimulate negative or defensive emotions, including release of cortisol, increased blood pressure, heart rate, along with emotions associated with guilt, shame, anxiety, and fear. This generally results in a person's withdrawing. It also decreases a person's ability to perform routine executive functions associated with planning, task-management, time management, and goal-orientation.

Intellectualizing your emotions away is a very common defense mechanism that is used during stressful or unfavorable experiences. The problem with intellectualization is that the emotion isn't erased. Rather, it continues to reside inside of you, waiting for the next opportunity to reveal itself. Your brain retains these emotions for as long as you continue to attempt to repress them. The process of intentionally, forcibly squelching negative emotions gives them power over you and actually consumes more energy than working through them to release them. The more you try to ignore or shove them away or repress them, the longer they'll remain a constant reminder of your unpleasant memory. Every time you consciously try to detach from your negative thoughts by pushing them down into your secret bad thoughts compartment, you are saying, "Hello!" because you are arousing them.

Quit saying, "Hello." In fact, don't say anything. Stop dwelling on your sad past. Don't deny it, don't argue with it, don't bargain with it, don't become depressed because of it. You don't have to constantly go through the first four stages of grief with your past. Go straight to acceptance.

When the bad thoughts haunt you, accept them for what they are—

things that happened that are no longer happening—so you no longer have to feel them. It's like mentally riding a bus filled with really bad stuff, bad people, bad air. The bus stops and you get off. The door closes, and you walk home. You are no longer in the bus with the bullies, the vandals, the abusers, the takers, the name-callers. The bus has passed. Even though you're still aware of the emotions you felt, the bus has left your neighborhood; and it's time for you to move on as well and no longer be stuck in the past. You don't have to take that bus anymore when you quit letting those thoughts run your brain.

They are going to fade away, as you will find out if you keep reading.

> Believe in yourself dear one for I have faith in you.

Transformation Tenets

- ◇ Focusing on the negative will not help you.
- ◇ Trying to think away your issues gives them more power and attention.
- ◇ Instead of avoiding or rejecting your past, acknowledge and accept it so that you can move forward.
- ◇ You are not your past—leave it behind you to make space for the present and future.

Neuroplasticity
and Transformation

"Our life always expresses the result of our dominant thoughts."
Soren Kierkegaard, 19th-century Danish philosopher

Did you know that your brain literally changes every day? It used to be thought that your brain was hardwired or static, except during the early years of development. We know now that our brains possess the remarkable ability to reorganize pathways, create new connections, and in some cases, even create new neurons (nerve cells) throughout our entire lives.

This critical information is the long-awaited light at the end of the tunnel for those of us with emotional, mental, or behavioral issues. It is a fact that we have the capacity to change at any age or stage of life.

The brain's ability to change, called neuroplasticity, is pivotal to your capacity to achieve transformative change. Comprehending that you can change the way you think and behave by changing the "wiring" in your brain is the perfect starting point for you. There is power in knowing that you are not stuck in the quicksand that keeps pulling you back into the negative mire of your past. The reality is that with conviction, even someone that has lived eight decades can learn new behavior.

"The brain is like a muscle. When it is in use, we feel very good. Understanding is joyous." Carl Sagan, American astronomer, cosmologist, astrophysicist, astrobiologist, and author. As Sagan reminds us, enduring self-change will occur when we exercise our brain and help it do what it does best for us: keep us functioning on all cylinders.

It is truly energizing to understand that you can stop from spiraling into the vacuum of your habitual patterns of thought anytime you are ready. This is wonderful news; miraculous in fact. It makes me want to sing and dance and organize a "Celebrate Your Brain" day. My kids tire of hearing me talk about our magnificent brain, and how it is the most phenomenal, complex, powerful organic structure imaginable. It is the most extraordinary gift we will ever be given—and we actually have the power to harness this brilliance, to steer it where we want to go.

A bit of background. By the time of birth, a healthy infant's brain has approximately one hundred billion neurons. Within the first three years of life, a child's brain grows faster than it does at any other time of life. Genetic composition and acquired knowledge together form the template of your brain. Through observation and interaction, a child learns to mimic behavior. The brain's storage house of information amasses an amazing amount of data in these early developmental phases, creating a complex network of thoughts and emotions.

Patterns in our thoughts develop early in life. By the time we are five years old, our personality is shaped. We are programmed to seek approval from others, to crave attention as a survival tactic. The relationships we observe and interact with during our childhood are our models for behavior. The quality of attention we receive will determine our patterns of thinking.

As we develop and maneuver ourselves through the twists and turns of life, we become increasingly focused on the daily circumstances of our lives rather than on learning and evolving. It makes sense that we tend to our responsibilities and matters of importance. This external orientation to which I refer consumes our thinking and dominates our lives, and we are drawn to the drama of whatever takes precedence or captures our attention…the next agenda item, whether it be our job, family, health, friendships, finances. Our mindset becomes fixated on the outward details of living. We forget we have the power to re-set our brains to achieve whatever we wish. We go with the flow, but we're not in the flow.

Then something happens that triggers the painful thoughts we have tucked away. When we entertain one thought, a Pandora's box of negative dysfunctional views of ourselves comes tumbling out. Our self-worth, never healthy, plummets even lower. Accompanying the distressing thoughts and memories are old habits that trip us up and make us howl in frustration (internally).

But what if that didn't happen?

We have the ability to retrain our brains, to empower ourselves to live the way we wish. The brain's potential for invention and creativity is remarkable, inspiring, and not to be taken for granted. Use it or lose it indeed. You can live with your old neural pathways and sabotage yourself, or you can create new pathways, regenerate cells, and soar.

> Your brain relies on change to stay nimble and powerful. By learning new information and forming new ways of thinking and behaving, you will be regenerating brain cells and making neural connections that will reinvigorate and connect YOU to a beautiful life of health and well-being.

Transformation Tenets

- ◇ Our brain is not hardwired as once was thought. It changes constantly.
- ◇ Anyone at any age can change themselves through neuroplasticity.
- ◇ Thought and behavioral patterns develop early in life.
- ◇ The demands of life consume our thinking, causing us to become externally-oriented.
- ◇ Your brain has far more potential than you realize and thrives on change.

Changing the Brain

"(People) Man is free at the moment he wishes to be."
Voltaire, 17th-century French writer, philosopher, and advocate
of civil liberties

So, what does this mean to you in your quest to feel better about yourself, to build your self-worth and develop unconditional self-love? It's the salve that you seek, the affirmation that you can change. It's the empirical science that cannot be contradicted—that you possess the inner power to change yourself. You can free yourself from the doubt and fear that has plagued you. It is a matter of harnessing this power and guiding it in a healthy, positive direction.

Right now, envision how you would feel without that self-critical narrative running through you, causing you to feel bad about yourself. Imagine not punishing yourself each time you made a mistake or bashing yourself for gaining a few pounds? Think about how liberating it would be to expunge those harsh internal voices that are constantly reminding you of your perceived flaws or your painful past.

In fact, our brain relishes change, it actually thrives on it. Numerous studies and research on the prevention of Alzheimer's disease and the slowing of cognitive degeneration have revealed that significant positive changes in the brain occur by learning new information. The human brain thrives on absorbing stimuli, which allows it to create new neural pathways that lead to new thoughts and behavioral patterns.

ATTENTION: YOUR BRAIN IS PREPARED AND READY TO DO THAT NOW.

Transformative and enduring change is not instantaneous, of course. But inside of you there is a working universe of constant activity. This microcosm is responsible for navigating thousands of thoughts through electrical signals in the neural pathways of your brain. Most people don't think about what's occurring in their brain to enable them to think, feel, act, see, touch, smell, explore, laugh, love. Our brain is the greatest gift that human beings possess. You can choose any day, any time, any place, to commit to retrain your brain and rewrite the narrative of your internal self.

Your brain works for you and only you. It's not your parent, partner, or boss, and it doesn't take direction from others. You are the boss. You lead your life. Your brain functions according to your desires, habits, and intentions. It remains on constant alert, ready to take the lead from you. Whether it is to contemplate and analyze, be strategic or tactical, passive or aggressive, spirited or lethargic, loving or unkind. It stores and retains infinite amounts of information, enables you to pursue any field of study, learn any language, or play any instrument. It also has a moral compass that reminds you to act with integrity, be principled in your behavior; or contrarily, permit you to err, cheat, hurt others, be angry or spiteful. It signals you when you need sleep and when you need food. It is your compass for your life. What an extraordinary blessing we human beings have been given.

> Your brain is the link, the inimitable lifeline,
> to building your self-worth.

Your Brain Thrives on Change

◇ If you are alert and motivated, the brain releases the neurochemicals necessary to enable brain change. If you are distracted and inattentive, your neuroplastic switch is "off."

◇ The more you practice retraining your brain with positive input, the more connections are made from neuron to neuron and the more cell to cell cooperation and connection. Think of athletes who train and musicians who practice in order to reach the peak of and maintain their talent.

◇ Initial changes are temporary. At first, your brain is just recording something new. In order to make a permanent change, the brain will have to decide that what you are putting into it is fascinating and significant enough to refer to often and to repeat.

◇ Memory will augment your fresh thoughts and habits and you will see a progressive improvement in how you feel and act.

◇ Each time you repeat the good stuff, the bad stuff is going to recede. It will be overwritten and fade and quite possibly be completely replaced or erased. This is called synaptic pruning— elimination of the pathways you no longer need.

◇ Remind yourself that you are moving in a positive direction, one that takes time and practice, but will take you to a healthier, more joyful place.

Transformation Tenets

⬥ You always have the choice to commit to retrain your brain and rewrite the narrative of your internal self.

⬥ Actively engaging your brain has been linked to preventing cognitive decline.

⬥ Your brain works for you and only you.

⬥ Remind yourself that You Lead Your Life

The Good Life

*"As no one else can know how we perceive,
we are the best experts on ourselves."*
Carl Rogers

Carl Rogers was my friend. One of the founders of the humanistic approach to psychology, he did not know me—and I never actually met him—but I knew him through my college course reading, my reference books that hold a coveted spot on my desk, and I have enjoyed a platonic love affair with him throughout my life. If you are unfamiliar with Rogers, he is a psychologist that is worth getting to know.

I realized recently that he and I are indeed on the same page when it comes to self-worth, which is one of the three components of the humanistic approach, along with self-image, and the ideal self. I found myself returning frequently to his book, *On Becoming a Person*, as a resource for this book. He understood what truly lies beneath the surface of the human mind. His work had the most influence on my approach to redefining myself by learning to trust myself and others in my life.

Rogers believed that humans have one basic objective in life: to self-actualize. He defined self-actualization as fulfilling one's potential and achieving the highest level of what it means to be human, what he termed as fully functioning individuals. Rogers' theories appealed to me in my own quest to build self-worth because he understood that people are capable of solving their own problems. When one is in an environment that enables them to unconditionally trust, they are able to let go of their defense mechanisms and be open to self-discovery, self-acceptance, and self-trust.

Rogers acknowledged that this may not be possible for every human being. It might not be able to happen for those living in a destructive environment. We are each unique and are meant to develop in different ways to the best of our capabilities. A poor self-concept, or low self-worth, may override our innate motivation to self-actualize. Rogers believed, as I do, that childhood experience is the main determinant of whether we can self-actualize as a fully functioning person, but other events later in life also factor into this theory.

Rogers' guiding perspective was that people are inherently good and creative—a belief that I've always held as a universal truth, even when people mistreated me or were cruel to others. We are born into the world innocent, free of ill will, and it is only when we are exposed to unfavorable issues in our environment that our innocence begins to erode.

Rogers understood human nature. A person in touch with their feelings who inhabits the present rather than the past, will naturally continually grow and change. He identified five characteristics of the fully functioning person:

◊ Open to experience, both positive and negative.
◊ Existential living, which means able to live in the present rather than the past or future.
◊ Trusting of their own feelings, instincts, and decisions.
◊ Creative thinkers who incorporate risk-taking into their choices and are able to adjust to changes, challenges, and a variety of experiences.
◊ Fulfilled by their lives, happy and satisfied, but always open to new experiences.

It's true that these are Western concepts. Cultures that value the group over the individual would not agree. But ours is a society oriented to the individual, where the "self" is a term for who we are as a person: our inner personality or soul. The closer our self-image with our real and ideal self, the more congruent we are, the higher our self-worth.

The development of congruence is key to understanding the process of developing healthy self-worth. A similar word that I use is alignment. When our outer self is aligned with our inner self, our thoughts and actions are in sync with our intrinsic inner self, our soul. This is dependent on unconditional positive regard, which happens when we feel valued, respected, treated with affection, and loved. A state of incongruence is when someone's experience has distorted their self-image, perhaps by receiving only conditional positive regard—meaning love and attention are only given when a child or person behaves according to another person's standards for behavior.

Rogers called the achievement of self-actualization and being in a state of congruence, "The Good Life." I have borrowed these words as the mantra for my own life. The Good Life is not a fixed state of contentment, happiness, or nirvana. "It is a process, not a state of being. It is a direction, not a destination," said Rogers. Our lives are ever-changing, and as we evolve, we learn to adjust, grow, and learn more about who we are along the way.

So, this is where we are headed: The Good Life. If you will join me, we will go there together.

> Once we learn to trust ourselves, to be open to life's experiences, to accept the lows and rejoice in the highs, and continue to seek knowledge and growth, we will find our place of inner peace and equanimity.

Transformation Tenets

- ◇ The desire to self-actualize—to reach one's full potential—is the driving force in our lives.
- ◇ Human beings are inherently good.
- ◇ Rogers' theory of a fully functioning person included being open to all experience, living in the present, possessing self-trust, thinking creatively, and being fulfilled.
- ◇ Living in congruence or in alignment with one's total self is fundamental to building healthy self-worth.

Part Three

Preparation

Self-Reflection

"We do not learn from experience,
we learn from reflecting on experience."
John Dewey, American philosopher who promoted social and
educational reform and was founder of functional psychology

Note: I suggest that you evaluate whether you feel comfortable in Self-Reflection because many people have experienced traumas that are too grave to handle by themselves. If this is true for you, please consult a professional psychologist for assistance in this process rather than attempting it on your own. You may also enlist the support of a friend or family member who can help you remain calm and focused. If at any time, for any reason, you feel overwhelmed, melancholy, or physically unwell, STOP, and return at a later time. This process is not intended to hurt you in any way. Rather, the purpose is to detox your soul, cleanse your spirit, and liberate you physically, emotionally, and spiritually.

The John Dewey quote above reminds me of Aldous Huxley's sage words, "Experience is not what happens to you; it's what you do with what happens to you." Similarly, what do we learn from an experience if we do not examine it? In fact, Socrates said at his trial for "impiety and corrupting youth," which was really about the right to express your views in a democracy, that "the unexamined life is not worth living." And to prove his point he voluntarily accepted a sentence of death by drinking poison hemlock. What we experience in our past deserves examining when it helps us grow and become wiser in our present and future.

Our earliest Greek philosophers are the founders of existential thinking, as they were the first known to examine the human condition. The word philosophy is derived from the Greek words for love and wisdom. Philosophers during the pre-Socratic and Socratic eras dedicated themselves to pursuing truth and wisdom, knowledge and logic, and moral discipline. When I took my first philosophy class at Northwestern, it didn't take me long to develop a profound connection to the philosophers' intense curiosity about the universe and humanity's relationship to its grand design. During my own personal quest to build self-worth, and in writing this book, I realized that the most vital component of any personal transformation is to take the time to reflect and examine where you've been so that you can move to a better, a higher ground of self-understanding.

Reflection is a process of consciously thinking through and analyzing your thoughts, beliefs, and experiences as a means of learning about yourself. It offers you the opportunity to pause and detach from the busy nature of life and be able to evaluate what you have been through. Reflection also permits you to consider new or different interpretations of what you've endured because you have distanced yourself from it. This is an exceptionally powerful practice for self-discovery and self-understanding. When you are able to derive information about yourself through reflection, you obtain valuable knowledge about your past events and their influence upon you.

With careful consideration, the process provides you with meaning and insight that will enable you to better understand how the past has affected you. Concisely put, the Practice of Self-Reflection will enable you to look back with composure and calm to interpret how past relationships and events have shaped your thoughts and emotions.

When you think about what you've experienced, whether it is many years ago or earlier today, you have the opportunity to review your behavior from a distance. This permits you to think about what took place with a shred of objectivity or at least not as much subjectivity. With constructive Self-Reflection, you can turn your focus away from self-flagellation or self-pity to understand what occurred and how it made you feel. For our purposes, it's a chance to realize that the experiences that contributed to your low self-worth are in the past. They are not today or tomorrow.

I am the queen of Self-Reflection. Most people have not looked at themselves that microscopically; nor should you. But you do need a baseline from which to begin the process of building self-worth. Self-Reflection is fundamental to the process as it provides the bridge between what took place then and where you are now.

You already know how my self-worth was affected by my childhood. Because of my precociously sensitive personality, I began the process of Self-Reflection when I was still a child and have never really stopped. I do it any time that judgmental voice inside me gets triggered and I begin to feel uncertainty and whether I am brave enough to deal with life's vicissitudes. Even though I've changed the way I feel about myself, there are times in life, as is the case with everyone, when I feel shaken or turned upside down. I no longer suppress my emotions but remind myself of what is happening, why, and do what I need to do to move quickly past it.

What about you? What events in your life may have contributed to a sense of low self-worth. For example, did your mother or father call you names as a young child? Were you bullied by anyone? Did you have an accident or some other trauma that left an imprint on you? Be prepared to think about any issues in your life that may be the root of how you feel about yourself.

There are those of you who do not have a firm grasp on what happened in the past to cause your negative self-worth, but you still suffer from it. There isn't always a direct link to what occurred in your past with how you feel about yourself. Nevertheless, you cannot start the next chapter in your life if you keep re-reading the last chapter.

I'm not asking that you *relive* painful experiences, which we have already learned is counterproductive as focusing on the negative reinforces the negative. Your objective in Self-Reflection is to identify one of the root causes of your low self-worth each time you practice Self-Reflection, acknowledge how this event caused you to feel, take note of anything that continues to trigger negative thoughts, and replace that with positive thoughts or images.

Productive Self-Reflection enables you to evaluate what occurred. It brings out repressed emotions, but gently. There will be no suffering, no self-flagellation, no regret, shame, or guilt. That is not the intention here. It is a process that will enable you to know what has been causing your ongoing insecurity. It clarifies what, when, who, and where, in other words. It concretizes your thoughts and emotions, so they no longer are sticky cobwebs or biting devils hiding in your mind waiting to attack you. You will learn that you are not who you were in your past. Instead, you choose to live in the present in which you are an evolved and peace-filled being. You are going to let go.

> Self-Reflection is key to healing from the past as you learn how to develop healthy self-worth.

Transformation Tenets

◇ Self-Reflection enables you to learn from your experience in a constructive manner.

◇ Self-Reflection is the bridge between what took place then and where you are now.

◇ The process of Self-Reflection is not intended to relive painful experiences or to suffer through events of the past.

◇ Productive Self-Reflection clarifies and validates thoughts and emotions, enabling you to release them.

How Does Self-Reflection Work?

"Knowing yourself is the beginning of all wisdom."
Aristotle

What happens during Self-Reflection is that our baggage—trunks over-flowing with musty thoughts we have outgrown and images of the needy lonely scared child who has been our companion—can be emptied. We can also throw away that haunted house mirror in which we used to see our SELF, a distorted image—too fat, too thin, lopsided, stooped, unmanageable hair, face with a small blemish that seemed like a tu-mor. That mirror showed a person who had been lied to, betrayed, who was heartbroken, angry, lonely, and depressed. We don't see our Soul Self, our inner core being, until we are healthier and value our self. Even those people who are considered stunningly beautiful or fit still have a distorted self-perception and suitcases filled with various wounds and heartaches. What we see on the outside of ourselves reflects how we are feeling internally.

As I have mentioned, I suffered for several years over my beloved father's death. Losing the one person I knew would always love me unconditionally, who would fight for me and guide me through the tough times in life, absolutely shattered me. I hid myself away from people because I didn't think anyone could understand how much I was hurting. I spent a lot of time thinking about the past, and my loss. But I wasn't self-reflecting. I was just punishing myself.

I had been a runner most of my life. I loved getting outside and moving my body, establishing a rhythm with my shoes on the pavement or path and the music in my earphones. After a while, it would be an out of body experience. I was aware of what was going on around me and felt very present, but I could forget everything that usually cluttered my brain during the day.

After my father died, I stopped running. It seemed selfish to indulge in the beauty of nature, to nurture myself with my favorite form of exercise, to feel anything but heartache.

After eighteen months of reclusiveness and deep, lonely grieving, I decided I would try a run to see if it could revive my spirit, if I could even find my spirit. I had been disappearing little by little, and I knew I had to do something to pull myself out of an early grave.

It felt great to move my body, even though I was heavy-footed on the pavement. I was up, had clothes on, and was outside. All of a sudden when I was on a solid pace and in the heart of my run, I started crying, great heaving sobs that dropped me to my knees.

Kneeling on the cement gasping for air, the memory of the last conversation I had with my dad rose-up in a sudden torrent of emotion. He had died in August. We had always spent Christmas and the July Fourth holiday in Ohio with my parents. That July visit was the last time I would see my father alive.

The last conversation we had was on his back porch which is suspended over a pond filled with carp and blue gill; we were surrounded by peach azaleas and white petunias, lavender butterfly bushes and rich gold black-eyed susans—an exotic setting that was my dad's favorite spot to relax. We were sitting together, just the two of us, when out of the blue he asked me, "Annie, are you happy? Are you *really* happy?" Even as I write this now, tears flow down my cheeks. It was prophetic in such a profound way, though I didn't know it then. "Do you feel you've had a good life?"

He continued for a while with a few philosophical questions. We never had shallow conversations. Throughout my life, my father was my mentor and a stolid, unwavering source of support. When it was time for me to leave for the airport, I was being rushed out the door and my father was busy doing something. When I walked up to hug him, he was distracted, so I went to the car where my mother was waiting to drive me to the airport. Just before we backed out of the driveway, my father ran out and said, "Annie, you're breaking my heart by leaving." And, I got out of the car and gave him another hug. As I waved goodbye, I started to weep, quietly.

And that was it. The last time I was with my soul mate. I had not realized until that moment of breaking down during my run that my father's questions to me were just what I needed to hear to re-launch my life. I had spent years mourning his loss but had forgotten to answer those last questions he had asked me.

I had blocked this painful memory. But the moment I got out of bed, determined to save myself, and let down my guard while I was running, I felt a healing begin. Because I had experience with Self-Reflection, I was not scared of what I was feeling, although it was painful. Afterwards I felt cleansed by those tears. As if by magic, I was able to get out of bed every day and go back to running. I began to recover the life I had abandoned when my father died. Self-reflection is powerful when one uses it as a practice to constructively review events that hurt or troubled you and offers you the opportunity to move forward with an unburdened mind.

My spontaneous Self-Reflection had probably saved my life. I wanted more than anything to be able to honestly answer my father's questions with, "Yes, I am really happy;" and "Yes, I feel like I have had a Good Life." No more lying in bed. I was ready to do something to grow out of my grief and accept that living "a Good Life" was my choice.

That's when I began seriously developing my plan and practices for recovery from low self-worth. It was as if that memory surfacing took the pressure off my overstuffed brain that was in danger of exploding. I began sitting for short periods in Self-Reflection, clearing out the past.

My mantra for my times of Self-Reflection was *ruminate, release, restore, and recover.*

The more I engaged in Self-Reflection, the less power my experiences had over me. The memories became dimmer. I also replaced the bad memories with positive thoughts closer to the present: visions of an island vacation with my family, for instance, the stunning landscape and wonderful people I met.

Every time I felt like I was going down the rabbit hole where I would view myself from the perspective of my past, I would say, "I am not my past."

> Never fear Self-Reflection.
> This is your time to tune into your Self.

Transformation Tenets

◇ There is power in Self-Reflection that is derived from releasing suppressed memories.

◇ The practice of Self-Reflection enables you to ruminate or review, release, restore, and recover.

◇ Self-Reflection mitigates the negative energy of past experiences.

◇ Remind yourself that you are not your past.

A Human Mosaic Vignette

Eva Interrupted

My client Eva asked me to help her lose weight; she wanted me to teach her how to "eat wisely," as she put it, blaming the hectic pace of her life as the source of her quick-hunger-fix eating style. Adamant about wanting to get rid of the forty pounds she gained over several years, she was prepared to listen and learn. "I want you to teach me how to *like*, if that's even possible, and prepare on-the-go food that is good for me," Eva remarked. When we spoke on the phone, I told her that I was not a licensed nutritionist, however, she said she was aware of a mutual acquaintance with whom I had worked that lost a significant amount of weight through a program I developed called HQIN: High Quality Impact Nutrition "I want to try it," Eva said with assurance.

During our first meeting, I learned that Eva was an intelligent woman—top notch education, an executive, world-traveler, art and music lover—she appeared to have the IQ portion of herself in good standing. "My life skills are oriented towards making things happen, being productive. It's the other part I struggle with." Eva strained to get the words out. "Honestly, I'm emotionally flat. Totally flat," she said in a monotone voice.

Eva's Teflon demeanor was betrayed by the nervousness of her roaming eyes and the constant movement of her hands and shifting of her body in her chair. I agreed to help her with her desire to transform her eating habits, but, I made it clear that focusing on food alone might not be a lasting solution to unhealthy eating. "There might be," I suggested with delicacy, "Something deeper causing your behavior and relationship with food." I asked her if she would consider another approach to building new healthful eating patterns, one that would involve a few practices such as self-reflection and gaining perspective. "No thanks," Eva said abruptly. "Just meal plans are all I'm interested in."

Okay, so I let that suggestion rest for the moment, knowing there was far more to be revealed.

As we got to know each other better, I asked Eva to describe what she meant by "flat," the word she chose to describe herself. I wanted to understand what her definition of flat was so that we could have a mutual plane of understanding. "Well, ummmm, (long pause) let's just say that I don't allow myself to go there. No...I won't go there." Her eyes moved in every direction to avoid mine. "It just doesn't do me any good to go there." With someone as private as she, I realized that it might be helpful to schedule our next meeting outdoors, away from distractions, and outside of walls that could be—metaphorically—standing in her way.

Eva described herself by the list of things she accomplished during her day, in a detached, objective way. "My life is super hectic. At the end of the day, I am totally drained. When I get home, I go about my evening rituals, which include devouring potato chips and cheese and crackers. By the time I finally get into bed with my stack of fluffy satin pillows, all I do is toss and turn. No way can I sleep due to the hundreds of thoughts occupying space in my head. Work, dry cleaning, dental appointment, visit to my sister's, next project...I do all the right things. I read, listen to rainstorms on my sound machine, go to the kitchen for chamomile tea or a big glass of pinot noir, then return to bed, telling myself that tonight would be better, but it never is," she sighed. "I took sleeping pills for years, but they stopped being effective. I am an insomniac." This was the first time I noticed a slight difference in Eva's stilted responses. Baby steps, I thought to myself, it would take a series of tiny baby steps with Eva.

Part Three: Preparation

After our second meeting, I introduced Eva to the science of neuroplasticity, the brain's ability to change at any age of life, and she relished the concept that she could actually transform her own brain, having never known that before. For that to take place, I suggested that she focus on what she would like to change about herself, rather than spending energy on what she didn't like, such as the weight she'd gained.

"I don't know why I gained so much weight," Eva said, even after I told her to try not to think of the weight as the problem. "What if you try a different approach?" I asked her. At that point, I could feel that she was beginning to trust me, and she agreed to be open to my suggestions.

What I learned through my own quest is when you offer someone the opportunity to feel at ease, to become comfortable, to trust you, their defenses will begin to melt away; the warmth, compassion, and trust enables them to relax and open up. As we worked together, I noticed Eva started to look forward to our sessions. She told me that I was her social outlet. "I feel quite at peace with you, Anne. I don't want to be a robot anymore. I want to start to enjoy my life."

As the stiffness in her demeanor begin to soften, bit by bit, I asked Eva to start journaling, especially at night during her restlessness, to write about anything she could think of, anything she felt inside that might be creating the tension and insomnia. If she was okay with it, while she was journaling, I asked her to reflect on her past, as a way to rewind and perhaps find out if there was something that took place about which she was unaware, an incident or relationship that caused her to flatten emotionally. Additionally, we began to practice deep breathing exercises together before each session as well as afterwards. I asked her to practice deep breathing in the morning before work, anytime during the day she needed to relieve stress, and as long as she wanted to at night in bed. Baby steps led to medium steps.

As soon as Eva established a consistent routine of journaling and actively engaging in deep breathing, we introduced specific phrases into her vocabulary. These were calming terms that she liked, and that she would repeat to herself during moments throughout the day when she felt anxious, her go-to mantras. Eva also decided to join her condo's social group that met monthly. More encouraging steps forward.

Within five weeks, I noticed that Eva's energy was different, warmer, the tenseness in her body language was largely gone, and she was even hugging me when we got together! "I really like the foods I'm eating, and I am starting to sleep in three-hour increments!" Eva was giddy. I asked her not to weigh herself for six weeks, however, she couldn't resist, and told me she had already lost twelve pounds, and was feeling much better. That day we began walking together during our session, which lasted an hour, with pauses in between for water and stretching. While we walked, I let her talk about anything that came to mind.

At our next meeting, we sat and had a quick lunch, then went for our walk. "You know Anne," Eva began, "I want you to read what I wrote in my journal on Sunday. Ignore the curse words, but here you go." We stopped walking and she handed me a small brown leather journal, "Open it there," she pointed to the red bookmark. I suggested at the last meeting that she try to travel back in time, only if and when she was comfortable, and felt safe and strong enough to do so, as a way to recall any event in her past that had caused her to feel disconnected from herself, and everyone in her life. Tears drained from both of our eyes as I read about the trauma she experienced when she was seven years old—the terrible episode that caused her to shut down emotionally for her entire life.

It took place while she visited her cousins at their farm upstate. At night, while her cousins were sleeping, her uncle would crawl into bed with her. "He would massage my body, saying he wanted me to relax. He took his right hand and rubbed my entire body, from my head to my toe. I trembled with fear. I thought he cared about me, but instinctively, I knew what he was doing was wrong. My own father never did that." Eva was ashen. "He breathed so hard into my ear while he put his hand on my chest and between my legs, holding his penis with the other. I was too terrified to know what to do or how to get away, and he told me that if I told anyone, he would hurt me bad. I believed him."

Although Eva had seen psychologists throughout her life, she wasn't ever able to "go there." She blocked the trauma by forcing herself to believe it never happened. And the only way Eva could do it was to become emotionally dead, or "flat," she said. Through the process of becoming more open, more comfortable with herself, by allowing her inner thoughts and emotions to come to the surface, she was able to carefully tear down the walls in her head. The process of journaling made her understand how real and horrendous she felt when it happened, and how damaging it was to her identity.

Eva was learning to accept and trust herself. She allowed herself to gently reflect on the heinous experience without fear or judgment, because she was able to detach herself. Soon, it was time to start the process of healing. "My grief and shock at being molested interrupted my life. I stopped emotionally maturing when I was seven years old. I was dead to myself, dead because I felt so wasted and emotionless. I couldn't look at myself without feeling deep anguish and shame." Eva now knew that she was not the reason for what her uncle did to her, nor was she at fault for lying there next to him. She was an innocent young girl without a clue of what to do.

Eva and I worked together for eight months, and today, she is married, has one child, and, although her weight is not quite where she wants it to be, she feels alive, content, and liberated from the depths of self-loathing and shame. The heavy burden of the trauma that cut the life out of her life was no longer a part of her life.

The Ritual of Self-Reflection

"To reach a port we must sail, sometimes with the wind, and sometimes against it. But we must not drift or lie at anchor."
Oliver Wendell Holmes

Self-Reflection: Ruminate, Release, Restore, and Recover

Self-Reflection is a ritual you will perform daily for as long as you have the need. In the beginning, you will use it to shake loose the negative self-talk that has been going on in your head for much of your life. After you feel you have investigated and examined the root causes of your low self-worth, evaluated their influence, demystified their power, sifted through the ashes of what has consumed so much of your energy, you can move on to less frequent Self-Reflection and to exploring your feelings about events of the week, or about things that happened at work or in the family. This is a time to sit with your soul, and if it eventually turns into meditation rather than Self-Reflection, that's ok. What's important is to establish trust with yourself, knowing you are going to devote this time of morning or evening to building your self-worth. Once the invalidating content of your mind has been neutralized or emptied, you can also begin replacing it with beautiful positive content.

Treat yourself with kindness and gentleness at all times. There is no judgment here. This is the opportunity to get in a cozy spot with a velvety blanket around yourself, to take deep breaths, and think through the issues that have been causing you distress and unease. You will manage this process with care and consideration for what you've been through to get to where you are today, not to further malign yourself or feel bitter about your past. Be mindful of how you are feeling, which means you will be attentive and alert as you listen to your thoughts and emotions with sensitivity. This is a time to honor yourself, to treat yourself with grace as you let your thoughts flow inside of you. Always, always approach this practice with care and compassion for what you experience. This is a stepping stone to greater self-understanding and self-acceptance.

Advance preparation. In advance, prepare a set of questions that will help guide your Self-Reflection and keep you on track. This can be your system of setting boundaries for yourself during this process. Stick to the script, follow your questions, and keep moving. Focus on the details of what happened and not the emotions. When we think contextually, that is about the specifics such as location and people present, we are prone to move away from the emotional aspects of our issues and be more objective.

Examples of questions you might ask yourself:

- What am I feeling right now, at the beginning of Self-Reflection?
- What happened to cause me to feel bad about myself?
- Where was I and who was I with that left me with these thoughts?
- Are any of the people that have caused me to feel poorly about myself still a part of my life?
- How did this challenging experience impact me?
- Today, how does it continue to hurt me?
- What triggers precipitate these distressful feelings within me: a person, a place, a song, a certain food, an activity?
- Did I learn something valuable by what took place?
- What am I feeling right now, at the end of Self-Reflection?

Time and place. Morning people who arise at 6:00am to sip their coffee or tea and meditate or exercise have it made. Add an extra 20 to 30 minutes of quiet time to your routine, or, for now, substitute Self-Reflection for meditation. For night owls, eliminate or cut down screen time or reading, just for now. The quality of the time you spend on Self-Reflection is far superior to the quantity. If you are fully focused it may take only 15 minutes.

Select a quiet, comfortable location where you can be alone with no interruptions. If music or white noise helps you concentrate, include those. Always have a glass of water within reach and a notebook or journal.

Deep Breathing. Take several deep breaths in and out. Breathe in deeply for five counts, expel the breath for seven counts. Repeat this as long as you need to in order to relax and mentally prepare. If for any reason you begin to feel discomfort or anxiety, put it off for another day, and just focus on deep breathing.

When you are relaxed and ready to begin, ask yourself the questions you have prepared and remember to focus on objective details, which will help to dispel some of the intensity of your emotions. Focus on your breaths as you think and reflect.

Recording your experience. Take notes on your thoughts and emotions during your time of Self-Reflection. Or if you prefer to talk through your thoughts, use your phone or computer's recording app to keep track of your thoughts. If you feel nervous or wary of how you might react, ask a close family member or friend (one that is nonjudgmental and loving towards you) to sit with you and help you with the process.

As you write or dictate the answers to your prepared questions, make note of what actually occurred, who was involved, and when. Specify the details of what happened as much as possible. Even though intense emotions may be aroused, the act of recording what happened and how you felt and are currently feeling will help objectify your emotions. Let the feelings flow through you and remember that you have a job to do, which is to take down this information so you can use it to change the way you think about yourself.

Right now, you are just gathering information about yourself. Later, you will read over or listen to the notes you made to help you understand the sources of the negative messages in your mind that were internalized as low self-worth.

Keep in mind that the process of Self-Reflection is for you to ruminate, release, restore, and recover, so that you can constructively reflect, let go, renew, and heal during this time. It is not an exercise that asks you to relive your past, you have already lived your past. It is intended to address the events that continue to cycle through your brain and acknowledge them, accept them, and then grow beyond them.

If you begin to feel anxious or have any troubling physical responses such as increased heart rate, pause, have some water, and put your notes away. Come back at another time or the next day and begin again. If, at any moment, you feel that the subject or memory is too heavy for you to handle alone, then please seek advice from a professional, whether it's a psychologist, psychiatrist, or your physician. There are some matters that we may not be equipped to manage on our own, particularly those that are gravely traumatic. Seek counsel in these cases, and a support system will provide the appropriate level of care.

> Self-Reflection is an essential component of transformation, enabling you to identify what you are feeling about your past in order to move forward with a fresh perspective.

Transformation Tenets

◇ Establish parameters in advance of Self-Reflection that include preparation, time and place, and how you plan to record your thoughts.

◇ This Practice is to neutralize and empty the content of your mind so that you replace it with beautiful content.

◇ Treat yourself with kindness and gentleness at all times.

◇ Always be aware of how you are feeling throughout the process of Self-Reflection—stop if you begin to feel anxious, pause, and return when you are calm and ready.

The Result of Self-Reflection

"I will not let anyone walk through my mind with their dirty feet."
Mahatma Gandhi

One of the most refreshing outcomes of a consistent ritual of Self-Reflection was the clearing out of all the garbage and useless junk that had accumulated in my mind. I had a lifetime's worth of negative messages and images about myself that I needed to drop off at the dump site, including episodes from my childhood and throughout my life that kept coming back to torment me.

Releasing my toxic thoughts, restoring my self-worth, and recovering my true self were all a result of the work I did when I focused on Self-Reflection. I love Gandhi's quote, above because after you thoroughly cleanse your mind of destructive habitual thoughts, you are so much more aware of any new thoughts that try to enter and dirty your inner sanctum of peace. You will learn that there has always been a purpose to your life, before anyone had an opinion about you or passed judgment on you (including yourself). And you will recover that purpose.

Let me tell you how this can happen to you.

After you have established a regular practice of Self-Reflection, you will have accumulated a certain amount of data through your note-taking or dictation. When you are ready for the next step, you will revisit this data to identify issues, emotions, thoughts, and behaviors that are likely at the root of your low self-worth. Digesting this information, you will notice patterns that probably arose in childhood that are still being repeated. You don't need to have a degree in psychology or be as obsessive as I have been to do this. It will almost jump out at you.

For example, when I feel someone is lying to me, or not being honest with me, I sometimes overreact because my emotions related to the issue of being lied to go back to childhood struggles. I recall my father lying to my mother about where he had been and with whom; and witnessing my mother's reaction of falling apart because she knew he was not telling her the truth. I saw how deeply that hurt my mother. And, even though I worshiped my father's brilliance, it hurt me too. I knew that he conveniently rearranged reality to suit his purposes of continually betraying my mother and then trying to confuse her further by denying everything she knew in her gut to be true.

Revisiting and interpreting my voluminous notes from years of Self-Reflection, I realized sometimes I leap to conclusions with friends, family, or colleagues whom I feel have not been completely forthcoming with the information I asked for, or whom I find out later did something differently than what I was originally told. If I don't take a moment to pause before responding in this kind of situation, I can feel wildly out of control inside—as my mother used to feel—because of the injury done to her, and to me as her witness, when my father would fabricate stories and falsify the truth. If I don't breathe deeply and remember what I have learned from Self-Reflection, I interpret events and interactions in the present based on my past history.

Constructive Self-Reflection is a wonderful path to healing. When we focus our attention to what we experienced with an intentional objectivity, it allows our negative energy to flow through and beyond it to the point of releasing it. This will open space in your mind and heart for positive thoughts to enter.

> I no longer suffer silently from past experiences.
> If I am triggered, I pause to self-reflect and move on.

Transformation Tenets

◊ The process of Self-Reflection allows you to remove clutter from your mind, it is a Soul Detox.

◊ Self-Reflection leads to self-discovery and self-understanding.

◊ The process of reflecting enables you to uncover the root causes of your thoughts and behavior.

◊ Constructive Self-Reflection leads to healing.

Part Four

The Practices

What we have discussed to this point has been creating a tapestry of information for understanding self-worth as the lens by which everything in your life is filtered, including principles, the importance of the science of neuroplasticity and our brain's capacity for change, and important steps that will facilitate lasting change.

The Practices are entitled as such because practices are actions that depend upon you engaging, rehearsing, repeating, and applying them to your life as frequently as you wish, and for as long as they are beneficial to you. By providing you with an array of options, I am not suggesting that you engage in every single one, however, it is important for you to choose those Practices that you like and believe you will stick with, and those that best align with you and your lifestyle.

Give one or two that you gravitate towards, that you believe you can stick to and that you like, an investment of time. If you do not find those helpful, move onto others. We are unique, and our comfort level differs from person to person, therefore, find what you feel at ease with and go for it.

JOURNALING: It is very important to document your work with the Practices to listen, interpret, and learn from what you are experiencing. This is an invaluable exercise to measure your progress by noting any subtle or significant changes in your thoughts, emotions, and behavior. I cannot emphasize enough the value of writing, as a cathartic process, and one that is critical to your ability to work through and understand the causes of your issues, to accept them, and also observe yourself move beyond pain, anxiety, grief, or any emotions you have endured, and then build powerful, sustaining self-worth for your life.

This section of the book is intended as a reference for you to read and act upon when you are ready. Remind yourself that as you practice these exercises, you will become more proficient in them, and will have an easier time achieving your objective(s).

With time, patience, energy, and focus, you will find that if performed on a regular basis, the Practices will enable you to release the thoughts that have impeded your ability to feel joyful, and replace them with thoughts that bring warmth, comfort, confidence, and love.

Retrain Your Brain

"Knowing is not enough; we must apply.
Willing is not enough; we must do."
Johann Wolfgang von Goethe, German writer, statesman, poet

The disconnect that develops as we evolve from infancy into adolescence and beyond is a result of our perception of who we believe we should be based on early life interactions with family, friends, teachers, babysitters, and any individuals with whom we spend time. Each experience either reinforces our sense of identity or erodes it.

Envision yourself living without all that burden of negative memories and self-talk that has held you back from enjoying life to the fullest. The dynamic nature of being alive is that there will continue to be moments that challenge us. But by building self-worth, we will have the strength and stamina to address whatever comes into our lives.

The disconnect with our real self and our ought self (who we think we are or should be externally) creates a tension within us, an unnatural and distressing strain. The reason it is unnatural and creates discomfort within us is that, in our Soul Self we yearn for consistency in our thoughts and behavior. We desire internal harmony and congruence.

I learned about the term **cognitive dissonance** while in college. As soon as my professor began discussing the psychological ramifications that it has upon our psyche, I felt that I might be a target that was within close range of his words. This was me. I was cognitive dissonance personified. This term refers to the internal tension one feels when we perceive contradictory beliefs, values, or thoughts about who we are. The mental discomfort experienced results when our thoughts or beliefs conflict with new information that we obtain. Cognitive dissonance is manifested in internal inconsistency which causes psychological strain to the person experiencing it.

Why did I immediately align myself with this term? Because I recognized that there was a chasm that separated who I was in my soul with how I behaved in my life. My outside did not align with my inside. Inwardly, I felt one way, outwardly, I behaved another. Inside I was delicate and insecure, outside I was confident and self-assured. The rubber band that held me together was stretched to its limit. Any moment, it would certainly wear too thin to tolerate the tension.

That was my reality, but I was not about to change by finding a way to eliminate this internal dissonance since I was "succeeding" in all areas of my life. My efforts academically were yielding exceptional results and my social life was better than I'd ever imagined. So, why do anything different? And, I didn't.

I didn't change what was working for me because I hadn't arrived at the point where my internal pain threshold couldn't handle it any longer. That wouldn't take place for another two decades. That was a lot of time to live with the cognitive dissonance that was churning about my brain.

What happens when one lives with cognitive dissonance is that their beliefs and behavior are at odds with one another. With time, our beliefs cave to the demands in our environment, resulting in behavior incongruent with our beliefs. During the very early phases of my own journey to build self-worth, I did more soul-searching than seemed humanly possible. And, I knew enough about cognitive dissonance to realize that the only way to eliminate it was to transform the patterns that had long been the outside me, the Outer-Inness that I conveyed to the world—and to myself, moreover.

When I started my quest to feel better, both my inner and outer selves were false constructions. My outer self was who I thought people wanted me to be. My inner self was populated with secret negative messages that were my own and others' criticisms of who I thought I was. Neither was me.

I knew I couldn't transform my patterns by thinking my way out of this labyrinth of lies I had constructed about myself. Logic and reason were not the ingredients to remedy this schism I had lived with my entire life. Every time you consciously try to detach from your negative thoughts by pushing them down into your secret bad thoughts compartment, you arouse them instead of quashing them.

So how could I go about this change without arousing the "beast" inside me?

I had heard the expression since I was at prep school, "Knowledge is power." By the time I was prepared to begin the work of building self-worth, I understood at the deepest level what had to be addressed within me. I also understood that I had the ability—as we all do—to retrain my brain. But I had to figure out in what way. Knowledge is power, but until the knowledge is applied to one's life, its value remains dormant. Using knowledge is not the same as trying to think away your issues. Knowing what is troubling you is important in order to transform yourself but knowing isn't solving. I knew better by this point.

Acknowledging all my past wounds was the beginning, but until I figured out a way to take that information and incorporate it into my life through practice, it was just information. What was residing in my brain would not enable me to transform at this point. It was theory.

To bring the storehouse of information that was in my brain to life, I knew that I would need faith and perseverance to lean on. Information is good for understanding oneself but using it to create a life of purpose and meaning would be extraordinary. I had to bring all my knowledge to life by applying it, living with it, and practicing it.

I had done so much Self-Reflection and facing my fears, how much more could I absorb? A lot more, it turns out. I had started a journey toward building my self-worth as a foundation for the powerful positive life I wanted to live. I had to keep going. I had committed myself to transformative change.

To keep on track, I created a program for myself called *The Practices*, because that's what it takes to retrain the brain: new practices. Repetition is the key to learning, unlearning, and re-learning. Athletes, dancers, and musicians know this because of their rigorous training.

Repetition creates long term memory by eliciting strong chemical interactions—new proteins—at the synapse of your neuron (where neurons connect to other neurons). This is a self-perpetuating cycle and this process also creates new synaptic growth, like adding a branch on a tree, to strengthen and increase the neural network.

When we are seeking enduring transformative change, our new thoughts must be repeated for a longer length of time than you would expect in order to override old thought patterns that caused our old behaviors, which must be held in check. Consider asking the millions of people who have tried to adopt healthier patterns of eating or engaging in a regular exercise practice when they have never enjoyed plant-based foods nor perspiration, they will tell you that they gave it a chance, but it didn't last long. It takes more than a few weeks to train the brain to form new patterns of thought and behavior. But what you derive from a relatively short period of time will forever change your life.

Triggers

Understand and Pay Attention to Them

One major hitch in maintaining our practices so that eventually our new thoughts will be automatic is our emotional response to our "triggers." A trigger, also known as a cue, is something that leads you to feel a certain way based on past experience. A trigger is a stimulus that evokes a particular thought or emotion from the past. This could be a specific word or phrase, a person or social situation, anything that destabilizes the progress of practicing your new thoughts. Triggers can occur without warning and take the wind out of your sail.

Part of staying on track is identifying what triggers invoke the emotions that reinforce your low self-worth. Once you do that, they will have less power over you. Knowing your triggers is key to the process of change. Your triggers might be the sound of waves rushing against the shore, because the last time you were at the beach, you experienced a break up. A trigger could range from something prominent in your life, such as a person that is still a part of your daily life, whether it is your boss or a family member that has derided you over the years, or it could be something subtle, such as a smell, or a particular food, or a song. Pay attention to anyone or anything that invokes unsettling emotions within you and make a note of it. Understanding what things cause you to feel bad about yourself is an important part of self-understanding and self-awareness, as well as being able to accept how they make you feel and move beyond them.

For me, hearing about the onslaught of bullying that is occurring today takes me right back to when I was eight years old at camp. Today, however, I only feel for the victims of the bullying, knowing how damaging it is short-and-long term, and worrying that they may not have access to resources that can help them deal with their emotions—I no longer relive my experience, due to my journey towards self-worth.

The other aspect of dealing with triggers is having a plan in place to deal with them as they arise. After you have identified what triggers reawaken your wounds, knowing what to do with that information, taking the knowledge and putting it into action is pivotal.

How to Manage Triggers

- Ask yourself why the trigger has power over your thoughts and emotions.
- Pause and begin taking deep and steady breaths.
- Separate the emotions you are feeling from what happened by detaching yourself from your past. You are not living in the past. You are centered on the present.
- Choose to understand that the trigger is only effective when it negatively jolts your memory. Recognize that you are allowing the trigger, a song or a season, to absorb your mind and mood, and be resolute in your desire to diminish its power on you.
- With time, the trigger will diminish as you continue to practice awareness by your conviction to leave the past where it belongs. History, nothing more than history.

Criticism was another huge trigger for me. Well, nobody enjoys criticism, let's lay that out in the open, but I was so vulnerable—so naked and afraid—of criticism. I interpreted critical remarks as explicitly attacking, not my actions, but who I was, my essence. I perceived it as a form of rejection, and that brought up all sorts of fears and toxic thoughts. I even used to be negatively triggered by good memories. When I heard the song, The Girl from Ipanema, I associated it with my father and the love he had for Brazilian music. Instead of embracing the song fondly, I mourned my father intensely, which was a dangerous place for me to go because my grief absolutely knocked me out for two years. I learned to turn the song off, if possible, in order not to provoke a trigger that could bring me down. Today I listen to that song often and with joy in my heart.

Similarly, when I hear about young people committing suicide because they were bullied, my empathy can overstimulate my old patterns of thinking and dredge up my past experiences in a matter of seconds. As much as my heart goes out to the friends and families and victims of bullying, I need to either put my feelings into something productive—like reminding myself that my efforts to help others to build self-worth may be able to rescue someone from the results of bullying, or prevent it altogether—or quickly disconnect from these stories before I am dragged back in time.

This is why making the commitment to enduring transformative change is so important. Change is difficult and time consuming. It is so important to allot enough time for constructive Self-Reflection, examining, understanding, and letting go of the origins of our low self-worth. All those sessions of sitting for twenty minutes are the best preparation for the practice of building and maintaining self-worth. Please believe me that feeling better about yourself is worth the time and energy you put forth. There is nothing more important than knowing your life matters. Your presence as a compassionate human being adds value to the world, perhaps now more than ever.

> Commit to being a lifelong learner by retraining your brain to continue developing and changing as your life progresses. Never stop learning and growing.

Transformation Tenets

⬦ The inner tension that develops between your outer self and your Soul Self is known as cognitive dissonance.

⬦ It takes practice to retrain your brain, repetition is key to learning new thoughts and behavior.

⬦ A trigger or cue is a stimulus that evokes a thought or emotion from your past; it is important to familiarize yourself with your triggers.

⬦ Create a plan so that you are prepared to respond when triggers arise.

How CDV Affects our Self-Concept

Children of Domestic Violence (CDV) — An Interview with Linda Olson, Psy.D, Clinical Psychologist and Psychotherapist

Dr. Olson and I formed a friendship when I was well into the last phases of writing this book. The information she shared with me during our first meeting provided me with an entirely new understanding of my own struggles with conflict, rejection, and distrust. I wanted to learn as much as I could as I realized that Dr. Olson's area of study—to which she has devoted more than thirty years of practice and research—has profound correlation to the subject of self-worth.

The acronym, **CDV,** which stands for Children of Domestic Violence, was one I had not heard before meeting Dr. Olson. Clearly, this area of psychology pertained to children who had been physically and emotionally abused, however, I had no idea until I spoke with her that I was, in fact, a child of domestic violence. My parents' turbulent marriage affected me deeply, but I was not aware how intensely it shaped my self-concept.

"When you are exposed as a young child to a hostile environment, whether it involves physical abuse or emotional abuse, or both, the impact upon a child is long lasting and severe," Dr. Olson stated. "I have met many, many adults who don't know why they feel worthless, angry, and alone. It is not until they reflect on their childhood that they realize how much the childhood adversity they endured at a young age is responsible for their negative thoughts and emotions as adults. CDV is the single most unknown, unaddressed childhood adversity. It is the missing piece of the puzzle. If we are truly going to help people, we must focus on the root cause!" Dr. Olson remarked with passion.

Dr. Olson is a world-renowned expert in the field of CDV and has pioneered much of the research behind this growing area of psychology. "Growing up with childhood domestic violence teaches us to believe a set of lies about ourselves. These lies tell us we're worthless, fearful, angry, alone, guilty, sad, hopeless, resentful, unattractive, and unloved." Dr. Olson explained that what we absorb during our childhood has immense ramifications on our overall sense of worthiness.

"Our beliefs and self-concept are formed in childhood and become the filter for every experience and interaction we have later in life," Dr. Olson explained, reinforcing what I describe in my book. "When we are raised in an atmosphere of violence, we become programmed to see the world through a skewed, fragmented frame of mind that steals our true identity and ensnares us in a warped self-concept." Dr. Olson shared that when a person's self-concept is poor, they pivot towards information and experiences that reinforce their negative feelings about themselves and others.

When a child grows up with domestic violence, they are made to feel worthless, afraid, sad, angry, hopeless, unloved, and are likely to continue feeling this way as they age and throughout their life. "This distorted self-concept impacts all aspects of their lives, reminding them about how weak, damaged, or inadequate they are. They live with these lies in their head, unable to see themselves in a true light. Growing up with domestic violence causes the negative memories of the past to dominate and disallow a person from reaching their full potential," Dr. Olson stated. From the research I had done on early childhood development, I understood that magnitude of influence that parents and guardians have on children, however, this interview and subsequent others I had with Dr. Olson provided me an entirely new understanding.

"As you point out in your book, Anne, the amazing component to being human is that we have the ability to recover through the quality of resilience, which is how we survived as children. We learned to survive the terror of observing or being subject to painful events, to get through gut-wrenching experiences. Childhood taught us to be resilient, to keep persevering, which is why as adults, we can dig deep and release these false illusions." Dr. Olson talked about the importance of "unlearning the lies," we learned as children, and reprogramming our brain through the power of human resiliency. "Your childhood does not define you; you have the ability to move beyond where you have been through resilience."

With every issue we hold onto internally, that blocks our ability to live with an open heart and mind, we owe it to ourselves to find the root cause in order to understand why we feel inadequate, then we have the ability to accept what took place, heal from it, release those memories, and transcend to a place of peace and equanimity.

Helping individuals who have suffered from CDV has been a lifelong mission for Dr. Olson, one that has been inspired by her personal experience. Like millions of others, Dr. Olson says that the domestic violence she witnessed as a girl led her to enter (and remain in) a marriage that replicated this destructive pattern.

Research has found that growing up in a household affected by CDV is the most significant predictor that an individual will find herself or himself in an abusive relationship later in life, and/or be the perpetrator of this behavior. "All of these negative beliefs that you develop as a child become internalized, and they exert an unconscious pull on the individual," Dr. Olson remarked. "The individual feels compelled to repeat what feels familiar, because at some level the brain thinks this is what's right, and that this is what a 'loving relationship' looks like. It also provides certainty because this is what seems familiar from childhood."

After enduring an abusive marriage for more than twenty-two years,

Dr. Olson commented, "I finally realized the impact this was having on my sons, and that gave me the courage to leave. Thirty years ago, this life-threatening crisis was something that no one dared talk about with others, and – tragically – not much has changed over the years. Most people still think that 'domestic violence' refers to the physical abuse experienced by adults, most often women, and they don't realize the damaging and lasting impact that is inflicted on children who witness this behavior, even if they aren't touched themselves." This turning point in her own life led Dr. Olson to find ways that she could help others affected by CDV, hoping to spare them from the pain and tragedy she experienced.

Further fueling Dr. Olson's commitment to making a difference in the lives of others affected by CDV is the memory of her two sisters, who both died as a result of this horrific crisis. Her sister Mary endured a series of abusive relationships and died homeless, and her sister Ann was stalked and killed by an abusive ex-boyfriend. "The severe impact that CDV has on a child has dramatic, long-term impact, even death," Dr. Olson stated, as was the case of her sisters. "Seek professional help so that you can change the pattern of thinking and redirect your life," urged Dr. Olson.

> If you have severe issues related to childhood events, please contact a professional that specializes in CDV or childhood trauma. Dr. Olson's contact information is below.

Dr. Linda Olson is a Licensed Clinical Psychologist and Psychotherapist who has been working for over 30 years in the area of Childhood Domestic Violence (CDV). This refers to children who grow up living with domestic violence, and domestic abuse, and trauma. She has also specialized working with eating disorders, sexual abuse, obsessive/compulsive disorders and anxiety, and self-regulation issues.

Dr. Olson's intensive training has been in Cognitive Behavioral Therapy (CBT), Dialectical Behavioral Therapy (DBT), Mindfulness, Exposure Response Prevention (ERP), and Attachment theory.

Dr. Olson's email information: www.drlindaolson.com

Dr. Olson is Founder and Georgia Chapter Chair, Childhood Domestic Violence Association (www.GeorgiaCDV.org).

Gain Perspective

"Science is a way of life. Science is a perspective. Science is the process that takes us from confusion to understanding in a manner that's precise, predictive, and reliable—a transformation, for those lucky enough to experience it, that is empowering and emotional."
Brian Greene, Director of Columbia University's Center for Theoretical Physics

The story of why painters before the 14th century had no perspective in their art is interesting in relation to why those of us with low self-worth must gain perspective on our situations. It is generally thought that artists before the 1300s did not know how to paint their subjects in three dimensions, using shading—light and shadow—to portray how things really look. It is presumed that painting with perspective—instead of painting as if everything were flat—had to be discovered.

This is not true. James G. Harper, professor of Renaissance and Baroque Art at the University of Oregon, has pointed out that artists demonstrated a knowledge of perspective as early as the eighth century. The real reason medieval period artists did not paint with perspective was because they didn't have the desire to make lifelike images. Western Civilization was in shambles after the fall of the Roman Empire. It was the Dark Ages of the plague, hunger, and oppression. Like the rest of the population, artists were only concerned with surviving and not with passing on the knowledge of perspective.

Part Four: The Practices

When life became interesting again, sparked by the Renaissance, classic works of philosophy regained popularity and thoughts once again focused on the individual self. Artists began paying attention to accurately reproducing the curvature of our beautiful human form and perspective became part of an artist's training again.

Similarly, those of us who have been living with low self-worth have been living without perspective. Essentially, we have seen ourselves as static figures, motivated to perform outwardly as shadows of ourselves; while inwardly we were living in our own Dark Ages. It is not surprising that one of the great mind-transforming practices in building our self-worth is gaining perspective, recognizing we are made up of both shadow and light.

When something occurs in our lives that causes us to feel distraught, there is a wave of intensity that distracts us from everything else in our lives. For most people, with the passage of time, the emotions connected with the incident become less intense, and we begin to feel a separation from whatever caused the initial wound, whether it was words or actions.

Those of us with low self-value, however, get stuck in a pocket of no perspective and sucked right back into that original wave of intensity. The further we can remove ourselves from the drama of our emotions, the more objective we can be about the reality of what is happening right now in the present. This is what gaining perspective is about.

Perspective enables us to view anything, no matter what, with greater clarity (as if you are seeing in three dimensions instead of two). This is pivotal to the process of building self-worth. It provides us with better vision and greater understanding into what actually occurred, how it made us feel, and what negative effect it has on our current wellbeing. As a result, we can modify our feelings and realize the differences between then and now.

Another brilliant factor that perspective brings into play is that we are more apt to want to find a solution to our ongoing issues if we are thinking clearly. Obviously, ongoing suffering has not helped in any way. With perspective, you become open to new experiences that will replace past experiences. You can equip yourself to be stronger and more resilient through sheer optimism once you shift your perspective from the past to the present.

Where does perspective come from if your inner self has been subject to a plague of self-doubts and hungers for approval and attention from those for whom you perform?

Perspective comes from the understanding and compassion you have developed through the practice of Self-Reflection. Each time you sit down to reflect, you are communing with your soul. Remember how I said in the beginning of Part Three, Self-Reflection, that this is something that you may have to push yourself to do initially, but it will become something that you want to do, that you crave. That is why I emphasized the ritual of Self-Reflection as preparation for the practices. You will use Self-Reflection in every phase of discovery and recovery of yourself as you embark on a new way of living.

Perspective is inordinately important to the ability to detach emotionally from something that has caused you pain. Having perspective enables you to see your past from a different point of view, one that in time extinguishes the intensity of past wounds.

To gain perspective, I asked and answered these questions (not more than one a session) during my 20 minutes of Self-Reflection a day. These were specific to me and my experiences. You will ask and answer your own questions in order to understand and have compassion for your past self and move on to a joyous present.

As we move forward in our journey to build self-worth, we actively use the science of neuroplasticity to create long lasting, sustainable change in our brain. This is what it means to retrain your brain. We let go of former negative patterns of thought and behavior, and by accepting them as past, and thereby, no longer a part of us, we can move forward and rebuild our inner self.

Part Four: The Practices

RETRAIN YOUR BRAIN: Leverage the Power of Neuroplasticity

Provide answers to your own questions of why your thoughts and behavior have been consistent with low self-worth. Define the dilemmas of the past, use perspective to see things differently and to change your thinking.

My Questions

Why do I compulsively seek acceptance and approval from others as if they are a prize I have to earn over and over no matter the circumstances?

- ◊ I felt such loneliness and isolation as a result of being rejected by authority figures like my elementary school teacher, so-called friends and peers, and, later in life, when I was betrayed by colleagues, although I tried my hardest to do my best.
- ◊ My parents were so caught up in their turbulent marriage they could not freely give me the acceptance and approval a child needs or pay attention to what was happening to me.
- ◊ I have a need to receive affirmation from others as a result of my low self-worth, which left a void in my core being that could not be filled with my own acceptance and approval.

Note: With the gift of perspective, I realize I am no longer being singled out by a teacher for talking in class or by childhood bullies because they are jealous. I do not allow colleagues to bully me. I am an adult and am confident of my ability to communicate and perform my work well. I no longer live with my parents' turbulent marriage. I realize my father loved me very much and I have accepted my mother's fragility during my childhood and understand that she loves me and is present to support me now. I no longer need outside affirmation to be liked and accepted because I love and accept myself.

Why do I permit people to mistreat me?

- ◇ I dislike conflict.
- ◇ I feel it is safer to act as though abuse doesn't bother or hurt me than to reveal my pain.
- ◇ I feel suffering and heartache as a result of a loved one's abuse is a normal part of life, as that is what I saw as a young child.
- ◇ I don't know how to stand up for myself without becoming over-emotional and losing it all together.
- ◇ For whatever reason, I subconsciously feel I deserve to be mistreated.

Note: With the gift of perspective, I am no longer afraid of conflict because it is a normal consequence of living a busy and enriching life. I realize there is more than one viewpoint and more than one right answer and not everything depends on my having the perfect solution to a problem. I now know it is better to share my feelings in the moment than to stuff them down inside me until I feel like I am gagging on them. As an adult now, I believe that my mother paid too high a price in suffering in her marriage, and that both she and I deserve to feel happy and peaceful and not suffer in silence. I can stand up for myself in any situation because I value who I am and will not allow anyone to abuse me with my consent. I am neither a victim nor a perpetrator.

Why am I ineffectual at setting boundaries?

- ◇ I have no history of or role models setting boundaries.
- ◇ I am often afraid to tell the truth about how I really feel and risk angering or hurting someone.
- ◇ I have the need to be needed, so I allow others to walk over me.
- ◇ I believe it is not pleasant and perhaps even rude to say no to someone.

⬧ I don't respect myself enough to define appropriate time management for myself, let alone do I allot time limits to others.

Note: With the gift of perspective, I understand that boundaries are a way to maintain harmony in relationships, and that it is up to me to set clear boundaries in regard to my expectations of others and their expectations of me. I will speak my truth as that is part of being my authentic self. I accept that I am a "helper" in this world, and enjoy being needed, but I will not allow others to tread over me in order to get from me what they should be able to do for themselves. That benefits neither of us. Boundaries are a way to show respect for myself and others. Setting boundaries provides much-needed space to do things for myself, rather than always being available no matter what time of day or night.

Why do I have to be the best in everything I do?

⬧ Being "perfect," or better than anyone else, was a way to gain my father's respect and attention.
⬧ I wanted to be recognized for my achievements and intelligence in order to be valued by others because I had trouble valuing myself.
⬧ I have been extremely hard on myself because I have believed if I am not the winner, my identity is as a loser.
⬧ I have an intrinsic competitive drive that will not give me a break, even when I go to bed at night.
⬧ Being good is not good enough. I have to strive for excellence.

Note: With the gift of perspective, I accept that I do not have to be the best at everything. I have removed the word "perfect" from my vocabulary as it does not exist for me nor anyone. I no longer have to impress my father or anyone else. I am the leader in my life, the authority figure, and I recognize myself for my achievements every day, no matter how small. I am intelligent and accomplished as I am and continue to learn and grow. Part of my compassion for myself and others is to let someone else have a chance to be the best. It shouldn't be the same person winning the medal or taking the prize every time. I enjoy seeing others reach their potential. I remain competitive but have a grounded understanding of what is important and what is not. I am comfortable being who I am because I know I am a consistently good, kind, and loving individual.

This process was groundbreaking for me in that it allowed me to be open in a more honest and pure way than my previous attempts to let go. I was able to not only recognize what and why I had been troubled, but also to reframe my past with positive actions to follow. I was not just feeding the negative and poking the bear, which could stimulate potentially harmful consequences by alerting the sympathetic nervous system to release hormones. I was replacing the negative with positive intentions. I have no way of knowing for sure without functional magnetic resonance imaging, but I believe my brain began to be more in balance as a result of this process. At least I felt more in balance. I was moving from focusing on the problem to focusing on the context, or what I want to happen.

This was a valuable practice because putting the past in perspective allowed me to stop lying to myself about me. I was not the victim I saw myself as in the past. I felt energized, excited, and most of all, ALIVE in my core being. My Soul Self was undeniably engaged in my quest for self-worth, directing me to keep moving forward.

Putting your problems, feelings, and all human behavior in perspective is a practice that can help relieve anxiety in almost any situation. Don't make a mountain out of a molehill, some of us were told as children. As time goes by, things in your past are supposed to be smaller as they are farther away. And once today is over, the challenges that appeared so overwhelming won't loom quite so large as the earth continues revolving around the sun. The ability to see yourself with new eyes sharpens the clarity of your vision.

The goal of the practice of perspective is to teach yourself that life issues are manageable over time, and overreacting to events will not help you. With repetition, you will become seasoned in the art of perspective which will allow you to understand that what you suffered through in the past will no longer have power over you in the present or future, due to the fact that you have been able to understand the nature of these circumstances and move forward with a renewed and cleansed mind.

The process of perspective is to gain a shift in consciousness. When we step back we are able to see the big picture; conversely, when we lean in, we can perceive details that we did not see before. Sometimes perspective comes in a flash, and instant, and sometimes it requires time, however, it always causes a shift in which you are able to change gears and move in a new direction.

The practice of perspective is useful anytime you are wrestling with something. It takes time, however, as any mental practice does. Just as any other practice we apply to our lives, the amount of time it takes varies from person to person. Be patient with the process and feel assured that you will reach the point at which gaining perspective becomes a natural part of your repertoire of self-care.

Having gained perspective on your past, you are ready to be wonderful you, who has been inside this whole time, safe in your core, Soul Self.

> Gaining perspective provides us with the vision to see things as they are and not as we fear they are.

Transformation Tenets

◇ Perspective is a way to view anything with greater clarity and insight.

◇ Perspective is a powerful practice to detach emotionally from something that has caused you pain.

◇ Having perspective enables you to see your past from a different point of view, that with time, will extinguish the intensity of past wounds.

◇ Perspective is a way to reframe your past and replace wounds with positive thoughts and intentions.

Colin's Story

My youngest son's formal name is Richard Colin Boudreau, but he's gone by Colin since his birth. His full name, however, is listed on every official record, including the school directory. Colin was my introverted, shy, tender child, who painstakingly avoided any kind of controversy. When he started fourth grade, a child in his class began to call him names. The one he used the most was "dick," which can be a nickname for Richard or mean something else. "Dick, dick, dick…you're such a dick," he'd say to my son, enough times to sting. The boy's taunting was amplified, of course, by the other kids who were listening. This kid would also steal Colin's lunch on a daily basis.

At first, Colin said nothing. It went on for weeks before it finally became too much for him to bear. After a particularly bad day at school, Colin came home extremely sullen, with noticeable black circles under his eyes. He didn't say a word as he started doing his homework. When I was able to get him to open up to me about it, I could see that he was terribly distraught by the entire situation.

Colin begged me not to get involved, believing this bully could beat him to a pulp. After a lengthy conversation, I was able to convince him that bullies have to be stopped. I was too familiar with the fact that bullying is deeply toxic and can be life-altering, leaving a wound that is difficult to heal even over time. It also can be life threatening if adults ignore a child's need for assistance. I called the boy's mother and explained what he had been doing to Colin for weeks. I mentioned to her that if my child were taking someone's food, and worse, using his name as a curse word, I would want to know. Fortunately, I didn't have to go to the school with the issue as the boy's mother handled the situation with earnestness, as did the boy in the end.

This experience took a harder toll on me than it did on Colin. I knew Colin was resilient as he had faced other challenges in his young life and rebounded. After all, he had perceptive parents who attended to his needs.

I took the situation to an entirely deeper level. Not only did I internalize what happened to him, how he must have felt at school, the suffering that was unjustifiably thrust upon him, I continued to envision the scenario in my mind over and over. I kept checking with him to see if he wanted to discuss it, asking him how he was feeling, and was determined to keep on top of whether this bully had changed his behavior or not. It became an obsession with me; while for Colin the indignity of the incident had long since diminished.

I finally realized that my internal anger and anguish in response to what Colin had endured was one thousand times magnified by my experience when I was the same age. I was suffering with post-traumatic stress from the bullying at camp that went on for sixteen months unchecked when I was in elementary school. It felt nearly as raw and real as it did all those years ago. What unsettled me was that even with all of the work, interviews, research and writing I'd done about self-worth, those painful memories remained crystallized in my brain. Did this mean that I hadn't really developed self-worth? Was my own personal quest all for naught? As much as I knew about the topic, why wasn't I able to erase the past?

This incident prompted me to revisit the tools I had created, particularly the practices I'd developed to release toxic thoughts and emotions. Clearly, I was still clinging to some negative feelings from the past. I saw myself in my son, and knowing how anguished I had been, I didn't want him to experience anything remotely similar to what I had endured. But, Colin is not me. He has from birth grown up in a stable, nurturing environment, one rooted in unconditional support and love. This was about my projecting my own experience of bullying onto him. I knew what to do.

I dove right into my techniques for cleansing and replenishing oneself. After a few days, I was back on the path of positivity. I also learned a meaningful lesson. Even though every single person can build their self-worth, life has a way of constantly testing us. It is during the difficult periods that knowing you are worthy is pivotal. The inner strength and resilience that is derived from building healthy self-worth enables you to recover, renew, and move forward with courage and confidence.

There will always be moments that challenge what we know to be true about ourselves in our core, even after we have accepted that it doesn't matter how the outside world perceives us. It is who we are on the inside that is important. Like exercising, you have to keep doing it for your muscles to remain strong and not atrophy. Just like maintaining your car, you have to keep changing the oil and following up on the warning signs to ensure a smooth ride. Who wants to break down at the side of the road on a rainy night? Much easier to do what you know you need to do as soon as you become aware of a problem.

Realizing the need for a review, I went back to the basics of my discovery of what self-worth is and why it is the vital lifeline for every single one of us.

Detach from Your Thoughts

"Attachment is the great fabricator of illusions; reality can be obtained only by someone who is detached."
Simone Weil, French philosopher, mystic, and political activist

My friend has a magnet on her fridge that reads "Don't believe everything you think." It's a reminder that not all our thoughts are true. To detach from our thoughts requires that we understand *our thoughts are just thoughts.* They are not reality. Some thoughts are important, but many are not.

A number of articles on the internet claim that the average human has between 40,000 and 60,000 thoughts per day. No one can find the actual source of this figure, but what scientists seem to agree on is that the quality of our thoughts tends to be consistently repetitive, and that the overwhelming majority of our thoughts are negative. We know from fMRI studies that negative thoughts have a more powerful and lasting effect on the brain than positive ones and stimulate areas that contribute to depression and anxiety. Therefore, there are probably more people walking around in the world with low self-worth than we even imagine.

It's good to know I am not alone, but it is tough to think of all the suffering that results from these loops of doubt, dread, and discomfort. Thoughts, after all, come with baggage. They stimulate and reawaken the emotions originally felt when the thoughts were deposited in our memories. So, we're dealing with thinking and feeling, a double whammy.

Thankfully, we now know that we can change these thoughts and their tag-along emotions that define us and our world. And we know that we must.

If you observe your problems, fears, and challenges as a witness instead of a participant, your turbulent thoughts and negative emotions will lose their grip on your mind. They will not be able to distort your sense of self-worth and well-being. Essentially, they wither and die. My hope is that they at least provide compost for growing new, healthy thoughts.

How do you throttle back after so many years of being attached to your thoughts as reality, investing in them as if they were valuable stocks? You detach.

What does that mean? Probably not what you think. It does not mean separating yourself from anything other than expectations of outcomes. You are still involved in the rushing river of your life. But detachment allows you to step out of the river and sit on the riverbank or a rock in the middle of the river and observe. You do not have to find yourself on a raft paddling for your life over rapids. You do not have to risk falling in and being swept away and over powerful waterfalls around the bend. You step out of that picture and rest your mind from all the possibilities of disaster. After doing so, you might decide to avoid the river when it is that rough. Find a way around it. Or stay where you are if that is comfortable. It is entirely possible that the rushing river that is your life will become calmer in time and you can float comfortably or swim strongly when required.

Practicing detachment allows you to give up your habitual thoughts and the emotional charge that comes with them and give yourself the freedom to explore other options in your mind. Practicing detachment means recognizing your thoughts are just thoughts, not reality.

But, still, the question remains how to detach?

Meditation

One major avenue of detachment is the supportive practice of meditation, which has successfully provided detachment, clarity, and peace for overburdened minds for thousands of years in many Eastern cultures. Now mainstream in Western cultures, too, meditation is accessible to all at any age or stage. My friend's son's first grade teacher even used meditation techniques to calm active 6-year-olds before having to give out the state's mandated standardized testing materials. It is used for cancer patients to control pain by moving the mind beyond it. Meditation's calming and healing applications are vast. In recent news, we learned that the coach of the Thai boys' soccer team trapped in a cave for twelve days taught his team of boys how to meditate, helping them remain calm and also conserve energy during an extremely challenging period of time. Meditation was a brilliant and highly effective way to quell what might have been an unbearably traumatic experience for the boys.

Meditation is easy to learn, a simple process, it does not cost a dime, and can be done anywhere at any time. The positive effect of meditation is both immediate and long term, and it has amazing benefits to the whole person — mind, body, and spirit.

The benefits of meditation are expansive, and researchers are learning more about its powerful efficacy in numerous health-related areas. To name a few of the physiological benefits, meditation reduces blood pressure and heart rate, improves blood glucose levels, reduces inflammatory proteins, and has positive effects on the brain such as decreasing production of cortisol (which is a key ingredient in sparking fear), increasing brain connectivity, reducing atrophy in the hippocampus, and slowing the aging of the brain.

Meditation reduces cognitive rigidity, increases problem solving capacity and motivation, reduces compulsive tendencies, elevates clarity, and promotes the intuitive process. It reduces anxiety and negative thoughts, increases optimism and lessens depression, enhances self-acceptance and self-worth, and engenders resilience. Perhaps most importantly, meditation heightens awareness of the inner self, the discovery of consciousness beyond the ego, and a connection with one's true being. It actually provides the opportunity to feel at one with yourself and the world.

The practice of meditation is a means to reach awakening or enlightenment and to end suffering. When we are in a meditative state, our mind is relaxed, inwardly focused, and in a higher state of consciousness than when we are awake. The rewards are many, but in regard to positive self-worth, regular meditation results in greater clarity about ourselves and instills a natural tendency to treat ourselves and others with compassion and loving kindness. It supports the practice of detachment by enabling you to separate from your emotions, expectations, anxieties, insecurities, and enables you to connect with your true self, your Soul Self. This enables us to feel a sense of calm and peacefulness that is pure.

Let's begin.

RETRAIN THE BRAIN: Reap the Amazing Benefits of Meditation

Is there any more useful activity you can do for yourself for any rhyme or reason in your life than meditation? You start sweet and short with as little as ten minutes a day, and transition to longer times and different meditation forms and styles, if you like, when you are ready. It is a beautiful, life-altering solution to much of what ails all of humanity. When you practice meditation long term, you are re-sculpting the brain and changing its physical structure to promote peace.

You can join meditation groups or do meditation as a closing to an exercise program of yoga, for instance. There are many online meditations possibilities as well. You can get meditation apps that will give your phone a tap at a certain time and guide you through a meditation. When my daughter, Sophia, was very ill, I would play guided meditations for her so that she could rest her brain and body, while also enhancing her immune system. It was an extremely effective and immediate way to calm her during her painful healing after surgery. The best aspect of this powerful practice is that you can do it yourself, anytime, anywhere.

Beginner's Meditation Relaxation Response. This is intended as an introduction only. It is to help counteract the response to fear that increases anxiety, heart rate, and blood pressure.

Sit quietly on a cushion on the floor with your legs crossed. I like to close the shades or curtains, dim the lights, and light a candle or incense to create a space that feels more sacred to me. You can also meditate sitting in a chair or on a couch or lying down in a bed if you have physical limitations. I do not typically recommend lying down as some people will fall asleep rather than meditate. You can meditate while sitting in your car if you need to (while parked), train, airplane, anywhere you feel comfortable.

Close your eyes and focus on your breathing. Breathe in through your nose, out through your mouth and listen only to your breath. Count five in and eight out. Do this for 5-10 minutes. When thoughts enter your mind, let them flow through you as you continue to focus on your breath. You can also silently repeat a sound, word, or phrase, or simply count your breaths. Allow yourself to fully calm down and flow into the process. The focus on breathing or on one thing helps regulate and calm your mind and heart.

When you are ready, gently open your eyes. Keep seated for a few minutes. It is important to enjoy the process and not be concerned with the result. Practice this breathing technique twice a day but be sure it is two hours before or after any meal as the process of metabolizing food tends to interfere with relaxation.

Mindfulness Meditation. Being mindful is the state of being present, connecting with your Soul Self, which is a conduit to melting into the universe.

Before you begin, decide how much time you would like to devote, that way you won't be distracted by how much or how little time has elapsed. Use a timer with a pleasant chime, or your phone, so you won't have to pause to check the time.

Sit in a comfortable position with your upper body upright. Relax your head and shoulders. Put your arms and hands parallel to your upper body and rest your hands on the top of your legs. Let your head fall naturally forward a bit and lower your eyes before you close them.

Listen to your normal breathing patterns. Focus on the physical sensation of breathing. By listening to your breaths in a quiet and comfortable pose your brain will start to send signals to your body to relax and calm down.

As we try to stay in the present moment and not gravitate toward thoughts of what we should be doing, let thoughts and images flow through you. Focus on observing them the way you would a breeze that sways the trees. The breeze flows through the trees as the leaves move about. Listen to your thoughts, emotions, or other distractions as they rise up within you but just be an observer not an active participant, so they can keep moving like clouds.

Sometimes it helps to get grounded in the present moment by silently naming what you hear in the present (car traffic, a lawn mower), what you feel (a movement of air that lifts the tiny hairs on your arm), what you smell (sandalwood incense).

As you sit with thoughts coming in and out of your mind, tune back into your breathing. The reason this meditation is called mindfulness is that it is a practice of returning, again and again to the present moment. Return to your breaths. The more you practice returning to your breath, the calmer you will be, and the thoughts will begin to diminish over time. Mindful meditation is a way to quiet your mind without forcing thoughts away or judging them, just observing them.

When the timer sounds, gently open your eyes and notice how you are feeling. Pause and take in the experience. Some people clear their mind; others have dream like images that project on the mind like a movie. The goal is to clear your mind of the normal clutter of 40,000-60,000 thoughts a day. Detach from your thoughts. With time and repetition, you will reap the amazing benefits that meditation offers.

Practicing twice a day for 15-20 minutes is a worthy goal that can happen in time. Remember, you are reshaping your brain through meditation, any opinion, judgment, or criticism diffuses into a peaceful presence.

Our over-active mind is like living with a chorus of chattering gossips who never stop talking about when you said this or did that, and then you felt x, y, z because so and so acted like a, b, c, and on and on. It happens to everyone and given time and practice, you will be able to quiet the chatter.

You can tame the thoughts in your mind—the well-worn thoughts that bounce around in your head like pinballs. When those thoughts feel they are being listened to and paid attention to, they settle down. Observe, acknowledge with good humor, not frustration, and the gossips will move on.

The Power of Keeping a Journal — A Reminder: Rely on Journaling to Keep Track of Your Thoughts

As I discussed earlier, one of the most effective and powerful ways to observe and learn about yourself is by writing about your feelings and thoughts. It offers you a nonjudgmental form of communing with yourself that is instrumental in your quest to build self-worth. By detailing what took place that triggered specific thoughts, and describing the what, when, where, and how it made you feel, you will gain tremendous insight into what you have been thinking and feeling.

I hope that you have indeed been keeping a journal, whether it is an actual physical journal, one that is private to you, or if you prefer, use your computer, iPad, or phone to record your thoughts. Having the ability to see your thoughts concretely helps you identify issues that are reoccurring or that cause you undue strain. Documenting your thoughts also enables you to recognize subtle changes in your thought patterns and behavior.

Please do not permit this process to cause you excessive strain. If it is still too stressful to write about past events, put it aside for now. The work of building self-worth is inwardly focused, so being able to express yourself in writing is a wonderful venting mechanism that will give you an understanding for how you are feeling in the moment and as you go from day to day. Writing is an unparalleled vehicle to measure your progress and evaluate what is working and what may not be working. You will be able to look back at your writing and note the growth and transformations that have taken place more easily since they are tangibly captured.

Write for wisdom about yourself, for the cathartic mental and emotional release, for the insight and clarity, and for relaxation and anxiety reduction.

Label Your Thoughts. I used another technique for detaching from my thoughts and expectations. I would choose one specific memory or unpleasant thought and give it a name. Label it. For instance, rather than continue to replay the bullying incidents that happened to me, review the details over and over, focus on me as a victim, and remind myself who the perpetrators of maliciousness were, I objectified the experience by calling it **SHIT—Stuff Hell Into Toilet.** I know that sounds immature and silly, and quite frankly, it's atypical of me to speak this way, but that is how I felt at this point in my journey: debased and humiliated. Therefore, I decided to flush this experience down the toilet whenever I thought about it. Within weeks—I kid you not—I found myself laughing whenever I encountered those particular thoughts and mentally flushed them out of my system. Since I've always believed curse words to be a lazy way to express oneself, it was even more humorous that I was calling my "crap" SHIT.

Labeling memories is a way to separate yourself from what took place.

The intent of the exercise is not to draw more attention to the thought, instead it is to create a distance between you and what took place. With time, this memory becomes an object that you look at from a distance, and eventually, you will be able to throw it in the garbage, not the recycle bin! The act of labeling and throwing out your negative thoughts can be highly cathartic. It was for me. Give it a try.

Your thoughts are ideas floating in your head. Just because they appear in your brain, you can choose not to accept them. I was in the midst of reflecting upon why I had lived for so long from the outside in, my state of Outer-Inness—basing my worth on what others thought of me and what I believed about me—when I began reading voraciously, seeking sources that might help me understand myself better. Interestingly, I found a trove of profound wisdom and guidance in the writings of our founding Greek philosophers. Ancient Greek philosopher and scientist, Aristotle,(384 BC-322 BC) once said, "It is the mark of an educated mind to be able to entertain a thought without accepting it.

Aristotle's quote weighed heavily on the list of my favorites as it caused me to dig deep and ask myself questions—deeper questions—that would allow me to stop the constant thrashing inside me. A thought is not a command, nor a rule to be enforced, it is merely an idea, opinion, or concept. Aha, then a thought is not a fact. And, if it's not a fact, then it also may not be the truth. As simplistic as this may sound on the surface, what it meant to me was that just because I had spent many years of my life with distorted thoughts about myself didn't mean that they were necessarily true, or that I had to accept them any longer.

It was up to me to choose what I wanted to think or believe about myself. It is my life, I had to remind myself, and it is up to me to decide how I wish to think and feel. Of course, Aristotle's quote also meant that one should not be easily influenced by others' ideas and beliefs, rather they should have trust in their own ideas, and this is also true as it pertains to you and your self-worth. No one's opinion of you should matter as much or more than your own.

Part Four: The Practices

Cognitive Defusion: A Practice of Letting Go

It was soon after my immersion into all things "self" related that I learned about Cognitive Defusion. Cognitive Defusion is another approach to reduce and detach from painful thoughts and emotions. When one is fused to their thoughts, they have immense power over their life. The aim of Cognitive Defusion is to transform a person's relationship with distressing thoughts and emotions by learning to observe them, rather than believe they are one with their thoughts.

Begin by taking deep breaths. As you unwind, let your thoughts come and go without holding onto them. This is not a process of eliminating your thoughts, rather letting them flow through you. This enables you to create space from the thoughts that are causing you distress. It also allows you to reframe what is bothering you until it loses its meaning and no longer impacts you in the same way.

Do this every time you catch yourself thinking a negative thought, either in real time, or if you are in a meeting or somewhere you need to focus on other things, discreetly write down your thought and deal with it later. If you have the thought "I am a worthless loser," for instance, reframe it as "I am having the thought that I am a worthless loser." In other words, *it's only a thought. It's not real.* Say it out loud for good measure. If you'd like a boost, follow your reframing statement with this: "The truth is that I am a winner, the fabulous exceptional Anne Boudreau, and I am creating new neural pathways."

Having detached from your judgmental inner critic who broadcasted blame, doubt, and shame on your self-loathing channel night and day, you can listen to and observe your thoughts and emotions with compassion and presence of mind. You will draw closer to your Soul Self as you silence the toxic voices in your brain. You will give up the shrill voices and sharp traps that tripped you over and over. And you will know peace in the temple of your mind and body.

Detachment does not mean you don't care. It is an objective nonjudgmental state of mind that allows you to separate from old destructive patterns.

Transformation Tenets

◊ Practicing detachment means recognizing your thoughts are not reality; you have the power to change your thoughts at any time.

◊ Practicing detachment enables you to let go of habitual thoughts and the emotional charge that comes with them.

◊ Meditation is an excellent practice for detaching from thoughts with amazing holistic health benefits.

◊ Cognitive defusion is an effective process to observe your thoughts and transform your relationship with them.

The Mandala

A Lesson in Detachment

A few years ago, I had the pleasure of viewing the creation of a breath-taking, stunningly beautiful mandala made out of colored grains of sands. This tradition practiced by Tibetan monks is a ritual to signify the transitory nature of life. Mandala, in Sanskrit, means circle. For Tibetan monks, it is a spiritual symbol of the universe.

No two mandalas are alike, and the designs are very complicated, consisting of intricate geometric patterns and ancient symbols that represent the world in its divine form—perfectly balanced, precisely designed. The monks, clad in deep crimson robes, hunched over a table while trickling sand out of tubes and funnels onto a template. The colors of the sand (a special dense and heavy sand that won't get blown around) are striking and deeply hued. The monks worked together for ten to twelve hours a day in a meditative state, with little reprieve. The calmness and serenity in their demeanor was mesmerizing. I felt peace, honor, respect, and love in their presence.

When the mandala design was finished, the monks prayed over it and then, to my astonishment, completely destroyed it during a closing ceremony. Sand samples were offered to those present and the remaining sand was taken to a nearby river where it was submerged to share the monks' blessings with the world.

The process of creating the mandala was to call the community together in meditation and awareness of something larger than their own small world. But the mission of the tradition of creation and destruction is to remind us that nothing is permanent. Change is constant. We cannot be bound to even the most beautiful things.

This is why Buddhists meditate: in order to detach from our material world because nothing is permanent. The only thing that is real is peace through enlightenment.

After viewing the monks in their ritual, I found a scroll with a message from the XIV Dalai lama that I would like to share with you on your journey to self-worth.

True Meaning of Peace

The most important factor is maintaining peace within oneself. In the face of any difficulty, is one's mental attitude.

If it is distorted by such feelings as anger, attachment, jealousy, then even the most comfortable environment will bring no peace.

On the other hand, if one's attitude is generally calm and gentle, then even a hostile environment will have little effect on one's own inner peace.

Since the basic source of peace and happiness is one's own mental attitude, it is worthwhile adopting means to develop it in a positive way.

Accept Who You Are

"The worst loneliness is to not be comfortable with yourself."
Mark Twain

The day I first found this quote by Mark Twain, I felt instantly acknowledged. When you don't accept or value yourself, that discomfort is always there, inside of you. You can try to run from it, but you cannot hide from what is inside you.

After about four weeks of working through the period of Self-Reflection, during which I spent focused time rewinding and recalling the major issues that had been spinning relentlessly in my head, I had a revelation. There were only two choices: either I would remain as I was, living with constant inner tension and self-doubt, or I could choose to acknowledge that my past experiences would not forever define me. I could teach myself to believe that my life was worthy, even if to no one else but me.

There was no permanent marker that left indelible tattoos in my brain that said distrusting, self-demeaning, unworthy—to name a few of my thoughts about myself. I had studied much on the science of neuroplasticity and understood that I was capable of rewiring the neural pathways in my brain with new, self-assuring, and invigorating thoughts. But I still wondered whether I could truly rid myself of the heavy messages that burdened me throughout my life. I had often heard people talk about finding themselves or finally learning to love themselves, and then one year later they were back in rehab or worse. Was it possible, quite literally, to re-create myself internally?

The only way to find out was to carry forward with what I had learned, knowing that any constructive changes would be worth my time and energy. I knew that I had to accept myself fully, taking into account all of the past pain, mistakes, and fears, as well as forgive those who played a part in causing me to feel low self-worth. I needed to accept all of me. Yet how could I do that when I was still holding self-deprecating thoughts inside? I knew from reflection and evaluation what those thoughts were, I was able to objectify and detach from them. But I continued to see myself in the mirror with those exacting eyes.

The one certain way to stop the self-critique was to STOP. And, I did.

I decided to just be fine with the way I was and accept all of me every single moment of every day for the remainder of my life. This meant that I had to accept that I had it all wrong: it's NOT how other people see you that makes you a success, it's how you feel about yourself.

I could feel my heart racing with joy at that very moment. Of course, the excitement was just in the imagining me without defenses, without having to push thoughts down, and most of all, with no self-doubt. It was the most exhilarating thought imaginable.

I had sought approval my whole life from others, although I did not feel any better about myself when I got all those lovely compliments about my talents, skills, beauty, and intelligence. I had felt lonely and isolated as a result of being rejected by my peers, even though I caused them no trouble. I had permitted people to mistreat me because I didn't know how to stand up for myself and because I thought I was so good at tolerating my suffering. After all, it didn't bother anyone but me—which was ok because I was used to feeling bad about myself.

I felt strong, but weak; confident I was going in the right direction, but still confused about where I would end up. I knew I was going to be alright, but what did that look like?

Through all my years of introspection, I knew that I could count on my obsession to not give up on myself. I was consumed by my own persistence to get to the bottom of why someone who had grown up with all the advantages money could buy, who was by all outward signs a success, would feel low self-worth—which brought me to this very point.

I had researched self-worth, committed to change, self-reflected—journaling all my questions and answers—attained perspective on what occurred and why, detached from my sad past and the lies I had told myself about me. I felt I knew myself pretty well. But I really only knew the me who was emerging from the slime. I was a lovely—turtle—at this point, poking my inquisitive neck out, but carrying a heavy shell. It was time to be me. I would have liked to emerge from the shell as a hummingbird, but that was not on the agenda. I was going to be me. Who was Anne, Annie, wife, mother, sister, daughter, friend, executive, coach, me?

All of these years I was standing still inside of myself hoping for someone or something to come and rescue me. But all along the path of my life, there was no one who could change me but me. I had to lead my life in the direction that would give me what I was seeking.

I am the leader of my life.

Self-acceptance turned out to be a warm bubble bath. It begins with compassion for yourself. You know what compassion is: concern for the sufferings or misfortunes of others. I had felt compassion all my life for others, often nicknamed, bleeding heart. Where was that empathy, mercy, kindness, tenderness for my imperfect self?

It was in the wings, ready to fly. I just had to give it the freedom to do so.

RETRAIN THE BRAIN: Your Time to Create New Thoughts and Behavior—Be Your Own Best Friend and Advocate

Among all your close relationships, the most meaningful friendship you will ever have is with yourself, for all the reasons we've discussed in this book. No one understands better than you how to calm yourself, detach from difficult people or circumstances, restore yourself through positive self-talk, exercise, meditation, and other powerful practices. No one but you knows what you are really thinking and feeling. Therefore, you deserve to be able to comfort yourself as you would a dear friend. When you become your closest friend, there is nothing powerful enough to make you feel alone, abandoned, undesirable, afraid, or unloved.

By accepting yourself, you have made an agreement to treat yourself with unwavering support, even when you err or take a step back, just like a best friend would. *You have become your own best friend.* Naturally, you still enjoy your friends, family, colleagues, and others, but you have developed your own source of strength, power, and resilience that no one will ever be able to crush or take away.

Learning to accept yourself is a lot like treating yourself as if you are your closest friend. If you are chilly, you get yourself a soft warm blanket. If you notice anxious thoughts beginning to form, respond with gentle reassurance: "I don't like this feeling, but it will pass." Maybe, despite your best efforts, you feel emotionally vulnerable. You let it flow through you, ask yourself why, then make hot tea. Soon enough, your self-compassion will enable you to move on. No more drama. You are committed to practicing loving kindness for yourself.

When you are out and about living your life and run into a situation that would have formerly thrown you for a loop—your colleague criticizes you, you are late to pick up your child and feel like a terrible parent, you run into someone who is toxic and are momentarily flummoxed—treat yourself as a best friend would. Be understanding, don't beat yourself up. Recognize what happened was not intentional and move on with no negative residue. You will be amazed by the resonating affect that self-compassion and kindness, self-respect and self-care have on you and your life. Issues that used to irritate you will not be problematic, as you are focused on more important matters. People or situations that made you feel uncomfortable or insecure will be manageable now because you know that you can handle anything that comes your way. You know who you are, and no one can tell you otherwise. Your safety net is you.

You can even precede each reminder to yourself with the phrase, "As my own best friend." As my own best friend, I am reminding myself that I am fine just the way I am, and if there is any merit in my colleague's criticism I will sort it out as informational feedback, not as crippling rejection. As my own best friend, I realize that I have been on time for 99 percent of my child's needs and that being human does not include being perfect. As my own best friend, I understand that I can greet someone I know and take my leave quickly and cordially. I owe nothing to someone who in the past has sucked me into their wasp's nest. I have learned that "No" is a complete sentence that requires no follow-up paragraph of explanation.

You no longer cringe when someone says something that makes you feel somehow at fault. You are not afraid to disagree with someone, fearful they will reject you or fearful of conflict itself. You have a best friend who always has your back. You!

Please yourself. Why have you been denying yourself in order to please others? Once I accepted myself, I no longer felt the compulsion to be a people-pleaser, but instead, focused on pleasing myself. I loved staying home and spending time with my children more than going out to yet one more social engagement, so I started giving myself permission to follow my soul's desire. Instead of putting everyone else's needs first, I began to honor my own. Remember to listen to your gut-check response, your intuition, and you will make the decision that best suits you. The more often you practice pleasing yourself, the sooner it will become a habit to which you look forward—and deserve.

Set boundaries. You know you need them in place with others, not just in your head. Because I was finally accepting who I was, I found my relationships with loved ones strengthening. My love was free to pour out instead of being held back by resentments. With healthy boundaries, I could enjoy my family and friends even more.

Kindly but confidently state when it is convenient for you to get together and when you need to leave in order to get your sleep or do the things you want to get done. Once you start, you will realize how others took advantage of you because you did not have boundaries and tried to be all things to all people. When you treat yourself with respect, others will too.

Realize that you are enough. You don't have to be the smartest in your class or the fastest runner. You don't have to be told you are a great friend or boss to feel okay. You don't have to be the best-dressed or most perfect guest or hostess. When someone came over and my house was messy, I felt fine, which was a fresh take on being comfortable and living without stress or fear of judgment. I did not have to be "on" every minute I was being watched. Sometimes I could just be casual Anne who will pick up the slack some other time.

When I say relax your standards, I don't mean that you should have no standards. It's just that you have been so tough on yourself, it's time to give yourself a break. You don't have to measure yourself against "the best of the best." Or against anyone. Be as you are—yourself.

I know this is easier said than done, however, when you choose to commit to self-change, your commitment includes releasing negative thoughts about yourself and valuing who you are with no judgement. This takes time, but with time, you will begin to judge yourself less and less, to be more aware of triggers that awaken toxic thoughts, and as they arise in you, you will enable them to flow right out. You will begin to praise yourself for the simple things you do and not let mistakes shut you down. You will feel alive and filled with peace because for once in your life you are okay just as you are. Your unique footprint on this earth deserves to feel worthy and spectacular. With time, accepting yourself will feel like the only option.

My whole world was powerfully enhanced as my self-imposed barriers about what was correct and approved began to come down. I finally put away the magnifying glass I had handy to examine my every flaw and fault.

Look in the mirror and tell yourself "I love you just the way you are." Do not evaluate, analyze, or question. Think about how lucky you are to be alive. You are extraordinary from every conceivable angle. You have everything you need to feel fulfilled.

When your mind starts to wind up for its usual blast from the past critique, your brain can now see right through those old stories. You can almost blow them away. Having accepted yourself, you have the power. The ball is in your court. You have possession—of your self—accompanied by your best friend self. A formidable pair of winners.

It has been a lovely interlude, getting to know and accept yourself, but we are going to walk a little further down the path to make sure this is all part of lasting transformative change.

> You are a glorious mix of everything that made you who you are today:
> genes, history, environment, knowledge, love,
> and acceptance.

Transformation Tenets

- ◇ How you view yourself is paramount to living a fulfilling life.
- ◇ Self-acceptance means accepting all of you, and being your own best friend: YOU ARE ENOUGH.
- ◇ Pleasing yourself is an important aspect of developing healthy self-worth—it is a way to honor who you are.
- ◇ Set boundaries, your time is precious and valuable.

Generate Positive Self-Talk

"You're braver than you believe, stronger than you seem,
and smarter than you think."

—Winnie the Pooh

Your mind is always generating conversations. And, depending on what is happening in your life, there is a possibility that you are carrying on several different monologues at once. One is attending to what you are doing at the moment, such as writing words on the computer and thinking about those words. A different one is reminding you of your appointment in two hours, another is reflecting on your argument with your husband last night, and there is one telling you that you didn't sleep well, look tired, and need to call your mother soon. As all these intersecting thoughts navigate through your active, complex brain, you are anything but, in the moment, or fully present to your life. The fact is that we all have times when we allow our minds to wander into the busy traffic of our lives, which allows the moments when we are fully present and awake to be even more meaningful.

Aside from the to-do's that occupy space in our brain, there is the ever-present internal conversation we have discussed throughout this book that distracts us from the present moment, blurring our today with our yesterday and our tomorrow. The inner voice that no one but you can hear. We know with certainty that you are who you believe you are. If what has gone into your head is positive, you will value yourself and flourish. Negative messages lead to a negative self-image. That is not your fault. It's the way you were molded. Fortunately, we now know we can change a negative internal script, and our brain, by retraining our pattern of thoughts.

Self-talk, that conversation that goes on in your head all the time, is the script for your life. If you feel that you have been inhabiting a bad movie for some years now, it's quite possibly because the script that has been literally written into your brain is simply not a good one. Your thoughts, which are expressed internally in words, though not necessarily sentences, are the source of your emotions and attitudes. The conversations you have with yourself can be destructive or beneficial. They influence how you feel about yourself and how you respond to events in your life.

Inner speech develops alongside social speech, according to Charles Fernyhough, author of *The Voices Within: The History and Science of How We Talk to Ourselves*. It is produced 10 times faster than verbal speech, at an average pace of 4,000 words per minute, so it is quite a significant language load that we are absorbing every waking hour. And, as stated before, it's not just a solitary voice chattering in your head. It can be a monologue or a dialogue, or a conversation with different perspectives.

Parents, caregivers, and educators must be very careful about what they say, not only around small children, but around all ages of development. Whether positive or negative, humans internalize the speech around them, as well as give themselves their own messages they construct from their experiences. We experience this as adults as well, doing something as simple as reading or listening to the news. If we do not pause to think about what we are consuming and feeding our brain, we can start or end the day feeling like it is the end of the world according to what is being reported. Even people with healthy self-worth need to continually monitor the messages going to their brains if they want to maintain a positive outlook on life.

RETRAIN YOUR BRAIN: The Power of Positive Self-Talk

Positive self-talk is about flipping the conversation in your head from negative messages to positive ones. After years and decades of negative self-talk, it takes time to change. First, you have to create new content to send to your brain. Don't leave this to chance, thinking that now that you have made progress in so many areas of building self-worth, positive self-talk will come naturally. It will not, not at first. Second, your brain has to create new neural pathways and connections that will override the old reliable ones that carry all your collected negative history. This requires unlimited repetition, just like all the other practices. The good news is your brain loves to learn new things so never despair. Practice positive self-talk daily and in three to six months, you will be doing it automatically.

Although it takes time and practice to replace the former critical self-talk, as soon as you begin practicing your new internal script, you will feel the uplifting effect. It is similar to the way you feel when you read an inspirational quote or watch a heartwarming movie, you feel the spark of optimism. Feed yourself full with soul-enriching words and phrases that encourage and nourish you.

Write down personal affirmations. Record, if you haven't already, all of the attributes you like about yourself. I chose a half dozen personal affirmations about myself and quite literally paused twice a day when alone and said "I am a patient and loving parent. I am a creative person who enjoys writing, art, and music. I am compassionate, kind, and loyal. I like the fact that I am analytical. I am taking the time to build my self-worth, which will change my life." Although it takes only a minute to say your affirmations, positive self-talk was so foreign to me it was like learning a new language. I was more used to chastising myself for the things I had done wrong. Choose the words or phrases that you believe and like about yourself, not those that others use to describe you. Remind yourself that you are focused on removing the critic in your head and infusing yourself with positive, affirming, and inspiring words that will make you smile inside and out. Apply this exercise to your daily life as it is effective and transformational.

Collect positive quotes for inspiration. With the internet at our fingertips, finding inspirational quotes takes little time. I have shared many with you in this book and have also written several of my own—that have personal meaning to me. There is a reason I feature a meaningful quote at the beginning of each section of this book, and a positive takeaway thought at the end of each section. I try to bookend conversations in my head with this kind of discipline on a daily basis. Even simple statements influence the way we feel, such as I am amazing! I choose to live with optimism and joy! Every moment offers the chance to feel great! My life matters! I am Love! Life is Incredible! I am the leader of my life. I am blessed to have a best friend inside of me. I am resilient and have inner strength to heal and renew!

Even my mother, who is now eighty-four, keeps uplifting phrases on her bathroom mirror, after years of suffering with low self-worth, she has gained inner strength and peace. Books of daily affirmations for a year are a wonderful investment, providing you with a positive reference point for every twenty-four hours. They are short, pithy phrases that pack a lot of sentiment and wisdom.

Choose a short mantra to shift your mood or attitude. I also decided to develop a mantra for myself that would be my go-to word, or a phrase if you prefer, to shift my consciousness. Each time I would start to go into a spiral of doubt and fear, I would bring that word into my head and repeat it until I calmed myself. I will not share my personal word with you as it is one I still depend on as needed. Find your own word or phrase that inspires you. It can be based on anything that brings you joy and light, anything that soothes you. In addition, I wrote myself notes that I left on my desk, kept in my wallet and in the car. In the beginning, I had them everywhere I turned.

Here are some examples of powerful words and phrases that might help you center yourself. Sprinkle them around your environment so you are always running into something uplifting to say and hold in your mind for a moment.

Be aware of your negative thoughts. You have heard the phrase, keep your friends close and your enemies closer. It just means you must be vigilant about your thoughts. Even though you have worked hard to examine your negative inner thoughts and figure out why you have them, they will continue to rise to the surface because they have been with you for so many years. They are still your brain's default response in stressful situations. It takes time to reprogram your neural pathways and negative thoughts are sneaky and covert.

Take a few moments to listen to your thoughts. Write down what is going through your head right now. Is it positive, negative, or neutral?

Now listen to the people around you having conversations, or speaking directly to you. What kind of messages do you hear? Negative messages that you hear around you can penetrate into your brain as well as your own thoughts. Remove yourself from a situation that involves negative and judgmental commentary if you can.

Use prepared phrases as a script for yourself. When you feel you are absorbing others' negative energy or that you are giving off negative signals yourself, you can halt a downward spiral with phrases that have the force to transform your energy. Power Phrases. At first, my self-talk was focused on addressing the negativity that was occupying vital space in my brain. I developed a way to listen to my thoughts, take a deep breath, and blow them out with an exhale, and replace those thoughts on an inhale with hopeful, optimistic words. Eventually I could do it while watching my children play sports in public, or at work during a tense meeting or verbal exchange.

I wrote down certain phrases to repeat over and over:

I am calm and prepared to handle this situation with dignity and grace.

I feel vulnerable now because of how this person spoke to me, but I am okay and will be okay.

He/she can say things that might hurt me for a few minutes, but I heal quickly.

I know who I am and that no one can touch my soul.

This emotion will pass, and I will renew myself through the power of resilience.

I do not take the comments as critical or judgmental, because I know who I am and that their opinion does not have to be my opinion.

I do not fear—I choose to go boldly forward.

Another approach I would take as soon as the "you're not good enough" pattern of thinking arose within me was to stop, pause, take some deep breaths and tell myself this:

I am intelligent, loving, generous, and a GREAT human being. I have power inside of me. I will use my power to lead my life in a direction that strengthens and sustains me.

Here is another phrase I repeated to myself often, and still frequently do:

Anne, move away from toxic people. People can say what they like, and I am free to feel anyway I wish. I wish to be filled with joy and calm. Life can be just as I have always dreamed. I lead my life with hope and courage and faith.

These self-talk "scripts" have been lifelines for me during unsettling times. It is amazing to know with resolute confidence that you can take minor steps each day to replace toxic thoughts with encouraging ones. Remind yourself that with awareness, practice, and repetition, these positive thoughts will become embedded in your brain, and will eventually replace the old critical ones. I've done it, and so can you!

Reframe negative statements into positive ones. At the most basic level, do not call yourself, or allow anyone else to characterize you with what you feel is a negative description. Change "bossy" to "natural leader"; "compulsive" to "efficient" or "excellent focus on details"; "fearful" to "careful," "clumsy" to "graceful," "impatient" to "patient," "disheveled" to "composed and together."

You can do this even with everyday responses to daily requests or questions. Instead of saying "No problem," when asked to do something additional, say "I definitely will do that!" When clerks ask how your day is, don't even think about saying "ok," "good," or "fine." Say "Outstanding!" "Fabulous!"

In addition, do not repeat negative beliefs about yourself. Stay away from using the words "never" or "always," which indicate whatever you say is a generalization and, therefore, false. Do not negative futurize—as in something bad is going to happen instead of something good is going to happen. Find the opportunity in the challenge: for example, "I am not retreating, I am just advancing in a different direction."

> These new, revitalizing thoughts that you translate into positive self-talk will transform how you feel by uplifting your soul and energy to a place of peace and equanimity. You truly are the leader of your life.

Transformation Tenets

- ◊ Positive self-talk is a superb source of motivation and sustenance.
- ◊ Use short, pithy phrases or power-packed, inspirational words to shift your mood—create personal mantras that mean something to you.
- ◊ Develop a script for yourself to review, absorb, and to use for positive outcomes.
- ◊ Be aware of negative thoughts that are triggered within you and reframe them into positive ones.

Exercise!

"Physical fitness is not only one of the most important keys to a healthy body, it is the basis of dynamic and creative intellectual activity."
John F. Kennedy

Exercise is indisputably one of the most effective sources of holistic health in the way that it affects our mental, emotional, physical, and spiritual being. No matter what your view has been in the past, now is the time to learn a new hobby that will help you sustain and enhance your positive self-worth. Routine exercise is one of the best and fastest ways to improve energy, focus, mood, and overall health and wellbeing. Exercise nourishes every part of us. Even if you have loathed any form of exercise in the past, I pledge to you that by the time you have read this chapter, you will want to stand up and start moving. Keep in mind, humans were made to move, not be sedentary.

So, for those of you who do not exercise because you don't like to, don't feel you have the time, or perhaps have a disability that does not permit you to, here is a point I would like you to consider: Every single human being can come up with an excuse not to exercise, that's easy. It takes more drive to do something you don't want to do or think you can't do. By now in our quest together, however, you possess a deep appreciation for the power of your brain and know unequivocally that your brain will follow your lead. Believe me when I say that movement, no matter how small, activates your mind and body in ways that are infinitely beneficial.

Think about when you are at a concert and one of your favorite singers is on stage belting out a song you love. Whether it is John Mayer or Renee Fleming, your body starts to gyrate, your hands clap along the with the rhythm, your shoulders are swaying back and forth, you shift with the music without even realizing it. Your energy is high, and your heart is singing. You feel great. You feel alive. You are moving!

I know unequivocally that when you make the decision to include some form of exercise in your daily life, you will experience dramatic changes in the way you feel, think, and behave. Exercise is one of those no-brainers, cannot do without, sprinkle-me-with-endorphin-fairy-dust practices.

You might be wondering what the connection is between exercise and self-worth? Pure and simple, it is a stimulant for growth and transformation. Because exercising makes us feel better in so many ways, it is a monumental motivator for change. It increases our productivity as it improves our clarity and focus and detoxes us mentally and physically. The endorphins generated through exercise replace negative thoughts with positive ones, reducing anxiety and fear.

We have learned in recent years through studies on the brain that when we exercise, new neurons (nerve cells) are formed in the hippocampus through a process called neurogenesis. The hippocampus is a brain component that is linked with the ability to form new memory and also affects our long-term memory. As new neurons form, they are thought to have unique codes for memory that enhance our existing memory and enable new thoughts to be stored. When you move, you are fostering the growth of new brain cells! Exercising improves your ability to learn new information and—ready for this—helps to regulate your emotions.

Friends have said to me, "It's easy for you to work out because you love it." My response has always been that it is not so much that I love going to the gym or running outside, it is that I feel great afterwards. Exercise is one of the mightiest of all strategies for quick mood transformation.

There is no down side to exercising, although I advise you to start slowly in the beginning.

OK, ok, I hear you saying, "but I don't like to exercise," "I don't have time to work out." "I have knee problems that won't let me exercise."

There are many types of exercise and many ways to move that neither take a lot of time nor strain the body. Be creative in the form you select. It doesn't have to be a heavy burden. Incorporate exercise into your life in clever, smaller increments, if you've been unable to commit in the past. There is no mandatory amount of time or type of exercise. Just know that your brain and body thrive on movement.

If you enjoy being with people and feel that exercising with others is a smart incentive, find a facility that offers classes that appeal to you. Those who take classes such as yoga, Pilates, water aerobics, strength training, circuit training, body pump, cycling, and many others, love the motivation and camaraderie that exercising in a group offers. If you prefer to work out on your own, take a walk or jog, or exercise to videos at home. DANCE.

The key is to begin in small chunks of time, especially if you are a person who doesn't like to exercise. Choose something that you firmly believe you can stick to. It can be a five-minute walk that expands to 10 minutes, 30, 45, and perhaps an hour. It does not have to be strenuous or time consuming. In fact, much of the data recently reported states that moderate exercise may be healthier for the long-run.

The point of exercise is to support your body's metabolic functions, skeletal framework, muscles, and of course, your mind. My mantra is **ACTION DELIVERS A CHAIN REACTION.** How can you consider these benefits of exercise and not jump up and dance?

Mental and emotional benefits of exercise

- ◊ Improves Memory and Recall
- ◊ Aids in Mental Resiliency and Recovery

- ◇ Improves Mood and Attitude
- ◇ Mitigates PTSD and Trauma
- ◇ Improves Sleep
- ◇ Provides a Sense of Accomplishment
- ◇ Decreases Depression
- ◇ Boosts Focus and Concentration
- ◇ Increases Self-Discipline
- ◇ Increases Relaxation
- ◇ Enhances Creativity
- ◇ Prevents Cognitive Decline
- ◇ Increases Endorphins and Serotonins
- ◇ Helps with Addiction
- ◇ Decreases Anxiety and Stress
- ◇ Manages ADHD and ADD
- ◇ Boosts Self-Esteem and Self-worth

Physical Benefits of Exercise

- ◇ Increases Energy
- ◇ Manages Weight, Reduces Obesity
- ◇ Lowers Blood Pressure
- ◇ Increases Production of Neurons via Neurogenesis
- ◇ Improves Cardiovascular System
- ◇ Reduces Blood Pressure
- ◇ Slows Aging of Cells
- ◇ Reduces Risk of Heart Disease and Stroke
- ◇ Reduces Risk of Type 2 Diabetes
- ◇ Manages Blood and Insulin Levels
- ◇ Strengthens Muscles and Bones
- ◇ Improves Osteoporosis
- ◇ Decreases Back Pain
- ◇ Supports Posture

- ◇ Improves Skin Health
- ◇ Improves Sleep
- ◇ Improves Flexibility and Balance
- ◇ Decreases Recovery Time from Injury
- ◇ Improves Strength
- ◇ Enhances Sexuality
- ◇ Increases Longevity
- ◇ Improves Vascular Function
- ◇ Lowers LDL(bad) Cholesterol and Increases HDL(good cholesterol)
- ◇ Reduces Risk of Diseases: Heart Disease, Stroke, Alzheimer's, Blood Clots, Kidney Damage
- ◇ Reduces Risk of Endometrial Cancer, Lung Cancer, Colon Cancer, Breast Cancer

RETRAIN YOUR BRAIN: Exercise for Longevity

How do you even start if you don't want to do it? **Self-talk.** Do you think athletes want to jump in the pool on a cold day or practice sprints in the rain? They use self-talk to motivate themselves to get out there. You're only starting with 5 minutes or 20 minutes, or a class at the gym—in air-conditioned or heated comfort. Just tell yourself you want to do it. If that doesn't work the first time, get dressed and show up. Where the body goes, the mind follows. And once you start, your body will begin to crave physical exertion and activity because you feel so good afterwards.

My mother, Patricia, hasn't exercised in thirty-five years. She, by her own admission, is lazy by nature. My mom is eighty-four. Her legs are exceedingly weak, but her mind reminds her that she must keep walking to prevent becoming wheelchair-bound. So, she walks in her home, around her kitchen and through the hallways, three-times a day for ten minutes listening to the news. Do not delay, get going today!

Tips to Begin a Healthy Routine

**Before beginning any type of exercise, be sure to check with your physician first.

- ◇ **Find out what your friends do for exercise and join them.** A social connection is one of the easiest ways to develop discipline. I used to see two of my friends walking at dawn before work in good and bad weather. How do you do it? I shouted out my window on a frigid day. "I know she's waiting for me," they both said pointing to each other. Meeting someone at the gym for a class or workout circuit provides the obligation to show up.

- ◇ **Choose to do something that will keep you coming back.** My friend raves about machine Pilates, which uses equipment called a reformer and a backboard with springs attached. Because it is rather expensive, I asked what kept her signing up for more classes. "I can lie on my back on the reformer" she laughed. "That's my dream position for exercising." She found something that was easy to get into each day before working up to the more strenuous exercises. Plus, her classes were at a small studio where she knew everyone, contributing to a family atmosphere.

- ◇ **Move throughout the day.** I highly recommend standing up every hour and shaking out your whole body from head to toe and then taking a little walk around the house, even walking out the front door and running around the house before going back to your chair (for those of you who work at home). I noticed a woman at the airport going through an exercise routine when our plane was delayed. If nothing else, I know I can use the wall to stretch out my body. I can enhance a quick walking break outside by doing walking lunges. I can dance to music while cooking dinner. There is no end to how you can stretch and strengthen your body during the course of your daily duties.

◇ **Choose a time of day that suits your schedule.** If you are most energetic in the morning, awaken thirty minutes earlier to exercise. If you prefer evenings or lunchtime, then that is your time for yourself.

◇ **Make an appointment with yourself.** You wouldn't cancel an appointment with your doctor or your cousin who is flying through town, nor should you back out of your commitment to invest a bit of time in your health and wellbeing. When you commit time to exercise, after a few weeks, it will become an activity to which you look forward.

◇ **Be mindful of how you feel after you exercise.** Check in with yourself and listen to your body. If something feels off, then reassess what you are doing and find an alternative.

◇ **Start today!** Change your mind, body, and soul through exercising on a regular basis.

> Physical activity retrains your brain just like the mental practices you have employed to build new neural pathways to generate powerful positive self-worth.

Transformation Tenets

◇ Begin to exercise today to support and accelerate strengthening your mind, body, and spirit during the process of building healthy self-worth.

◇ Physical exertion, no matter how much, energizes and cleanses. Exercise is a Soul Detox.

◇ Find a form of exercise that suits you best and that you enjoy for long-term sustenance.

◇ The benefits of exercise are extraordinary and life-changing.

A Human Mosaic Vignette

The Power of Human Resilience

Joel and I met when we worked for the same company. I was single, and the position required frequent travel, which I enjoyed. Our company held semiannual meetings in Manhattan, where Joel and I first met. He was based in Delaware and I in Atlanta. During our national meetings, the younger staff members hung out together and socialized. Joel stuck out because he was gregarious, witty, and charismatic. He assumed the role of social coordinator for our group, arranging our nightly dinners and après dinner festivities. We formed friendships that spanned a geographic reach across the U.S., except for Joel and me. Our chemistry was strong, so strong that even my boss commented on how *well* we worked together, in his unabashed, sarcastic manner.

Our romance was intense, but short-lived. We were young and had no interest in keeping tabs on one another or maintaining a long-distance relationship. About twelve years later, we bumped into one another at a restaurant. I hardly recognized him, in fact, I wouldn't have noticed him if we had not passed each other on the way to the bathroom. Joel was skinny, bald, and pale. We hugged one another, spoke briefly, and exchanged phone numbers. Joel was not the same person. That energy and spirit that was magnetic had vanished. He was quiet, solemn, awkward, and definitely not the warm and vivacious person I knew in my twenties. Something was not right, but I didn't ask.

My former boss and I kept in touch throughout the years and when he was in Atlanta for business, we would have dinner and catch up. I asked him if he had heard anything about Joel, mentioning that I had seen him several months ago. He was shocked that I didn't know, thinking that he and I were still in touch with one another. "Joel lost his mother in a head on collision about six years ago, and soon afterwards, his father died of prostate cancer. If that weren't enough, his older sister had a serious stroke that left her impaired, and, I am sorry to be the one to tell you, Joel was diagnosed with leukemia," he said in one long, miserable, heartbreaking sentence. I couldn't think about anything my former boss said after learning about Joel. I had to end our dinner abruptly, and don't remember driving home.

I immediately called Joel, praying that I still had the right number. He didn't answer. I left him at least four messages before he finally returned my call. We had dinner the next time he flew into town. He told me his leukemia was in remission—thank goodness, but that he was, in his words, "I am a zombie in a shit-show."

Just a few years earlier, I had begun working as a consultant specializing in marketing and communications and rebranding companies, giving my clients a new identity. I had also started a small coaching practice with friends and former colleagues. My clients were companies and individuals seeking a sizeable change and a new brand that would increase their base of business or help them with personal issues. I loved the variety of work; no job was ever the same. I shared this with Joel during our conversation to distract him. When we were about to say goodbye, Joel asked me to help him, saying that he would pay me whatever I wanted. He wanted to, "Rebrand himself and his life, to find a purpose, and to feel a spring in his step again, if that were even possible." He also said he needed to be with someone he wholly trusted, and not a stranger or another therapist.

Joel had been the inspiring leader of all leaders—robust, energizing, full-of-life, smart, funny, kind, generous, and he always wanted the best for everyone. The series of tragedies he suffered, including having his own former healthy self fall victim to leukemia, ripped his heart out, stole his fervor for life, and, he was functioning at a very low level, mentally and emotionally. Even the sound of his formerly deep, husky voice had changed. There were no visible markings of the Joel I knew when we were in our twenties.

I agreed to work with him, how could I say no? Although most of the time he and I spent working was over the phone and via email, we did meet whenever he came into town for meetings. Joel had been through months and months of intensive therapy with two different professionals, a psychologist specializing in grief, and a psychiatrist who could counsel him as well as prescribe appropriate medication. Joel knew all about the phases and stages of grief, which he had lived through, however, now he needed to know how to transition back into his life, to stop wanting to hide from the world, and maybe, hopefully, find a way to smile again—he emphasized that he longed to "smile internally."

The initial program I prepared for Joel that was based on a routine of daily exercise—not just a brisk walk, but a vigorous workout with visible perspiration, and a three-day, forty-five-minute weight lifting session. Of course, Joel had to discuss this regimen with his oncologist and internist before beginning. He had to start slowly, in limited increments of time to build his strength back. As healthy as exercise is for one's body, it is also beneficial to one's brain. A workout program catalyzes the endocrine system to release hormones and the brain to release chemicals that have a hugely positive impact on one's vital organs.

Aerobic exercise catalyzes brain boosting chemicals such as endorphins, serotonin, norepinephrine, epinephrine and dopamine, all of which stimulate energy, focus, concentration, productivity, motivation, and happy or feel-good emotions that are often called the "runner's high. Joel would derive immediate benefit from a consistent regimen of exercise, particularly for his mental and emotional frame of mind.

Exercising would also help Joel gain weight through adding muscle mass that he lost while grieving and battling leukemia.

Together, we created a food profile that included fruits and vegetables, whole grains, beans, healthy fats, unprocessed meats with no nitrates, chicken, salmon, and eggs, and an abundance of fluids, especially water. Joel admitted that he had not been eating much at all in the last four years, other than an occasional yogurt or sandwich. There was no question that the lack of food was heavily depleting his mind, body, and spirit.

Within two weeks, Joel told me that he was feeling much better. "Although I am still not sleeping well, I am at least sleeping some, and I have more energy than I have had in ages." We then worked together to establish a routine practice of breathing exercises, mindful meditation, massages, acupuncture, and journaling. Not all at once, of course, but each day he would exercise, eat to refuel his cells, meditate, and write as much as he desired. As he engaged in these practices, Joel began to notice that he was having longer periods of calm, less anxiety, and better concentration. His work performance dramatically improved and his appetite tripled.

During our conversations, we discussed the fact that he would need to focus on new patterns of thinking for his brain to begin generating new neural pathways. He had always loved Italy, and I suggested he begin listening to Italian language courses online, as well as taking up yoga.

In five weeks, Joel began reflecting and writing about the losses he experienced and how they had affected him. We began working on the practice of Gaining Perspective, because he had been drowning in a sea of sadness with no beginning, middle, or end. Since he had lost his sense of who he was during the mountain of challenges he endured, we also spent time creating positive messages and phrases that he could repeat to himself throughout the day and night to remind him that he was on a path to growth and transformation. He also dove into the practice of listening to and understanding triggers that caused him to feel melancholy and alone. He would write specific notes about the triggers and how they affected him. The more he became aware of these, the less impact they had upon him. What was significant about identifying triggers was that Joel was able to sort through how he felt emotionally each time they arose, and as he let the emotions flow through him, they lost power.

After five months, Joel gained greater mental clarity and physical strength. Now he could work on his spirituality by tuning into his inner core, his Soul Self, which he had forced down and away. By asking himself questions that related to his internal core being, he was able to begin healing spiritually, emotionally, and mentally, while also renewing and "rebranding" his identity based on the changes he had experienced. This included joining a synagogue near his home, praying and meditating more frequently, and joining a few organizations to expand his social life. Although Joel was extremely reticent about going out on dates and going to parties, he was willing to be open to all of it—everything he could do to fill the tsunami that had nearly drowned him. He was ready to live and breathe in hope again, with the awareness that there might be more difficult times ahead, but that what he had survived made him understand the fragility and beauty of life, and had given him the strength to heal and transcend the past.

Human resilience is a divine quality, one that enables us to survive illness, tragedy, heartbreak…"I am beginning to rise up from the dead," Joel said. "I had a big personality two decades ago, and, although I'm not that person now, I'm starting to smell again, taste again, and notice when it's raining, and that I might need an umbrella."

Coping Strategies to Support the Practices

"Nothing great is created suddenly, any more than a bunch of grapes or a fig. If you tell me that you desire a fig. I answer you that there must be time. Let it first blossom, then bear fruit, then ripen."
Epictetus, Greek philosopher, (55-135 AD)

We greet each day knowing that something is going to be different. Whatever it might be, life moves forward and presents us with new information, new experiences, new people. Challenges are inevitable. An integral element of possessing self-worth is having the flexibility and stamina to adjust to changing or challenging circumstances.

Your ability to manage your responses to ongoing issues that cause you to feel anxious or uncomfortable can be supported through the practice of some simple coping strategies to keep you on track. There will be days when you don't want to take 20 minutes for Self-Reflection, or pay attention to negative messages in your environment and make a change, or to write in your journal, or to be your own best friend. Any one of us attempting to improve our lives can get to the point of diminishing returns, especially if work has been demanding, you or your children are sick, or your roof needs replacing at the same time your house is sinking and you need to shore up the foundation.

Don't give up. Taking a break is fair play. Sometimes we need to do something else to take our minds off where we are in our lives. Take a nap. Meet a friend for lunch. You don't have to do everything at the same time. Make a start. Plant the seed. Water the soil. But don't forget the sunshine. Take every opportunity to feel peace and joy.

Deep Breathing

If you watch an infant breathing, you will notice its abdomen going up and down. This diaphragmatic or abdominal breathing results in deep, even breaths that are calming to your system. Inhale slowly through your nose with your shoulders relaxed, expanding your abdomen (put your hand on your belly to make sure it's your abdomen rising and falling and not your chest). Exhale slowly through your mouth, keeping your jaw relaxed. Repeat for several minutes. If you are distraught for any reason, focusing on your breathing will help you calm down.

Deep breathing is proven to slow your heart rate, lower your blood pressure, and reduce anxiety and nervousness. It relaxes you by signaling your parasympathetic nervous system to calm down. It delivers oxygen through your blood stream and into every cell in your body. It detoxifies your body by using your lymphatic system and cleanses your lungs while improving your lung capacity. It improves your concentration and energy, releases endorphins, elevates your mood, and even prevents panic attacks and minor nervous breakdowns.

Breathing also has a way of giving us perspective. When you are in the heat of a distressing situation, pause, begin your deep breathing, and within a few minutes, you will feel better and more able to handle whatever situation you face. I always focus on pushing the air out of me with exaggerated force, it helps me immediately.

Nature Breaks

We spend so much of our time indoors: at work, cleaning, organizing, and cooking at home. And, we spend way too much time on our computer screens, more than is really needed. So many of the practices I have asked you to do involve sitting (or lying on the floor) presumably inside. Lack of exposure to the natural world is a deficit we all have in this day and age. I have to tell myself, and I am telling you, GO OUTSIDE.

The natural world provides a direct conduit to your soul. We go through daily life unaware that we are living on the earth, with all its magnificent bounteous beauty: trees, grass, and flowers in our yards; parks with green space and meandering trails; meadows, hills, and forests within a drive; creeks, rivers, lakes, the ocean; and of course, the sun, clouds, and sky. All of this stimulates our senses that we take for granted. Just the fact of breathing fresh air can clear the brain.

The Japanese have a practice called "forest bathing" that is becoming popular everywhere. It simply means making a healthy choice to spend time becoming one with nature. Studies have shown that invisible chemicals called phytoncides in some trees can reduce stress hormones, lower anxiety, and improve blood pressure and immunity. The sun activates vitamin D and stabilizes melatonin levels that are offset when you spend a lot of time in front of a screen. In fact, we get exposure to many unseen elements in nature that positively affect our brain and body, like negative ions, which contribute to relaxation, as opposed to positive ions emitted from electronics that are detrimental to our health.

Nature offers wonderful opportunities for meditation, of course, as well as physical activity if you don't want to just bathe in the sights, smells, and sounds. It is the best example we have of the cycle of life, with all its ups and downs. It is nonjudgmental. And it comes with a soundtrack of birds, insects, frogs, and the rush of wind in leaves.

Eat for Health

What we eat dramatically affects how we feel about ourselves. Learning to eat for health and longevity goes hand in hand with all of the principles and practices included in this book. Providing proper nutrition for my family is a passion of mine, as well as cooking. In fact, I have done so much research on nutrition that I developed a program that focuses on food sources that have the greatest potency to nourish the entire being called **HQIN, Holistic Quality Impact Nutrition.** That is a subject for another book. I just want to make a few brief points here.

Food is a subject wrought with anxiety for many people. Just as we learn to develop our self-worth initially based on our early environment, we also learn our food habits as young children. Many of us grew up eating sugary cereals, cookies, cake, pie and ice-cream for dessert, high fat meats, and processed convenience foods. Now that we know better, we can do better.

In order for our cells to regenerate and perform optimally, they require proper nutrients on a consistent basis. Studies have proven that without adequate and appropriate nutrition, our cells die early which causes our immune system to weaken dramatically. Unhealthy foods cause hormonal imbalances which result in inflammation. Inflammation, our body's response to imbalance, deprivation, injury, and infection, can seriously impact our health. When our health is compromised, everything goes downhill—including your program to build positive self-worth.

It is well known that a diet high in sugar increases your risk of many diseases, including diabetes, which is like the first domino to fall in a progression of diseases because it affects so many organs. Not to mention sugar is a key factor in weight gain, which impacts the health and efficiency of every system in your body. Studies have shown that those who have a high intake of sugar suffer impaired brain function as well as more susceptibility to mood disorders. When unhealthy amounts of sugar are consumed, free radicals increase, and dangerous inflammatory cells can cause premature aging as well as illness.

Eating habits are just that, habits, and all habits stem from the neuronal connections that are formed in your brain by repeated thoughts and actions. When you gravitate towards a certain food type for taste or satiation, your brain begins to create pathways of association with these foods that over time become entrenched in the brain; i.e., a habit is formed to desire these foods. When we ingest a particular food that is high in fat and sugar, such as a donut, for example, dopamine is released by our brain that triggers the sensation of feeling happy. The more we satisfy these cravings through unhealthy foods, the more we desire them. What most of us don't realize is that dopamine can be released by eating healthy foods as well. To desire healthy food is only a matter of building those new neuronal connections to create new habits. Each time you repeat the behavior, the pattern is reinforced. With time the neurons form new pathways, and, your brain has learned a new way of eating.

Say Thank You

Developing an attitude of gratitude is a variation of positive self-talk. When we were at our lowest, gratitude was the last thing on our minds. We felt victimized, if not by others than by ourselves. By observing and being grateful for the positive things in our lives, we take back our power.

Don't just feel gratitude. Write it down in your journal. Express it in a letter to a friend. Make a note and drop it in a gratitude jar and re-read your notes whenever you are feeling negative or having a down day. Be specific. Rather than saying "I am grateful for my health," say "I am grateful I made it to exercise class this morning and saw Emily there." Note how good you felt hearing a favorite song on the radio on the way to work.

Practicing gratitude provides benefits similar to the other coping strategies. By generating higher levels of positive emotion and feelings of optimism, being grateful boosts our immune system and lowers our blood pressure. We are also more compassionate, more forgiving, and more outgoing. Looking for the positive, like walking on the sunny side of the street, brings more light into our lives.

Part Four: The Practices

Check in with Yourself Daily

This may seem elementary, but if you establish a habit of checking in with yourself daily, you are far less likely to succumb to negative messages and attitudes that attack your self-worth like a virus. Neglecting to do this is like waiting to take your temperature until you collapse on your feet. So many times, when we are dragging or not feeling up to par, we don't think to take our temperature until it is raging, at which point our bodies are inflamed and infectious, we have to miss work and cancel everything, and we are miserable. We might have been diagnosed and on antibiotics for a week already, or treating the problem with homeopathic remedies, if we had taken our temperature in the beginning.

Being proactive about things that might impact your ability to work the practices shows that you value your new sense of healthy self-worth. The quicker you discover your need to adjust something in your environment, or internally, the easier it is to stay connected with your core and be your authentic self. "Taking your temperature," or checking in with yourself, is a way to regulate your thoughts and behavior. As long as you remain calm and maintain your cool, you can self-regulate your temperament throughout the day with a minimum of fuss.

Go to Counseling

I have cautioned many times throughout this book to seek professional counseling if you feel you have issues that are troubling on a deep level that you cannot manage yourself. There are talented psychologists and psychiatrists everywhere. Simply make sure your counselor is licensed as a psychologist (MA or PhD), psychiatrist (MD) or social worker (LCSW). Do your research and ask your friends for referrals. I make no claims to be a medical authority or licensed counselor myself. Only you know the severity of issues you face. Or perhaps your issues are not severe, but you would like the extra support of counseling. Any time during this process that you feel overwhelmed by your emotions to the point that you are alarmed, please get the proper support from a professional. Often churches offer free therapy groups for various issues, and hospitals do as well. If you are unable to afford counseling, there are options available that are at low cost or free.

RETRAIN YOUR BRAIN: Coping Strategies for Sustained Wellbeing

Expel toxic thoughts with your breath. I engage in repetitive deep breathing interludes to literally blow toxic thoughts out of my brain and out of my body. Sometimes I forget that my body can help me expel negative thoughts, just as positive self-talk can replace negative messages. Practicing deep breathing every day not only calms me but reminds me that I can also retrain my brain to automatically cue my deep breathing when necessary.

Combine visualization and breathing to reach a deep state of relaxation. When you desire to feel safe and peaceful, do your deep breathing to relax yourself. Then tap into a memory, or construct a new scene, of the most soothing place you can think of in the world. I visualize ocean waves, feel the heat of the sun on my skin, and my feet sinking into soft sand. Breathe in and out with each wave.

Progressive muscle relaxation. Another relaxation modality to deal with the stress of staying on task with your practices is progressive muscle relaxation. Start with your breathing to calm your mind and body. It's best to be on a mat or carpet on the floor for this. Focus on relaxing your muscle groups, one at a time from your head down. Open your mouth and relax your jaw. Pull your shoulders down and slightly back and consciously relax the muscles in your shoulders and neck. With your arms beside you on the mat, relax your triceps and biceps and your hands. Go back to your core and relax your diaphragm, abdomen, and pelvic area. Sink into the mat as if you are sinking into the earth—in fact if you can do this outside on a mat or towel on the grass it is even better. Relax your thighs, knees, calves, ankles, feet, and toes. Let yourself drift and keep sinking until you feel you are floating. When you are ready, start wiggling your toes, rolling your legs side to side, resume deep breathing, and so on up to your neck and jaw. Roll to your side before standing up. Then shake your whole body out. You will feel refreshed and energized.

Nature date. Make a nature date with yourself or a friend every week. Pick out a park, trail, arboretum, or botanical garden close by. As you walk pause to close your eyes and fill your senses with the sounds around you, naming them. Sit in front of a flower and meditate. Find a tree to claim as your own. Learn to orient yourself with your senses instead of following signs.

Eat healthier. One day a week, challenge yourself to prepare new recipes or to order new dishes at your favorite restaurant. One day a week restrict your sugar and do not have that Danish for breakfast. Eat fresh fruit and yogurt or eggs without toast. Little by little your taste buds will wake up and you will start looking forward to your breaks from the same food you have been eating your whole life. You will want to experiment and be more adventurous in your food selections because you feel better, and the brain rewards doing new things. Your brain will crave what is best for you when you train it to enjoy healthier choices.

Make a gratitude inventory. One day a month go all out on gratitude. Keep a running list all day of everything that that comes into your orbit for which you are grateful. Describe it in the tiniest detail. Perhaps you are grateful for the sensual aroma of your husband's aftershave lotion. Or, you are grateful that your son took out the garbage without you asking him. You don't have to tell him, just breathe it in and smile. See how many things you can come up with and read them over before you go to bed. I guarantee you will sleep sounder and longer.

Monitor your temperament. Schedule an appointment with yourself for a few minutes every three to four hours to notice how you are feeling. If you think you feel fine but notice a slight difference in mood when you check in with yourself, ask yourself what it is you are feeling, identify what may have triggered this emotion, and determine the real source of what you are experiencing. Give yourself a mental rating from one to five, with five being "this could ruin my day" and one being "I can let go of this right now." Take full responsibility for your emotions and don't blame others. By assuming ownership, you are the one that has the power to transform how you are feeling.

Address changes in temperament in real time before they affect your equilibrium.

> Knowing that you want to change, understanding what you would like to change, and moving forward with specific practices is the bridge from knowledge to action to brain change.

Transformation Tenets

◊ Life is filled with highs and lows and learning to cope with challenges is key to your equilibrium.

◊ Develop proper coping skills to reduce your anxiety and enable you to transcend the emotion.

◊ Being self-aware and checking in with yourself is a proactive approach to being mindful of any potentially challenging issues.

◊ With deeper, more troubling concerns, please seek a professional counselor who can provide you face-to-face coping therapies.

Part Five

The (Optional) Plan

Dear Reader: I developed "A Reverse Resume" as a process to unload what I had undergone, to write it all down, all the issues that were constant sources of pain. This allowed me to see how far I had come from my early childhood traumas, and literally and figuratively, thrust them out of my life so that I could start with a fresh template for growth and renewal.

The mosaic of my life was being rehabilitated and restored with new facets, rich and vibrant colors that reflected my exuberance, optimism, and inner faith and strength. Developing a reverse resume was a concrete approach to view my progress and move to a new zenith in my life.

You may choose not to engage in this particular activity—this is absolutely up to you and whether you feel it is a constructive use of your time. As with the Practices, these are opportunities to better understand who you are by having the ability to reflect, write, and move forward with a cleansed palette.

A "Reverse Resume"

"My mission in life is not merely to survive, but to thrive; and to do so with some passion, some compassion, some humor, and some style."
Maya Angelou

This quote by Maya Angelou feels as though I had written it, or perhaps always envisioned this message in my head. Maya Angelou had profound wisdom and depth about human nature. To create a life that is meaningful to YOU is a beautiful reason to make time for self-care and self-improvement. Life is precious and fleeting, and to live the way you truly wish and deserve is a compelling impetus for every human being to invest the energy into developing self-worth.

I had a wealth of data to refer to when it came to evaluating what I learned about myself from Self-Reflection. It was second nature to me to compulsively write about each major episode in my life that caused me to feel low self-worth—and there were a lot. I don't expect everyone to go to the lengths I did in trying to make sense of my low self-worth because I can make this process easier and shorter for you. But for those of you who are inclined toward getting all you can out of the process of examining the negatives from the past in order to replace them with positives, here is what I did. This was the prelude to organizing a "business plan" for myself as a way to structure my pursuit of healthy self-worth, which I used in addition to The Practices.

I did something rather surprising with the knowledge of the life events and episodes that had crushed my sense of self-worth. I created a "reverse resume" of what had held me back—not from being successful, which I was—but from enjoying my success and accomplishments. Once I had compressed and highlighted these items on my reverse resume, I saw them for what they were: things that had happened in the past that had altered my inner identity that I no longer needed in my life.

Here is a sample of the resume I put together of episodes that contributed to my low self-worth. My objective in doing this was to be able to examine what happened in the past and officially let it go. I was, in essence, firing myself from the job of continuing to revisit my old negative thoughts about myself. Having learned new skills that would promote positive thoughts about myself, I could let go of these experiences I had clung to for many years. What follows is just a sample from my resume.

Anne Ockene Boudreau

Addresses: Atlanta, Georgia; Chicago, Illinois; Lakeville, Connecticut; Brussels, Belgium; Bonn, West Germany; Akron, Ohio; Rye, New York; Santiago, Chile

Personal Objective: To build healthy self-worth by replacing the past, my "ought" self, with the present, merging my real and ideal selves

Major Episodes of Low Self-worth

Overdose on baby aspirin at age three: Santiago, Chile

- ◊ Experience: rushed to hospital, stomach pumped; others—screaming, shouting, crying, threatening; me—violently shaken and frightened

◇ Feelings afterwards: shamed and made to feel guilty by maids who were supposed to be watching me

◇ Impact on me: guilt, fear, felt responsible for other people's incompetence, sense I had failed

Fourth/Fifth Grade, Rye, NY, Camp, Two Girls, and entire 5th grade class

◇ Experience: bullied mercilessly by jealous "friends" at camp who were cruel and vicious; carried into 5th grade school year; others—made fun of me, spread lies, ganged up on me; me—was singled out and alone, sad and scared

◇ Feelings afterwards: humiliated, confused, lonely

◇ Impact on me: to try even harder to please friends and adults, and be perfect; to try to act like nothing bothered me when I was being ridiculed and devastated

Parents' fights over Father's betrayals and Mom's nervous breakdowns, everywhere we lived, with parents

◇ Experience: hearing and/or seeing fights where things were thrown; others—shouting, threatening, crying, denying truth and telling lies; me—frightened, crying, begging to stop; not able to understand or rationalize why my mom was bitter and angry towards my dad, and spent so much time in bed sleeping

◇ Feelings afterwards: confused about loving hero father even though he lied and was unfaithful, and standing up for mother, who was being hurt but would then result to drinking, drugs, and withdrawal

◇ Impact on me: poor role models for healthy relationships led to feelings of total distrust; my norm became strife and instability, and internalized confusion, but acted as though everything was normal; ignored feelings and continued to worship my father and largely ignore my mother; withheld turmoil of family dysfunction from others

Sometimes we feel if we detach from our most intense life experiences that we are cutting off a part of our self, as in amputating a piece of who we are. It is true that you will have some emotions about letting go of these things that have taken up so much of your time and energy. But believe me when I say life is so much sweeter without all that bitterness that was hard to keep swallowing. You make room for so many new gifts and blessings to enter your mind when you let go of the past. You will even begin to remember the good things and kind people who had been pushed out of your memories. One of the most wonderful results of all my Self-Reflection has been forgiving my mother knowing she did the best she could at the time and forging an exceptionally close relationship with her. Our closeness now has nurtured both of us.

> The path to positive growth involves accepting your past and letting go of the pain; you will transcend where you've been and how you've felt, and evolve to a place of joy and peace.

Transformation Tenets

◇ Creating a Reverse Resume of the events and people in your life that contributed to your low self-worth helps you acknowledge and accept what took place in order to transcend the past and grow beyond the memories.

◇ Accepting what precisely occurred and seeing it in writing legitimizes your thoughts and concretizes them.

◇ Writing about how these events made you feel is a powerful way to release them and let go of the pain associated with them.

◇ Letting go of the past opens you up to living with a liberated mind and heart and letting the beauty of life enter you.

Your Plan for Building Self-Worth

Note to Reader: Sustainable change occurs through a structural framework that encourages preparation along with an organized, tailored working plan. Even if you have never used a plan in your life, there is no better time than now to develop one that is specific to you and your experiences. If it feels overly cumbersome to you, just extract some of the essential points and create your own template for transformation. The key is to follow a plan and stick to it.

Plan for Transformation

"Plan your work and work your plan."
Napoleon Hill, *Think and Grow Rich* (**1937**).

After writing up my "reverse resume," which cleared out the negative voices and memories I had been hanging onto, I knew I needed to create some positive momentum with an action plan. Because I was determined that building my self-worth would be a successful enterprise that would sustain me in all areas—personal, professional, and social—for the rest of my life, I approached the situation as if I were an entrepreneur launching a new venture. Having worked in the corporate and nonprofit worlds, I knew the first step in creating a successful business, organization, or any kind of enterprise was to develop an effective and inspiring business plan.

Moving forward in this way further separated me from the person who had been so victimized by my feelings of low self-worth. I went from living in a subjective state, being tumbled about by feelings of unworthiness, to an objective state where I was choosing to engage my brain in making positive changes.

In considering the framework for this plan, I knew I had to base it on who I really am and not on who I thought I should be so that the world would love and accept me. I knew it had to accommodate my busy life as a wife, daughter, mother of three, a coach, consultant, woman with many important relationships, and a marketing executive. This was going to be a master plan for positive growth and transformation that I was ready to enter into with whole-hearted commitment. I knew where I had come from but needed to be more specific about where I wanted to go. What were my goals and how would I get there?

Just as in the corporate world, I needed a practical plan that would cover strategy and details of what needs to happen when, who is in charge which was easy—me—but I had to be able to accept new responsibilities. Having worked for global corporations and nonprofits, I knew the plan had to actually deliver results within reasonable parameters. I also knew that company culture was vital to the success of a strategic business plan. This meant staff (or in this case my family and close friends) had a stake in sharing the core values and objectives of the company.

Most business plans include the following components: a vision statement, a mission statement, core values outlining the key company principles, a SWOT analysis (Strengths, Weaknesses, Opportunities, and Threats), long-term goals, short-term goals, yearly objectives, and action plans that break down the vision, mission, and goals into realistic and attainable time and revenue expectations. Of course, goals may be adjusted based on economic conditions or other unexpected factors, however, the corporate vision typically remains the same as it is based on a longer-term perspective.

When I did some online research with the hope of finding a business plan that I could borrow for my own personal effort, I only found generic templates that didn't seem helpful—at least not for the sort of process I was going to undertake. I ended up creating a parallel template to those I'd used in my past jobs and populating it with my personal details and goals.

My plan had to be simple, but inspiring enough to keep my focus. It needed some tracking and measurement systems as an accountability element, as well as some sort of "reward" system to sustain me. The most important prerequisite was that it would continuously reinforce my desire to feel better about myself.

> Each of us is the CEO of our life. It is our choices, beliefs, and actions that drive our development as a productive human being.

Your Vision Statement

*"Someone's sitting in the shade today
because someone planted a tree a long time ago."*
Warren Buffett

What is your dream for how you would like to feel? For me it was to believe that I was lovable and worthy, not because I performed well or was a benevolent person, but because my life mattered despite what someone thought about me, whether I was a successful business person, writer, athlete, and so on. I wanted to feel okay about me without the external accolades I had needed all my life in order to feel worthwhile.

Your vision statement serves as the pinnacle of aspiration for how you want to feel about yourself and how you will live your life. A strong vision will guide you in the short-term and sustain you with long-term inspiration. It should be a portrait of how you want your life to look in five, ten, twenty years, and beyond. The most effective visions are anchored in your core values and beliefs. They reflect the type of individual you are and what matters most to you.

The vision must be yours, not your spouse's, your parent's, or your partner's. You must own it, believe that you can achieve it, and know that it will transform the way you approach your life.

Begin by imagining yourself with self-worth and inner peace. How would that feel to you? Contemplate how it would feel to not second-guess yourself, to not feel self-conscious or insecure? Think about how extraordinary it would be to be able to manage the ups and downs of life, to have the inner strength to face any negativity in your life with the knowledge that you don't need to let others destroy your spirit, deplete your energy, and steal your joy. No one can control you or how you feel about yourself. You are the leader and visionary for your life.

Compare how you feel now with how you desire to feel in three weeks, three months, one year, five years ahead. Remember, that anything is possible as long as you are self-aware and in tune with your inner self. Take some deep breaths for a few minutes and clear your thoughts of anything other than what you are doing right now. Write down as much as you'd like, and then you can shorten your vision into a few sentences.

Vision statements are always written in the present tense and should be short and to the point. Here are some examples:

Each day is joyful as I am doing what I'm passionate about with people I love and respect. Every day that I'm alive I have the chance to learn and develop in new areas. I am resilient and capable of handling the vicissitudes of life. I feel worthy and that I matter.

I am loving and patient with my partner, friends, and family because I have high self-worth. I am able to honor and respect others as I do myself. I am the leader of my life.

I am comfortable with who I am, and I believe that my life has purpose and meaning. I turn inwardly for positive feedback and power and manage negativity with the knowledge that no one has the ability to make me feel bad.

Each day I am fully present, experiencing life as a gift rather than a battle. No one but me has the power to control my thoughts or emotions.

I believe that my life has value, and that every single day is an opportunity for growth. I know that I am not perfect, nor is anyone, I don't even use this word any longer, because I know that I have value and am worthy of love just as I am.

Once you have developed a vision statement that you love and feel energized about, copy it onto poster board or use your printer to make a diploma size notice. Place your statement in locations in which you spend time during the day. Also, copy it onto a small notecard, fold it, and keep it in your wallet or purse for times when you are out and about to use in the presence of a challenging situation or toxic people. Or text yourself your vision statement so it is always available on your phone.

Here is my vision statement, as it was then, and continues to be today:

Anne Ockene Boudreau — Vision Statement

My enduring strength and self-acceptance is rooted in my inner Soul Self, which sustains me through life's highs and lows by an omnipresent belief that my life matters. I am able to trust myself and trust others. I feel worthy without having to seek it outside of myself, as I know that I have inherent value and inner tranquility that is based on truth and wisdom, self-compassion, self-respect, and self-love, and this is sacrosanct.

> Your vision statement reflects you living with positive self-worth, knowing that your life matters, and that you have the courage and confidence to be at peace with who you are.

Your Mission Statement

"There is no passion to be found in playing small — in settling for a life that is less than the one you are capable of living."
Nelson Mandela

A mission is an important cause that you believe is worth pursuing because it is an invaluable aspect of what you believe matters for you as a person and to your life. Your mission statement is vital to achieving your vision. Use it to motivate you on a daily basis as your guiding principle while you work toward building your self-worth. It needs to be unique to who you are and aligned with your values, goals, and character.

A mission statement supports the vision statement. Whereas the vision statement is about what you aspire to in the future, the mission statement is what you are going to do to achieve your vision. It is your daily reminder and motivator for your thoughts, emotions, and behavior, and a key component of change, as it provides you with a direction and focus to your daily life. I relied on my mission statement as a daily and, at times, hourly reminder of my commitment to feeling better and living with inner joy.

My own mission statement is personalized to reflect my beliefs and life goals. I would love to know what others come up with. Please share yours on my website: selfworthforlife.com

Anne Ockene Boudreau — Mission Statement

I am a talented writer who is committed to providing inspiring prose to uplift others. My lifelong passion is to help others develop self-love and self-trust through building a powerful foundation of self-worth. My coaching work and writing will provide a platform for me to share my knowledge and experience of transforming negative thoughts into positive ones. My hope is to be a force for spreading positivity and love, and to help rid the world of bigotry, violence, and hatred. I will continue to be a loving and supportive mother and role model to my children as they develop their unique desires and goals for their lives.

That mission statement was and is short enough to carry around with me and refer to often. I also wrote an expanded version of my mission statement to keep with my "business" plan for building my self-worth.

Anne Ockene Boudreau—Expanded Mission Statement

I am a talented writer who is committed to providing inspiring prose to uplift others. There is nothing more important or meaningful to me than helping others love themselves for who they really are in their innermost being. I will write books and provide interactive forums for communication where I can support individuals in their efforts to build self-worth and self-love.

I am and will continue to be a positive role model for my children by teaching them to be independent and self-assured individuals. I will accomplish this by creating a loving, nurturing, and open home environment in which we can share our thoughts and emotions without judgment or criticism. I am teaching them it is okay to express their anger or frustration, hurt or sadness, and that they are loved with no conditions. I provide and will continue to maintain a home that is a haven from pain and sorrow. My role as a parent is to support my children in what they most want to do, rather than to prescribe or demand what they must do.

I believe that my life matters, and that I have a purpose here on earth. I awaken refreshed and reinvigorated each morning. If I feel other than that, I will spend time by myself in quiet thought or meditation to release any negative emotions and restart the day from a positive platform. My daily goal is to approach life with an optimistic perspective and feel that I am a vital force. I do this by being sensitive and aware, by eating healthy foods, maintaining an exercise regimen, and by being considerate and kind to family and friends.

I understand, and will remind myself if I forget, that my past is past, and it is behind me. I have a beautiful future ahead, a fulfilling and joy-filled life. When I slip, whether it is a huge landslide or a sidestep, I understand that it is okay and that sometimes those moments are necessary for new motivation to keep building stronger self-worth. I value time spent with nonjudgmental friends and loving family members.

I reduce my inner tension by accepting that I have work to do for myself. I have committed to a program for change that is allowing me to let go of all my layers of protective defense mechanisms and to retrain my brain with positive messages and images of self-worth. I know that in order to live with inner peace, I cannot try to be someone I'm not. I am a person with integrity who will strive to be honest about my mistakes and not lie about them. No longer will I pretend that I'm okay when I'm not. I am open to my emotions so that I can better manage them and have the capacity to release them. This is the way I heal and grow and provide a role model for my children.

I also have my business plan mantra with me at all times to echo and reinforce my efforts to respect and love myself no matter what is happening in my personal or professional life or in the world.

Anne's Mantra

My mission is to guide others to believe they matter by providing them with the assurance that they can change themselves and build self-worth.

Developing a mission statement that represents your beliefs and values, that provides daily motivation and focus to guide you to achieve your vision, is invaluable to your commitment to yourself.

SVOT Analysis

"The ones who are crazy enough to think they can change the world are the ones who do."

Steve Jobs

Business plans include a SWOT analysis, which is an assessment of a company's Strengths Weaknesses, Opportunities, and Threats. Since I am not a fan of the word "weakness," I have replaced it with "vulnerabilities." The word "weak" can have negative connotations in our society. "Vulnerability," however, is the susceptibility to be hurt or exposed. It occurs when one is open and sensitive to the extent they may feel pain or rejection. When a person is vulnerable to something or someone, it often means that they are in a position in which they subject themselves to someone or something unhealthy and potentially harmful. Therefore, SWOT is now SVOT in my business plan.

Additionally, I have replaced the word "Opportunities" with "Options." From a business perspective, opportunities are external, something a company strives to go after to increase their market share. Business opportunities may include taking advantage of changes in technology, government policy, regulations, uses of new products or services. I see these as "options" a company makes to improve their viability in the market or, in personal terms, the likelihood of carrying through your program to build self-worth.

This is a valuable exercise for businesses as it provides executives and employees with a realistic perspective of who they are, their position relative to competitors, what they do better as a company than others or what they are lacking, areas in which they can grow and expand, and what potential factors threaten their success. This provides the baseline for developing strategic and tactical goals.

Similarly, your plan for building self-worth should identify the specific areas of your life that fall into the SVOT categories. Be honest and thorough as you go through these steps. And think outside the box. Perhaps one of your strengths is that you have a skill very few people have. Although it hasn't made you money yet, it could be something that would make you happy. There are infinite options that could be your best choice for connecting with your soul. Brainstorm—what makes you feel better every time you do it? What is it that you believe makes you unique?

Strengths

Strengths are what we value most about ourselves. Ranging from character attributes to intellectual acumen to attitude, we all have distinct features about which we are proud. They are our inventory of what "sells." Here are some examples of strengths, skills, or competencies you may have.

Integrity	Curious	Intelligent
Honest	Compassionate	Productive
Open-minded	Loyalty	Leader
Generous	Creative	Problem Solver
Persistent	Supportive	Dependable
Empathy	Resilience	Efficient
Courage	Kind	Motivator
Witty	Patient	Articulate
Sensitive	Athletic	Innovative
Optimism	Organized	Resourceful

Vulnerabilities

Everyone has vulnerabilities, things to which you are susceptible. Vulnerability issues can also be equated to an insecurity about being in certain situations, such as a large social gathering or when you have to speak in front of your colleagues. There are numerous circumstances that cause us to feel our footing is fragile. The origin of these thoughts might stem back to your childhood. Try to identify what these vulnerabilities are and how they make you feel. Here are some examples of vulnerabilities that can be liabilities.

Distrusting	Critical	Compare self to others
Shame	Arrogant	Need to be loved
Guilty	Jealous	Impatient
People Pleaser	Fearful	Pessimistic
Resentful	Envious	Angry
Intolerant	Insecure	Tendency to gossip
Perfectionist	Controlling	

Options

In the language of building self-worth, options are similar to choices. We have made a choice to change our lives. Committing to change gives us options for more choices—actions to take that will help us build our self-worth, plus speed up the acquisition of positive mental, emotional, and behavioral habits.

Our brain is the most magnificent tool we have to increase our self-worth. As discussed, the nature of neuroplasticity is that our brains can accept new messages that focus on our positive well-being that will override old messages from the past that were negative and unhealthy. We also have the most powerful force in the universe inside us—our soul—which will provide anyone with the calming energy to manage any issue. When you permit your Soul Self to fill you with light and tranquility, you recognize that the choices you have are vast, and that you can respond to any situation on your terms in a manner that does not create more conflict or strain for you.

Our society has trained us to feel fear when we are unfamiliar with something, when we are in an adverse situation, or when we are facing a problem. Yet, when we fear something, we are channeling our energy toward that fear, and in our attempt to fight the fear, we pour more energy and focus into the fear itself. The negative energy that people put into arguing, controlling, criticizing, or condemning, acts as a boomerang that is thrown at someone and returns back to the person who threw it. Our best option is to keep making the choices that will help us feel connected to our inner source of peace—our Soul Self.

Each day presents the option to awaken with optimism, to feel invigorated and confident that you have the ability to change, to grow, and to know that you matter. Your life has purpose, and to honor your purpose is to seize the precious time you have to feel fulfilled. We are fortunate to have the ability to choose for ourselves how we want to feel, and pursue the path to healing, recovery, and growth. The opportunity to build self-love, which fuels self-worth, is not a finish line; it is an ongoing process of self-acceptance and self-compassion.

Here are some examples of options you have at any moment:

Pause: take a step back from a challenging scenario

Practice: meditation and breathing exercises will calm your mind and emotions

Perspective: be a witness not a judge; observe, don't pass a sentence

Rest: sometimes you just need to sit or lie down and close your eyes

Seek support: family, friends, professional counselors are only a phone call away

Heal: honor your body with yoga, massage, or acupuncture when it is crying for attention

Give yourself a hug: and a pat on the back; life is a learning process

Be gentle: treat yourself with tenderness and compassion

Reframe negatives into positives: everyone makes mistakes; focus on what was learned. Be active: walk, run, bike, swim

Get out in nature: hike through a forest, along a shoreline, sit under a tree

Plant: flowers, vegetables, anything that will give you connection with the earth

Prepare food: ditch the carry out and enjoy the rhythm of making your own meals

Listen to music: it soothes the savage beast

Hydrate: drink water all day

Threats

In business, "threats" refers to competitors, financial problems, losing market share, or other obstacles. On a personal level, threats abound in a world that is filled with negativity. Our culture has become riddled with bullying, bigotry, violence, global warming and other cataclysms—all sizable threats to our wellbeing. This is the part of building self-worth that is the most critical to prepare for and understand. Threats to our stability are everywhere.

In a landscape that is filled with these potential roadblocks, we add to it the experiences of our past, the memories that haunt us, the times we were hurt or lied to, cheated on, abused, neglected…too many to enumerate. Even though we have dumped our toxic waste, we will still face threats that trigger past pain.

By accepting this as a fact rather than expending energy trying to avoid or block it from affecting us, we can teach ourselves what to expect, how we might feel, and how we wish to respond. Everyone has their own threshold for what they feel threatened by, so it is up to you to reflect on those issues you have experienced and create your personal list. By articulating these and writing about them, you've already begun to deal with them.

Here are some examples of common threats we all face. The question to answer for yourself is how you want to change your old reaction to a new response.

Conflict

We face conflicts of varying degrees every day; not just arguments or disagreements, but choices about whether we want this or that. The end result is either anger or frustration. You can choose to avoid unnecessary conflicts by refusing to magnify the consequences of a conflict. Ask yourself how important is it? Is it life threatening? Will it affect your ability to earn a living? How will you feel about this issue a week from now? Much conflict in our lives is pure drama we enter into to engage our brain in some high level "exercise." Instead of drama, seek productive conflict. This can actually lead to collaboration if each party maintains some objectivity. Refuse to be drawn into the drama. This will reduce the number of real conflicts you face.

Temptation

What are the things that might derail your progress? Say you have a propensity to gossip as a way of seeking approval or attention. You think it's harmless, but you know bad things can happen as a result of it because more often than not it backfires. Know that is a vulnerability and therefore a threat, you need to be prepared. When you feel like gossiping ask yourself: Is this my story? Is this about my life? What will I get out of talking about someone else that can contribute to my inner self-worth? Nothing because you are fulfilling an external, not internal need. Do not sign in for your temptations. Leave them lined up at a gate you have closed. Eventually they will dissipate and go elsewhere.

Criticism

Someone you care about says something disrespectful or hurtful, or that you perceive as a negative comment about you. This can happen to anyone who has a family, circle of friends, or workplace buddies. What do you do with your knee jerk reaction, which is to feel betrayed or destroyed? Consider the source. Is this legitimate, constructive criticism that will make you a better person or help you in any way? If not, remind yourself that no one is an authority on your vulnerabilities but you. Are you getting a grade from this person who is criticizing you? If not, take a pass on whatever is said. Mentally drop it in the wastebasket.

Fear

Fear is a primal emotion that alerts us to danger. It is important to listen to and feel what our guts tell us is a threat, or when we are suddenly overheated in an adrenaline flush. In other words, the body rules when it comes to fear, and the body doesn't lie. Except when it is listening to the brain saying, "The sky is falling," when the sky is right up there where it belongs. Check your fear. Is it an emotional reaction to a stable situation or is your body literally telling you to flee or fight? Ask yourself, "fight or flight"? If it is neither, it is not an emergency and requires no more of your time and energy. Do not enlist fear to be your security guard. Fear is afraid of everything. You, however, have the ability to weigh the circumstances and turn down the invitation to be scared.

Toxic Relationships

This is such an easy fix, but so hard to do. It is essential to eliminate the people in your life who have contributed to your low self-worth if they have made no effort to change and grow. We all make mistakes. We are here on earth to learn and to love. But there is no longer room in your life for toxic relationships. Too many of us accept living with toxic relationships because we feel it is what we deserve or that we fear being alone. What we must grasp is that living in this type of relationship is poisonous to your self-worth. Just as you are working to strengthen your inner self, you can choose to create new, positive relationships that will support your personal journey rather than interfere, even prevent you from moving forward. Ask yourself, "What have I ever received from this person that made me feel good about myself?" If the answer is nothing, your response must be bye-bye. Your life is far too meaningful to allow yourself to be treated with anything other than reverence and love. You deserve this, and you are in charge of your life.

Your Action Plan

"Action may not always bring happiness;
but there is no happiness without action."
Prime Minister Benjamin Disraeli

Your personal action plan is the framework and steps to achieve both your mission and your vision. Just as you would make a list of all you have to accomplish in your day at the office, or in your personal life, your action plan will delineate short-term and long-term goals that support your mission and vision. Remind yourself that building self-worth will change your life, positively impact those with whom you share your life, and have a resonating influence on everyone with whom you interact.

1. **What is the first order of business you want to accomplish?** Keeping in mind my brief business mantra—My mission is to guide others to believe they matter by providing them with the assurance that they can change themselves and build self-worth—the first action I want to accomplish is to share my knowledge and experiences about building self-worth by writing a book.

   ◊ Person A might want to embark on a new career that had been put off because of low self-worth issues.
   ◊ Person B may choose to work on developing new supportive friendships to replace old social contacts who were negative influences.

2. **How can I accomplish my top goal?** I pledge to spend two hours a day researching, reading, and gathering information for this book and two hours a day writing down what I have learned beginning on Monday, with breaks when I need to attend my children's events.

   ◇ Person A decides to enroll in one course a semester at the community college.
   ◇ Person B makes a commitment to ask someone new to lunch once a week.

3. **What do I need to change about myself to make this happen?** To write the book I want to write, I have to talk about myself and others who were a part of my experiences honestly. That means I can't indulge in being a people pleaser and I will have to be able to handle criticism and feedback by those people mentioned, like my mother, former co-workers, old schoolmates. I will rely on my integrity and self-trust to handle these situations.

   ◇ Person A may need to rearrange social and family priorities for a while in order to have several free nights a week to go to school and study. It will be important to say no to people who don't want things to change but remember that these changes further a goal.
   ◇ Person B, who is shy around new people, shrinks from the action of asking different people on a lunch "date" to try them out as friends. Our gut intuition will help us make better choices in finding people on a similar path.

4. **What will motivate me to stick with this process?** Keep the vision and mission in front of you at all times. Have a plan in place for missteps. Consider having a family member or loving friend be your accountability partner. Journal about your feelings daily or as often as

you can so you can record your progress. Use supportive and inspiring tools to keep you on track such as affirmations, exercise, meditation, nature walks, music, anything that relaxes and enriches you enough to draw you back to your vision. One of my motivations was to get all the boxes of notes I had been accumulating for years off my dining room table, so my family could eat on it again.

⬥ Person A may find motivation in the content of what is being taught. Our brains love to learn new things and are energized by any new subject.

⬥ Person B feels motivated to continue as soon as one of the people chosen for lunch turns out to be a good social companion, sharing some of the same beliefs and values, but bringing new energy into this communion as well.

5. **Set a long-term goal.** Establish a long-term goal first, along with a timeline. We know that change is not linear, and that it may take more or less time than you thought, but it is always helpful to attach a date as an incentive. A long-term goal is typically based on a twelve-month plan. My long-term goal was to have my book finished in a year. (It has taken me six years! What did I do? Readjust my goal.)

⬥ Person A had a long-term goal of graduating with an MBA in three years.

⬥ Person B wanted to be able to host a New Year's Day party for new friends.

6. **Create short-terms goals.** These can be monthly, weekly, even daily. My short-term goal was to work through each section of my book in a timely fashion, which meant spending no more than two days writing a section and one day editing a section.

- ◇ Person A had to make completing homework the short-term goal, keeping a calendar with dates of papers and tests and times blocked out for study.
- ◇ Person B had short-terms goals of getting to know someone at lunch, moving on to doing something after work or on a weekend, and progressing to hanging out comfortably at each other's homes.

7. **Plan to recommit.** When you get off course, what is your contingency plan? For everyone it is to go back to The Practices: get perspective, detach in order to be objective, accept what is going on, and go from there.

8. **Have a system of personal rewards.** How will you reward yourself for sticking with your plan? I would buy myself a new scented candle or essential oil; sleep late after a productive day; get a massage to soothe my scrunched-up shoulders; go to a movie with my husband or kids. I also had a long-range goal of taking a vacation when I was through with my book project. My husband and friends also brought me gifts from time to time when I met a goal.

9. **Measure your progress.** Change of any sort is measurable. I would check in with myself weekly to note what progress had been made, even if I noticed a minor adjustment in my mood or responses. I would use a journal that I kept in my desk and write down the date and time of my entry. I also added it to my phone on the calendar. Anytime you observe yourself feeling a subtle transformation, make a note of it as it will inspire you to keep going!

To make a business plan for building your self-worth demonstrates how far you have come on your journey of transformative change— and that you are successfully retraining your brain. Congratulations on this major accomplishment. Keep moving forward toward The Good Life.

Part Six

A Human Mosaic: Healing, Renewing,
Recovering, and Rebuilding

A Human Mosaic

Healing, Renewing, Recovering, and Rebuilding: The Path to the Good Life

"Annie, are you happy? Are you fulfilled?
Do you feel you are in a good place in your life?"
Alan Lawrence Ockene, my father, confidante, and mentor

The last time I saw my father before he died we sat in his favorite place on the back deck of the house overlooking the fish pond, filled with carp, catfish, bluegill, and bass. His children, grandchildren, and extended family enjoyed many joyous events and celebrations in this same spot. I spoke about this earlier in the book, but I want to remember it as I close my journey with you to build healthy self-worth. That afternoon, just before I had to leave to return to Atlanta, my father asked me: "Annie, are you happy? Are you fulfilled? Do you feel you are in a good place in your life?"

I believe we both knew that his questions were intended not only for my Self-Reflection, but also to address his subconscious concern that I might not be fulfilled. He knew me better than anyone and saw his own image in me. He wanted to know whether I was living *The Good Life*.

Despite our intimate bond, I did not realize until after I went through the transformative change of acquiring positive self-worth that my father and I were more alike than I ever knew. We both suffered from low self-worth but had perfected the art of disguising it from the world and even ourselves. My father, who was the pinnacle of success—except for his treatment of my mother—may have lived with the same need to prove his worth.

We both performed on all the stages of our lives, achieving awards for being on top of our game in business, moving among celebrities in our fields from one event to the next, protecting our inner fears by gaining external approval and admiration. In all my years of adoring my father, I never considered that he may have his own insecurities, that he also may have been bedeviled by negative messages that he kept in a corner of his mind. I had spent all my childhood and so much of my life trying to be "Perfect," (the dreaded P word that I removed from my vocabulary during my quest,) so he would be proud of me. What if he had done the same thing in his life? In fact, perhaps all his acting out with other women was a way of demonstrating how flawed he was inside, even if his outsides were worthy of adulation.

I am sorry that I was not able to share with him my discoveries of how different life can be with self-love, self-trust, and healthy self-worth; with compassion for and acceptance of all my flaws and struggles; and with my connection to my Soul Self and the spiritual energy of the universe.

Today I can answer my father's question: "Yes, dad, I am living *The Good Life.*"

In the beginning of this book I said to you, reader, that you have one life here on earth. One life in your corporeal form. However, it is a fact that your unique and beautiful energy, your spirit, your soul, lives forever, only in different forms, as defined in the First Law of Thermodynamics. You will always, for eternity, have a place in the universe that is sacred.

The fact that you are here is miraculous, and the gift of being alive is one to be revered and treasured now, today, not when you've run out of time and it is too late. Being a human being is a gift that we must never lose sight of in our fleeting time on earth.

What do I mean by *The Good Life?* This philosophical question goes back to the Greek philosopher Aristotle, (384 BC — 322 BC). Aristotle believed that moral virtues are the principle means to having a Good Life because they allow us to make the choices that both constitute and lead to good lives.

Each one of us has the freedom to do whatever we desire and be whomever we wish. If we are open to all of life and permit its natural rhythm to flow in and out of us, as resilient human beings, we have the ability to grow, learn, and live with joy and peace.

When you assume responsibility for your thoughts and emotions, rather than have your outward environment dictate how you feel, you have the ability to "Let your own experience tell you its own meaning; the minute *you* tell it what it means, you are at war with yourself," as Carl Rogers wrote. In other words, when you impose your pre-conceived opinions or beliefs—those acquired through your parents, society, or culture—onto new experiences, you are not able to experience the richness and fullness of that experience. When you have an idea about how something should be, you evaluate it through that bias.

I am reminded of when I went to see an award-winning film. All my friends and the public raved about this remarkable film. Every superlative imaginable was attached to this movie. By the time I was able to see it, those words that were used to describe the film played out in my head, "Extraordinary," "One-of-a-kind," "Best picture ever!" My barometer for the movie was disproportionately high. And, of course, the only place to go was down from there, so I was not as dazzled as others due to my preconditioned mind. I went into the movie with a predetermined bias that blocked my ability to enjoy it with fresh eyes.

Yet, how can we actually do this after years of living with expectations and established beliefs in our head? With implanted ideas for how things should or should not be. The lens by which we view our life experiences has been clouded by preconceived notions. With healthy self-worth, however, you are free to experience the beauty of life with fresh, uncluttered eyes. When you don't feel burdened by toxic thoughts, you *can* be in the moment, to enjoy smelling the gardenias in your garden, smile as you see your child walk in the door, not lose your temper when stuck in traffic knowing you'll be late to your meeting, and more importantly, you feel alive, optimistic, strong, and ready for anything.

You have learned the value of listening to yourself and believing what you hear without criticism or blocking it out. You no longer live with self-doubt. You have the freedom to be fully open to experiences and relationships, knowing that whatever happens in life, you will be fine because of your resilience and your inner strength.

When you can be fully yourself, live in harmony with your Soul Self, you have the opportunity to discover the authenticity of your natural, unconditioned emotions, those that arise from the experiences themselves, not from judging the experiences.

A huge component to being you is to feel that you can rely on your own choices and decisions, that you are no longer dependent on others for validation or disapproval. When you accept responsibility for yourself you become self-directed. Rogers's fundamental question that I kept returning to during my journey has kept me moving forward with clarity: "Am I living in a way which is deeply satisfying to me, and which truly expresses me?"

My answer then was: NO, I am not living a life that is either satisfying or reflects me.

When I reached the defining moment of my life I refer to in Part One, I knew that I had choices for how to live the rest of my life. My personal challenge to myself to rid myself of past wounds so that I could enjoy my life became heightened when my children were toddlers. I felt a constant drag that signaled to me I was not fully engaged with them, or myself. I was always thinking about what I should or should not be doing instead of relishing every moment of my time with them.

I could remain going through my days feeling internal discord, distrusting others, and fearing rejection, continue living with a dichotomous mindset that resulted in discontent and frustration, or I could change my thinking. I no longer wanted to live with inner tension that caused stomach aches and held me back from feeling at peace. I didn't want to live in the shadow of my past pain and let former events rule and wreck the rest of my life.

As importantly, I knew that I couldn't be the type of mother, wife, daughter, friend, colleague or human being I yearned to be if I didn't change myself. Everything about me and my life was impacted by how I felt about myself.

Although I had no role model to follow nor mentor to teach me, other than Carl Rogers' guidance in tandem with research I had conducted, I knew without a doubt that I could rewire the pathways in my brain by learning new thoughts and behaviors.

Through a series of exceptional interviews and much research, I became consumed with learning as much as I could about neuroplasticity. Once I knew empirically that anyone can change patterns in their brain, I had all the impetus I needed. The fact that I understood the potency of neuroplasticity was a head start that provided me with the courage and confidence to move ahead at full speed. I had total conviction that this would be a process from which I could only benefit. It was a solid win-win.

When I began, I had these words in front of me at all times: *One Life Here on Earth*, and *I Am the Leader of My Life*. These were huge motivators to me when I was stuck, had a setback, or when I was not able to feel concrete improvement. After about five months, I felt something that I could only liken to the movie, "The Ten Commandments," when Charlton Heston parted the Red Sea. That feat was beyond me, but I felt I had gained a new set of eyes and ears. I looked at the sky and saw a color I had never before recognized. It was azure blue and was the most magnificent color I had ever seen. I looked at the cherry tree next to my office window and saw the radiant fuchsia blooms with eyes unfiltered by doubt and distrust. I awoke in the morning refreshed, not wanting to stay in bed and hide under the covers due to the internal stress I felt. I lit my candles, as I always had, but now I could smell the aromas and breathe in the bounty of my world. My senses were awakened and engaged in life.

I was free to explore, to enjoy, and to feel at peace. I was moving forward.

I was living The Good Life.

I recalled an experience I had while attending boarding school in Connecticut. One morning, my eleventh grade English teacher, Mr. Carlson, took our class on a walk to a trail in the woods by Lake Wononscopomuc. He never mentioned what his intention was as he didn't want us to have any preconceived ideas in advance.

We were in a line walking behind our dashingly handsome teacher when he abruptly stopped in the midst of the woods. He turned around and invited each of us to look around and comment on what we observed at that moment. One person said, "I see lots of trees with thick roots." Another person saw "tiny white flowers," and another "sun rays through the thick leaves." Mr. Carlson seemed agitated as he raised his voice and said, "None of you see anything but the obvious."

I am paraphrasing his talk, but it was something like this. "You aren't open to the experience of being out here in nature, integrating with the beauty and richness that is all around us. You've been preprogrammed to see only what is right in front of you, the obvious, and not the subtle beauty that is everywhere. You are thinking about something else and missing out on what we have here. Look around again. This time look closely as if you've never been on this trail before. Notice the monarch butterflies with their orange and black wings floating from flower to flower. Do you see that blue jay to the right of us? Do any of you smell anything at all? Can you feel the sweet coolness of the breeze?"

After a few minutes, we understood—at least most us did—the

purpose of our morning walk: to be observant and present to what is before our eyes. To drink in the details and not just skim the landscape. Mr. Carlson was trying to teach us how to connect with the Soul Self and to employ our senses to their fullest capacity, a valuable lesson that I've carried with me all my life, and that actually influenced the theme of this book. Everything we see and feel is through the lens of our brain, which ultimately forms our sense of self. But, we can change our lens at any moment, with the right set of stimuli, practice, repetition, and an openness to experience. When we have self-worth, we can be open to any experience without defense mechanisms or filters, without preconceived ideas or beliefs. We are free to be open to everything without the rigidity of self-imposed, or culturally conditioned, restrictions.

The Role of Resilience in Maintaining The Good Life

Within the span of five months or so of working through practices to build my self-worth, I noticed a monumental change in my physical health. My stomach aches and nausea disappeared. I began sleeping better, eating better, and I had much more energy, strength, and focus.

As this became my "new normal" I realized I was developing "resilience," the capacity to recover quickly from difficulties—in my case criticism, flashbacks to being bullied, and any number of fears I had covered up and hidden all my life. I was no longer subject to such intense stress when recovering from negative experiences.

I wouldn't say I "bounce back" from every challenge to my goal of feeling calm and centered. There are certainly things that still hurt me. But I no longer feel like I'm in a dark cave by myself. I now know I can recover from whatever is thrown at me in a timely manner.

In the past few years, for instance, a colleague I adored from my former firm committed suicide, and the father of a friend of my daughter's shot himself in his car. Then, my father-in-law died unexpectedly, followed by a dear friend dying of an aneurism and massive stroke at 48, then my Uncle died, and a close family friend. Five funerals in less than four months. How does one handle such a flood of sadness?

Because I had been working The Practices for some time, I knew enough to gain perspective. I realized that as I get older, I will be losing more friends and family to disease and other causes of death. I understood that there is little, if anything, I can do to control the fact of another's death. I knew that I would grieve, but that it would benefit no one to ruin my health as I had when my father died; and in fact, would set a poor example of resilience for my children.

Healthy self-worth ensures that we can have confidence that things will improve, and that all difficult things will pass in time. We can recover from loss and heal from our wounds. Suffering and sorrow do diminish with time.

Knowing Peace

For forty years, I tried to control everything, to manage outcomes, to seek acceptance, to force myself to be my ought self rather than my ideal self. On the surface, I appeared a gutsy go-getter who had it all together. That was one side of me. I had high self-esteem (not self-worth) in that I knew I could succeed in my endeavors. Internally, though, my brain provided me with a continual loop of messages about how I was not good enough. But no need to go back there because I have moved on.

Imagine you are seeing the ocean for the first time in your life. You feel the velvety wet sand molding your footsteps as you walk. You notice the bright colors as the sun's rays create a stark contrast between the sand and the ocean. You see the crabs racing in and out of the tiny holes in the sand as you breathe in the scent of salt water. You hear all the sounds as if you were at a symphony—the waves, the seagulls, the wind rising from the tides. This is what it is like to know myself without the facades that separated me from experiences. I am part of a whole.

I owe some of my progress to Soren Kierkegaard, Danish philosopher, theologian, poet, and author, who originated the expression "Leap of Faith," as this is what I did for myself. I took the leap that whatever I did to help me build self-worth would be far healthier and more fulfilling than remaining as I was.

After returning to my Soul Self and tapping into the essential energy that is the real me, I have the authenticity I always wanted for myself. I know who I am and that my life has meaning. I am finally **ALIVE** and able to live in the moment, with self-awareness. Being open to the splendor and beauty of living, I am in the flow of life and not harboring past regrets or worrying about the future.

To live in harmony with your Soul Self is to be in complete comfort and grace. Grace is the feeling of a natural sense of inner peace and stability, nothing forced, nothing contrived. I have a life that is filled with rich experiences that I can enjoy as they come and go. And, when difficult times enter into the picture, and they do, I know in my soul that with time, I will survive and heal.

Although my quest to build self-worth took patience and perseverance, it was the most meaningful work I've ever tackled. It has changed my life.

My Hope for You, Dear Reader

This book was based on my journey, but, as a wise friend once told me, if it helps one person feel their life matters, then I've done my job.

My hope for you is that you live **The Good Life**. Why good and not great? Good is better than great. Great is infrequent, rare, a once in a while thing, typically a state that is fleeting. Good is steady, resolute, realistic, enduring, and hopeful.

What I discovered about myself after my quest to retrain my brain to release past wounds and open myself up to inner peace is that The Good Life is not found outside of ourselves. It is how we interpret the world that matters. If you feel worthy internally, then all the pillars you leaned on that disappointed you, and the mountain of expectations you set for yourself, shrink down to human size endeavors.

The Good Life is not about material possessions or one's stake in the world. When our life ends, we are remembered by our character, not what we had or didn't have, what we achieved or didn't achieve. We leave a legacy with our loved ones by the good we did. The good is defined as our integrity and honesty, our empathy and compassion toward others, by our tolerance and openness to experiences, the reverence we conveyed to others, and through the absolute authenticity by which we lived.

We have been on a journey together to understand what we need to live the most fulfilling life possible. We have focused on reflecting on the events that shaped us in our lives, positive and negative. We have worked to let go of the toxic thoughts through practices that gave us perspective, taught us to detach from negative messages, encouraged unconditional self-acceptance, self-trust, and self-love, and reframed our negative self-talk into positive inspiration. My hope is that you will continue to learn about yourself and apply the concepts I've shared with you, always knowing that you are an incredible, uniquely special person. Remind yourself that life is dynamic, that you will continue to meet unexpected challenges, but that you have within you the power to face all that comes into your life with confidence and resolve.

I want to add that I hope that after reading this book you either are already started on or will create your own Good Life, the life you deserve.

Possessing knowledge about yourself and learning how to think differently will bring you greater personal power and peace than you can imagine. It takes time to rewire you brain, but you will notice changes within a matter of months. Your experiences to build self-worth will be different from mine, however, the vision is the same for all of us: to feel our lives matter. And they do.

Never lose sight of the gift of being alive; always cherish your capacity to live as you always deserved and dreamed.

And, remember that you are a multicolored mosaic of life experiences, ever-changing as you evolve through your life. Every facet of who you are contributes to your brilliance and to the energy you radiate. You are here for a reason and when you believe in yourself, you have the power and momentum to do anything you wish.

> You were born for a reason. Your life has purpose and meaning. Your life matters. To know this with every ounce of your being is my dream for you.

I would love to hear from you about your journey to develop self-worth.
Anneoboudreau@gmail.com

Epilogue

A Human Mosaic

During my senior year in college, I chose to write my thesis on Leo Tolstoy (1828-1910), not only because he is one of the greatest writers of all time, I was also fascinated with his dramatic life-altering shift when he turned fifty. After completing *War and Peace* and *Anna Karenina*, Tolstoy was at the pinnacle of his career. He was surrounded by family, with a wife and fourteen children, was in good health, and had amassed enormous wealth.

Despite his success and fame, at midlife Tolstoy became intensely introspective and dissatisfied with his life. He lost his purpose and descended into a profound spiritual crisis and deep depression. Despondent and directionless, Tolstoy wondered whether he would ever find meaning in his life again.

On the verge of suicide, Tolstoy decided to immerse himself in the study of philosophical and religious doctrines hoping that they might hold the answer to the quintessential question of humanity: *What is the meaning of life, if it leads to inevitable death?* Tolstoy engaged in a comprehensive examination of every document he could find to answer the one question left that was keeping him from ending his own life. "Without knowing what I am and why I am here, life is impossible," remarked Tolstoy during this very low period of his life. He worked tirelessly to find the answer outside of himself, when in the end, he understood that the only way to live with meaning was to fully engage himself in humanity. After studying Western and Eastern religion, philosophy, and spirituality, Tolstoy created his own philosophy known as tolstovstvo. Its core concept was that humanity should live in harmony, unity, and peace.

Tolstoy knew in the 1800's what we as a global community must embrace today: "Freethinkers are those who are willing to use their minds without prejudice and without fearing to understand things that clash with their own customs, privileges, or beliefs." What wisdom, truth, and relevance these words have to us today. The irrational violence, political divisiveness, religious and cultural conflicts, bullying, bigotry, suicides, drug overdoses, the savage manner by which people communicate with one another — all this colliding discord has caused a climate of extreme negativity and hostility.

Our world today is not harmonious, unified, or peaceful. We live with dissonance and fear that echoes from the depths of our souls. However, every human being has a role in changing the climate of our world by taking a higher path, by modeling behavior that is nonjudgmental, accepting, compassionate, and loving.

This begins with you.

If you have been suffering from past wounds, feeling unworthy or inadequate, it is not easy to raise your own positive energy, let alone that of others around you.

During our lives, we are challenged with surviving difficult times, then trying to recover and restore ourselves. Our life is not a linear path of least resistance, but one filled with peaks and valleys, twists and turns, highs and lows, stops and starts. We are a complex composite of all of the experiences and relationships that have influenced us during our journey. Each event and interaction we experience contributes to the colorful, multifaceted, and brilliant mosaic that is our life.

Every human being has the power to influence the present and the future. Our universal energy is connected; we know this as a fact through the First Law of Thermodynamics that states that heat is a form of energy, and thermodynamic processes are subject to the principle of conservation of energy. This means that heat energy cannot be created or destroyed. Your energy is infinite. Your energy will never die, it will change in form, but it will exist forever. When you absorb this scientific law of physics, I hope it provides you the inspiration and motivation to transform the negative energy within you into positive.

As Tolstoy wisely stated, "Everyone thinks of changing the world, but no one thinks of changing himself." This book is dedicated to those of you who truly want to change, to grow, to live a meaningful life, and to have a powerful, resonating impact on the world. This is possible when you learn how to accept, trust, respect, and honor who you are by building inner strength and developing healthy self-worth.

Abraham Lincoln, (1809-1865), 16th President of the United States once said, "My dream is of a place and a time where America will once again be seen as the last best hope of earth." His words were prophetic then and have a profound bearing on where we stand as a country today. These words bear repeating and should be taken seriously by every human being who cares and believes in our world.

Our uniqueness is our strength. We have within us the power to create the life we imagine, the life we deserve, if we learn to honor our differences. The power to affect positive change is within your reach, you just have to grab it, build upon it, and share it with others.

Think of the wonderful energy that will be released into the universe by valuing who you are and being a force of optimism and compassion for yourself and for others in the world.

You matter, and your life is miraculous. Always believe that you are meant to live with joy in your heart and equanimity in your soul.

> You are an illuminated, multifaceted,
> and uniquely magnificent mosaic.

About the Author

Anne Boudreau is an author, coach, and executive devoted to guiding people to develop healthy self-worth. The capacity to lean inwardly for strength, courage, and compassion has never mattered more than in our current world.

Anne's desire to focus on the topic of self-worth is derived from her life-long passion to address the array of mental, emotional, physical, and spiritual issues that impede a person's ability to feel fulfilled and enjoy inner peace. In addition to writing full time, Anne advises others in the areas of self-worth and self-acceptance.

Prior to her career as a writer, Anne served as director of marketing and communications for numerous global corporations. She has counseled corporate executives on how to rebrand themselves and their businesses. Anne is actively involved with several non-profit organizations.

Born in Santiago, Chile, Anne has lived in South America and Europe, traveled extensively, and is multilingual. She is a graduate of Northwestern University in English and writing. Through broad exposure to many cultures, she has gained a profound understanding of the importance of spreading acceptance, compassion, respect, peace, and love—as these are the sacred qualities that will guide human beings to reconnect with one another and harmoniously unite us as a global community.

Anne lives in Atlanta with her husband, three spirited children, and three attention-hungry canines who rarely leave her side.

Visit Anne's website at www.anneoboudreau.com

CPSIA information can be obtained
at www.ICGtesting.com
Printed in the USA
BVHW031514080419
544913BV00009B/1269/P